When in Rome

WHEN
IN ROME

A Journal of Life in Vatican City

Robert J. Hutchinson

Broadway Books

New York

BROADWAY

Broadway Books titles may be purchased for business or promotional use or for special sales. For information, please write to: Special Markets Department, Random House, Inc., 1540 Broadway, New York, NY 10036.

BROADWAY BOOKS and its logo, a letter B bisected on the diagonal, are trademarks of Broadway Books, a division of Random House, Inc.

Visit our website at www.broadwaybooks.com

Book design by Maria Carella

First Broadway Books trade paperback edition published 2001.

The Library of Congress Cataloging-in-Publication Data has cataloged the previous edition as:

Hutchinson, Robert J.
      When in Rome: a journal of life in Vatican City / Robert J. Hutchinson. — 1st ed.
        p.   cm.
      "A Main Street book."
    1. Vatican City—Description and travel.   2. Vatican City—Social life and customs.   3. Hutchinson, Robert J.   I. Title.
DG794.H87   1998
945.6'34—dc21   97-45569
                                                      CIP

ISBN 0-385-48647-2

14   13   12   11   10   9   8   7

For Glenn Ellen . . .

She is all States, and all Princes, I,
Nothing else is.

Contents

Go to Rome! Never mind the journeys!
Go! . . . Life is not the same afterward.

LORD ACTON

Romam venite, fidem perdite.

MARTIN LUTHER

A Legion of Decency Guide to the Vatican

Wherever the Catholic sun doth shine
There's always laughter and good red wine;
At least I've always found it so
Benedicamus Domino.

HILAIRE BELLOC

*O*ne of the advantages of being a Catholic is that you get to see a lot of beautiful naked women.

You may never have realized that before, but it's true. I never could understand why thick-headed, drooling Protestants would accuse us of being prudes when they gave the world the Puritans and the Moral Majority and we gave the world Rodin's *The Kiss.*

From Michelangelo to Madonna, Donatello to Salvador Dali, Cath-

1

olic artists have felt little compunction about letting it all hang out *ad majorem Dei gloriam*. The billboards outside our apartment in Rome, which each week featured a new topless model advertising perfume or a new brand of blue jeans, are merely carrying on an artistic tradition that goes back to Botticelli and Caravaggio, Titian and Bellini.

Everywhere you go in the Vatican, you see nudity.

The Sistine Chapel, of course—inside of whose echoing walls the cardinals elect the pope—is covered with naked men and women, all piled on top of one another in what looks for all the world like some sort of biblical orgy. In the Vatican Treasury there is a magnificent bronze tomb of Sixtus IV, the patron of the arts and founder of the Vatican Library, completely covered by a series of topless, buxom nymphs each representing one of the liberal arts (Arithmetic, Astrology, Music, Grammar, and so on). It's a testimony to the Catholic erotic sensibility, I think, that a pope's tomb is covered by a dozen bronze nudes.

The papal apartments in Castel Sant'Angelo are likewise decorated in frescoes that would have made Hugh Hefner proud: tall, lithe young women all raising their pendulous breasts with cupped hands to what one can only imagine were admiring papal eyes. The Stufetta of Cardinal Bibbiena, today the seat of the Vatican Secretary of State in the Apostolic Palace, features a colorful painting of a tumescent Pan about to pounce upon a naked blond nymph combing her hair. And in the oldest part of the Secret Archives, above the wooden cabinets filled with all those red-sealed papal bulls, are brightly painted seventeenth-century murals depicting scenes with bishops and popes—but interspersed throughout are full-sized decorative paintings of beautiful young women dressed in loose tunics that invariably fall off a shoulder to expose at least one jutting nipple.

Imagine the ruckus that would arise if a university or public library today decorated its walls with murals of topless teenage girls.

I bring all this up to explain why I found myself, at age thirty-nine—an aspiring if not very successful sinner better known for learned tomes on baccarat and seven card stud—living in Rome with my wife and three kids and poking around the sacred highways and byways of Vatican City. It is a long, somewhat bizarre story that is weirdly bound up with travel and religion and my own strange inability to stay put very long.

I first came to Rome when I was nineteen years old, my imagination overheated with the wonders of Renaissance architecture and the braless halter top. I was a tourist, of course, but also a pilgrim. I was then and remain now a practicing Roman Catholic—meaning I rarely miss Sunday Mass, becoming irritable and anxious if I do (a condition that my non-Catholic friends think should be treated immediately with good drugs) and take the trouble to read papal encyclicals before ignoring them. I ignore them not because I find any fault with their premises or logic—indeed, I'm always astonished by the lucidity and sane humanism of papal teaching—but just because I don't feel like living that virtuous a life.

The popes have written eloquently against social injustice, and, truth be told, I would do the world a whole lot more good ladling soup at a Catholic Worker kitchen than I ever would as a writer. But I *like* being a writer; it's a lot easier and more interesting than working for a living. Similarly, the popes have condemned as sinful some of my favorite activities in the world, from ogling nearly naked girls on California beaches to gambling. I was sitting in the Vatican Press Office one day when John Thavis, the bureau chief of the Catholic News Service in Rome, gave me a splendid summary of why the Vatican has publicly condemned state lotteries. Having written a bit about the subject, I was naturally very interested. I couldn't find fault with a single one of the arguments John adduced—at approximately fourteen million to one, state lotteries are not exactly a smart bet—but I also knew, as surely as the sun will rise tomorrow, that I wasn't about to quit gambling.

For most of my friends, though, that in itself is an irrefutable argument against Catholicism, with a logic as tight as an Aristotelian syllogism:

A. *The pope says it's immoral to drink to excess, indulge in wild promiscuity, and tell outrageous lies.*

B. *But I like drinking to excess, indulging in wild promiscuity, and telling outrageous lies.*

C. *Therefore, the pope is full of hooey.*

A pretty airtight argument, I have to admit. But not being trained as a theologian, I've never felt the need to come up with elaborate excuses to justify my vices, preferring, instead, to simply enjoy them.

However, I've never been quite able to shake myself free of my religion either. Like a moth hovering around the flame, simultaneously attracted to and repelled by the bright light, I've always lived my life within the spiritual orbit of Rome and the Vatican.

I quite literally grew up with the events of the Second Vatican Council—beginning Catholic elementary school praying in Latin and ending it singing bad folk tunes in Swahili. And during my high school and college years with the Jesuits, I was force-fed a steady diet of Karl Rahner and Gabriel Marcel, charismatic renewal and liberation theology, the St. Louis Jesuits and the United Farm Workers.

Even after college, I struggled to make sense out of the kaleidoscopic acid trip that is Catholicism, wrestling with the contradictory impulses that flowed out of Vatican II, dutifully reading liberal (Hans Küng) and conservative (Avery Dulles) theologians, trying to understand what Christianity in general and Catholicism in particular are all about.

Non-Catholics, with their traditional disdain for the alleged superstitions of Rome, aren't aware of just how ridiculously hyper-intellectualized Catholicism actually is, how the entire history of Western civilization is filtered, magnified, and reflected in its arcane symbolism

4

and interminable philosophical disputes. When you combine the relentless philosophizing with the mind-blowing imagery of the Church's liturgy and iconography, even in their vastly simplified contemporary forms—each Sunday being offered a cup of the savior's precious blood to drink, staring up at a vivid image of his dying body on a cross—you end up, quite frankly, with very confused individuals, but also with people driven by a lifelong desire to sort it all out.

And the center of it all, no matter what the Jesuits tell you—for good or for ill—is Rome, the Holy See, the Servant of the Servants of God. Just as Jerusalem is the heart and soul of the Jewish people—"If I forget thee, O Jerusalem, let my right hand wither!"—Rome is the heart and soul of the Catholic Faith.

It was here that a cranky fisherman from Galilee carried a tiny, flickering flame of a new religious vision, a flame that was passed from one person to another, one family to another, until it somehow grew to engulf the mightiest empire that had, up to that time, stood upon the face of the earth. The mystery of Christianity has always been how a tiny sect of semi-literate Jewish peasants, following a grubby carpenter with little formal education, could have so quickly transformed the life, and altered the entire course, of human civilization. After all, Christianity changed everything—religion, culture, politics, science, philosophy, art, technology, sexual life—in a way that its many competitors, from the cults of Isis and Mithra to the noble philosophy of stoicism, did not. How?

The answer, at least in part, is Rome. Christianity came to Rome. It's as simple as that. Rome was the cultural, administrative, and legal center of the known universe. By taking their new faith to the very center of civilization, by daring to preach to proconsuls and tribunes, eventually even to the emperor himself—and by being willing to be tasty hors d'oeuvres for the emperor's household pets—the early Christians conquered the world. Today, I suppose, you'd go to Hollywood and get eaten alive by movie producers, agents, and lawyers, but two thousand years ago Rome was where you went if you wanted to reach a lot of people in a hurry.

And the key to this entire cultural transformation—this "revaluation of all values," as Nietzsche put it—was the spiritual dynasty that always claimed to be descended from the apostle Peter, the Roman popes. As a matter of historical fact as well as of doctrine, the popes have always acted as a kind of center of gravity for the scattered, culturally various, and linguistically distinct churches, striving above all to maintain Christian unity in the face of tremendous political, military, and philosophical pressures.

That the popes largely succeeded in this "ministry of unity" is incontrovertible, despite a number of major and minor schisms, and thus the Catholic world has largely avoided that fracturing into thousands of tiny denominations, each with its own doctrine and liturgy, that befell the Protestant churches after the Reformation. Despite the anguished howls of liberals and conservatives alike, the papal primacy—*Roma locuta, causa finita est,* "Rome has spoken, the case is closed"—has preserved the Catholic Church intact for two thousand years and allowed a continuity of doctrine that is largely unparalleled in the history of religions.

Once, during my first teenage trip to the Eternal City, I overheard a tourist ask one of the Swiss Guards, "Pardon me, but which way is the Inquisition?" It was the only time I've ever seen a Swiss Guard look utterly helpless.

She meant, of course, the Sant'Ufficio, the Holy Office—by then renamed the more politically correct Congregation for the Doctrine of the Faith—found to the left of the basilica, next to the Nervi (now Paul VI) Audience Hall. But I thought at the time that this phrase would make a great title for a book, with all that it implied in terms of unstated assumptions and blissful ignorance. There has never really been a travel-ogue book, as such, written about the Vatican, if only because you can't really travel there the way you can to other countries.

Most books about the Vatican are just plain dull, often written by sexually confused ex-priests or former Catholics angry that the pope won't change two thousand years of Christian teaching on premarital sex, or the sanctity of human life, or divorce and remarriage. Worse, they rarely convey the personality of the place . . . the smells and the traffic . . . the rich delicacies of Roman food . . . the perils of the Italian language . . . the way Italian monsignori push their way to the front of the line, just like their lay countrymen.

Like most Catholics, I spent most of my life knowing practically nothing about the Vatican, despite twenty years writing, off and on, about religion in general and the Catholic Church in particular. Unlike most Catholics, I had visited St. Peter's, interviewed cardinals and bish-ops, studied encyclicals and other official documents. But I had never really taken a close look at the Vatican itself, the actual place, as the living center of the Roman Catholic Church. That didn't prevent me from writing about it from time to time, naturally, even though I had never really checked it out firsthand.

I had friends and colleagues who were genuine *vaticanisti*— journalists based in Rome who spent their lives reading the tea leaves and studying the entrails of the papacy. But their focus was almost en-tirely on the theological or political controversies *du jour* and, even more important, the tidbits of curial gossip, nearly all inaccurate or at least misleading, that they could glean from their sources. They seemed sin-gularly uninformed about, or uninterested in, the trivial, on-the-spot, touristy details I found fascinating. I was far less interested in who was plotting to get someone fired; I wanted to know how much money a cardinal made, what those silly capelike outfits were called, where the Swiss Guards went drinking on their days off, and so on.

Some *vaticanisti* already knew these details, but many, I was later to discover, did not, had never taken the trouble—just like any native of any city—to see the sights and ask all the dumb questions a tourist would ask. One journalist at Vatican Radio, a Brit married to an Italian newspaperman, who had spent a dozen years in Rome, conceded to me somewhat wistfully that she had never checked out a fraction of the stories and sights inside the Vatican to which she had access. As a matter of fact, she said, most people hadn't.

As a result, twenty years after my first visit to Rome I set out to rediscover the Vatican. I wondered how it would all seem, to a smart-aleck American writer and confused Catholic, to really poke around the place, talk to the people who actually run it.

I wasn't completely naïve. I knew the curial Mafia imposed a near-total curtain of silence around the inner workings of the Church. It would take a dozen years of carefully cultivated friendships to even scratch the surface. But I didn't have a dozen years—and the people who *had* spent a dozen years covering the Vatican didn't want to offend their sources by writing frankly about what they had seen and heard.

So, that was my idea: I would go to the Vatican, an innocent lay lamb among the curial wolves. I would see what I could see, talk to whomever I could talk to. I would ask lots of dumb questions. And then I would report back.

Simple.

II

All Roads Lead to Rome

For the present I know not where to start, overwhelmed as I am by the wonder of so many things and by the greatness of my astonishment . . . In truth Rome was greater, and greater are its ruins than I imagined. I no longer wonder that the whole world was conquered by this city but that I was conquered so late.

PETRARCH, *Rerum familiarium*

*O*f course, I had a plan.

Among my *vaticanisti* contacts was a friend I'll call Irish Bob. Irish Bob and I had written for some of the same magazines over the years. He had earned a Ph.D. in medieval studies from Yale University and had spent more than a dozen years in Rome, writing for and then editing a number of different publications. Eventually, Irish Bob had a difference of opinion with one of his publishers and, in a fit of manic exuberance and youthful optimism, started his own four-color glossy magazine about the Vatican. I had once been the managing editor of *Hawaii* magazine, where I had earned an international reputation as an authority on thong bikinis, and so Irish Bob would sometimes call me up late at night, from Rome, and ask me for advice on how to start a magazine. I told him what little I knew—which was practically nothing—and he told me his hopes and dreams for his fledgling publication.

Irish Bob and I kept in contact over the years, and his magazine, while not exactly prospering, survived. I had done a few small favors for him from time to time, and thought he might be able to help me research my book. He kept a beautiful apartment in Rome, up on the Janiculum hill, away from the hustle and bustle of the city. And his magazine and contacts would provide a nice "cover" for me.

I made him an offer: If he'd let me sublet his apartment and help me get inside the Vatican, I'd write some articles for his magazine. Incredibly, Irish Bob agreed.

There was only one possible complication: my wife. She's a devout Catholic—but an even more devout Californian. Would she like to move to Rome for a while?

Glenn Ellen, her big green eyes wide, merely stared at me. By then she was used to my wild ideas . . . but this was even crazier than usual.

"You mean, Rome, Italy?" Glenn asked very slowly in reply.

I nodded.

"As in the Colosseum, *la dolce vita,* and Gucci?"

"Precisely."

She thought about it for a moment. I could see her running little video clips in her mind of weekend trips to Florence . . . frolicking in the Mediterranean at Positano.

"Why?"

I explained: We were both in need of spirituality. The rampant materialism of California was eating away at our souls. We're both Catholic, I said, and going to Rome for Catholics is like making *aliyah* for Jews: It's a return to the ancestral salmon run of tradition.

What better place to find that old-time religion than in Rome? The

Eternal City. Home of popes and poets, piazzas and pizza. If you can't find God in the Vatican, He probably doesn't want to be found.

I quickly outlined my plan. We had two free tickets to Europe on Air France saved up—compliments of a monthly long distance phone bill roughly equal to the gross national product of Uruguay. We could rent out our town house. Our eldest son, Robert John, then aged five, could go to an Italian kindergarten. In a few months he'd know more Italian than we would.

Glenn looked skeptical. After all, we had three wild sons all under age six, and traveling with little kids is not for the weak of heart.

Good point. Little kids in a foreign land couldn't be easy. Perhaps we could hire a part-time housekeeper and cook to help out?

Still skeptical.

I saw this required desperate measures. "And," I said, "we can stop over in Paris for ten days and have a real vacation on the way. What do you say?"

Paris cinched it.

There was a lot to do. We had to find someone to sublet our town house. Ship our belongings. Get passports for the kids. Make sure all of our bills were paid off. Tell our eldest son's school that he was leaving the country.

I made a few "electronic pen pals" on CompuServe—ex-pats who lived in Rome—and they gave me some useful tips about setting up a household in the Italian capital. One, a wonderful British lady named Margaret, mailed me a copy of *Wanted in Rome,* a weekly English-language magazine that serves as a kind of pennysaver newspaper for the entire English-speaking community in the city. I placed, via e-mail, a classified ad for a "mother's aide" in *Wanted in Rome* and gave our new telephone number in Rome.

It took many months of preparation, but at last we were off. After a glorious week strolling around Paris with the kids, we flew to Rome. From the plane, the hills of Umbria were green and lush, dotted with hundreds of orange-colored tile roofs. The Mediterranean also seemed so close to Rome it looked as though you could walk to it (as I guess the ancient Romans did). It was just a two-hour trip from Paris on the Air France 737, but we seemed to have crossed multiple time zones.

After we were virtually waved through customs, we stepped outside into the warm sunlight and were immediately swept up by a typical unlicensed Roman taxi hustler (the kind any decent guidebook would warn you against) who offered to take me, my wife, our three kids, eight bags, and a baby stroller to our apartment for "just" 110,000 lire. (Later, I would learn to take the local train to the Trastevere station for 5,000.) The driver, a large, hairy fellow who looked like a leftover extra from the film *Saturday Night Fever*—all tight black pants and gold chains— spoke not a word of English. We looked up the street where the apartment was located on his map. He just smiled and said, "No problem." Before we knew it, we were careening down the autostrada at 110 miles an hour in a dark blue Mercedes station wagon toward Rome and our new home.

Just for the record: Our first sight in the Eternal City was not St. Peter's or the Colosseum. It was a gigantic billboard with two perfectly spherical breasts, each twenty feet high, with a baby's smiling face between them. It was as though someone had taken this month's Playmate of the Month, stuck the pages into a really big color copier—cutting off everything above the neck and below the waist—and plastered the result on a wall. A caption said, "Pre-Natal: Nuovo Generation," and it appeared to be some kind of promotional ad for prenatal care. We were definitely not in Kansas anymore. A billboard ad like that would cause a forty-car pileup on any American freeway.

Irish Bob's apartment turned out to be more beautiful than we expected. It was located on a private, gate-guarded street, Via Aristide

Busi, across from the Villa Doria Pamphili—a large, somewhat rustic park filled with grassy fields, lakes, and towering Aleppo pine trees. To open the gate that led into Via Busi, you had to insert a special plastic key, which Irish Bob had sent to me in advance, into a little box off to the side. Via Busi was actually up a steep hill, but at the top was a large compound circled by a twenty-foot-high red plaster wall, in which were found four four-story brick condos.

In the center area of the compound was a little park with a tennis court, and at the high locked metal gate (which required a different key) was a gatehouse in which lived the gatekeeper, or *portiera,* who watched over the entire complex and let you in when you forgot your key.

The *portiera* frightened me from the start. Like many Italian women over the age of ten, she had a perpetual snarl on her face. Plus, she looked as though she could beat me, *easily,* in arm wrestling. She was short, squat, strong, and fat all at once, with hair dyed neon red, thick black eyebrows, and a wispy mustache. She was called, by everyone, simply The Portiera. Like nearly everyone in Italy, she didn't speak a single word of English. She did, however, have a pet parrot, whom she called (appropriately enough, because it's the Italian word for parrot) Pappagallo. Every day as he walked through the gate, my three-year-old son, James, was to shout, "Ciao, Pappagallo!"

The interior of the apartment was far more elegant than our town house back in California. It was a huge three-bedroom place, with fifteen-foot-high ceilings, crown moldings, green marble and wood parquet floors, and crystal chandeliers. There were balconies off both the master bedroom and the living room that overlooked the central garden and tennis court. The kitchen was very small, with a refrigerator most Americans would put under their bar to stock beer and olives in, but not to store food for a family of five. There was a primitive washing machine, but, to my wife's horror, no dryer. The hot water heaters were about the size of a barrel and located above the shower in one bathroom, and above the bathtub in another. There was a bidet, of course, in the bathroom, and James, our three-year-old, quickly peed in it.

The Italian owners, Franca and Massimo, were there waiting for us when we arrived by taxi from Fiumicino airport.

They were an outwardly friendly, well-dressed couple in their late fifties who, we quickly saw, spoke not a single word of English. Irish Bob had told us that two or three people from his office in Rome would meet us to translate, but they had not shown up.

Fortunately, both Massimo and I were able to mimic some of the sounds of the French language and that, along with a lengthy and rather robust game of charades, allowed us to communicate adequately. He gave me a quick tour of the building, showed me where the circuit breakers were located (an ominous sign, I thought), and dropped the massive, almost medieval keys in my palm.

Welcome to Rome, he said.

The next day we set out to explore our new home. We went in search of a local *alimentari,* a grocery store, to buy some food.

We lived in what appeared to be a fairly affluent Roman neighborhood, far away from the hustle and bustle of the city center. Our private street dead-ended after a block, but there was a small gate to the right of our complex that led out to an empty lot and then, directly in front of it, to a small traffic circle, Piazza Ceresi. In the middle of the traffic circle were parked dozens of cars.

Three roads fed into this small traffic circle, with cars whipping around it at a velocity I never thought possible with land vehicles. I was nearly killed three times walking just twenty feet. When Italian drivers see you step onto a zebra crossing, they go full speed so they can beat you through it.

One road, lined with small shops and bars, led down a short hill to Via Vitellia, a large one-way street that ran along the high walls of the Villa Doria Pamphili. Another road veered off toward a very modern-looking church, the Shrine of Our Lady of La Salette, which had a gigantic brick tower visible for miles around; and the third went uphill to the Piazza San Giovanni di Dio, which was a major shopping area on the Gianicolense, one of Rome's major thoroughfares. Fronting the Piazza San Giovanni di Dio was a covered open-air market, like a farmers' market, that would figure prominently in our lives for the rest of the year. It was a loud, boisterous place full of pushy Italian matrons with their pull-along shopping carts. I loved it.

We could see immediately that Glenn was going to need help taking care of the kids while I was off lunching with the pope and whatnot. There was no way she was going to be able to get out, with two little kids and a toddler, and do any shopping. Italy is not a stroller-friendly country. The sidewalks are interrupted every ten feet by driveways that drop off like sheer cliffs, and are usually littered anyway with parked cars. And given that our refrigerator could only hold enough food to feed a cat, we were going to have to shop every day, the way Italians do.

Luckily, that very afternoon, after we returned from exploring the neighborhood, we received an unexpected telephone call. Glenn answered. It was a young woman calling about the ad I had so presciently placed a month earlier in *Wanted in Rome* for a housekeeper and cook. The ad read: *Writers need mother's aide (light housekeeping, cooking) 30 hours per week. Must speak fluent Italian, some English. Near Villa Doria Pamphili. Interview. Call (6) 534-———.*

Glenn hung up the phone. "Who was that?" I asked.

"Oh, just someone responding to your ad," she said. "A Swedish girl, twenty-seven. She's lived here eight years, speaks fluent English and Italian, and her last job was taking care of three little kids."

I smiled. Glenn glared.

"Sounds perfect," I said. "You said you wanted some help."

"Well, I was thinking that maybe an older *Italian* woman might be more useful. She'd know how things really work around here, and wouldn't mind shopping and all that."

"Yes, yes, that's true," I countered. "But it would really help to have someone who speaks fluent English. And the kids might be more comfortable with a nice Swedish girl than with a snarling old lady."

Glenn called the young woman back and made an appointment.

The young Swedish woman turned out to be a lifesaver. Her name was Anne, pronounced *ah-nay*. She made our time in Rome not only bearable but fun. She was blond and beautiful, it's true, but Glenn quickly forgave her her good looks when she realized that she was great with kids, a hard worker, and knew Rome inside out.

We spent the next week getting reacquainted with the city. Neither of us had been there for a long time. It was shabbier than I remembered, with more clutter and graffiti, but still magical.

Glenn, Anne, and I took the kids to all the obvious tourist sites— the Colosseum and the Forum, the Pantheon, the Mouth of Truth in Santa Maria in Cosmedin, the Piazza Navona, Trastevere, Trevi Fountain, the Spanish Steps. We had a marvelous time. The kids had their pictures taken with the Roman soldiers, in full centurion glory, who stand outside the Colosseum for the tourists, usually half bombed.

At that time I was avoiding tourist guidebooks and reading the travel books of great writers who had visited Rome—particularly Henry James's *Italian Hours* and Goethe's *Italian Journey*. As a result, I kept dragging everyone off to see more obscure literary sites, such as Goethe's house on the Via del Corso . . . or the room where Keats died. This bored the kids no end, of course, although at least the Keats House is located just two or three doors down from a McDonald's, where they could get Happy Meals. We stayed away from the Vatican, because we knew the kids would go there dozens of times in the months ahead.

Eventually we settled in. We figured out the bus system. We found the one *alimentari* in our neighborhood that stocked throw-away diapers (what the Italians call *pannolini*.) We located a local newsstand that sold the *International Herald Tribune* and a pizzeria, L'Arte della Pizza on the Via Federico Ozanam, that sold delicious prosciutto calzone for just a buck. We got to know our way around the open market—and such indispensable Italian phrases as "Just a half kilo, please" and "When do you think the ATM machine will be fixed?"

After a week, it was time for me to go to work.

III

The Code of Silence

We lived by a very simple rule. If you talk, you die.

JOE VALACHI

The first order of business, once we were settled in, was for me to get press credentials at the Sala Stampa della Santa Sede, the Vatican Press Office. I took a taxi from our apartment down the Gianicolo hill—not having figured out the bus route yet—to St. Peter's Square. The Sala Stampa was and still is located at 54 Via della Conciliazione—one small part of two massive, four-story buildings, the Palazzi dei Propilei, which face each other across the piazza in front of St. Peter's Square. The same building that houses the Sala Stampa also houses various Vatican offices as well as souvenir stores on the ground floor.

On the day I arrived it was pouring rain. Hundreds of tourists were crowded into the large covered portico that stands out in front of the offices in this building. In front of the door stood two guards in blue uniforms, but they didn't try to stop me as I sauntered in.

I had heard horror stories, of course, about the Sala Stampa. When one famous priest-journalist, Andrew Greeley, began researching a new book on the Vatican back in the mid-1970s, it took him nearly two years of regular visits to Rome before the press office finally deigned to give him press credentials. And without press credentials—or an uncle who happened to be a high-ranking curial cardinal—the chances of getting past the Swiss Guards into the inner sanctums of Vatican City were, it was said, next to nil.

Also, even when you did manage to get accredited, the Sala Stampa staff was said to behave in the same paranoid and controlling manner as the Kremlin's Intourist "guides" did at the height of the Cold War.

Apparently, the Vatican is under the not-unfounded impression that journalists are a group of ill-bred, sarcastic pagans who would mock the holiest aspects of Catholicism if given half the chance. So why give them that chance?

To make matters worse, there are actually two overlapping agencies in the Vatican that attempt to control all information about the Holy See that appears in the media. The first is the Sala Stampa, which has become slightly more cooperative over the years, especially following the appointment of the taciturn Basque journalist Dr. Joaquin Navarro-Valls as its head in the mid-1980s. He helped win independence for the Sala Stampa from the second agency, the Pontifical Council for Social Communications, located in a bland office building inside the Vatican, near the Piazza Santa Marta.

The council functions in effect as the chief censor of the Roman Catholic Church, for it tightly controls what information may be released to the media and, more important, which media agencies are allowed access to that information. Like most Vatican departments, it is supposedly run by a bishop or archbishop, who changes every few years, but the real power is exercised by a permanent executive staff.

Irish Bob sent me a last-minute message with a piece of advice for dealing with the Vatican. I quote: "Please be jolly, witty, friendly, amiable, and leave a generally positive impression; don't be cantankerous, irritable, demanding, pushy, like I can be—it leaves a bad impression and the Vatican has a long memory. . . . Trust me: You'll get further if you do not inspire paranoia!"

The Sala Stampa itself is a bright, modern office complex with gleaming black marble floors and sliding glass security doors in front. I showed the guards a letter the Sala Stampa sent to me in the United States, instructing me to "present" myself upon my arrival in Rome, and they let me in. The staff was expecting me.

After I sat for a few moments on a couch, a plump middle-aged Italian nun with bifocals introduced herself and had me sit down in her office while she looked through my portfolio of magazine articles. She spoke so softly I could barely hear her, but her little birdlike eyes watched me intently, as though I might be a rare species of snake that could strike at any moment. Her name was Suor (Sister) Giovanna.

Suor Giovanna asked me to provide her with two color photographs, a photocopy of my passport, and a letter from my "director."

"You can get a letter from your director, yes?" she said firmly in broken English, more a command than a question.

I explained that well, actually, being self-employed all my adult life, I had no "director." I didn't even have a boss, unless, of course, she counted my wife.

The nun didn't smile. I cleared my throat. Obviously, the thought that someone might be utterly beyond the control of a "director" apparently struck her as suspiciously unconventional, even a bit bohemian.

Perhaps I could talk a magazine editor out of some kind of letter, I said. Would that do?

The good sister looked doubtful, but it was obvious that someone had already decided to grant me accreditation, against her better judgment, based on my past performance as a magazine writer and a letter from my publisher that I was under contract to write a book.

Suor Giovanna then explained the rules.

They would let me use their facilities, such as phone and fax provided I paid for them. I could conduct interviews within the Vatican precincts provided I was able to find someone who would be willing to talk to me. I could read the official press releases (the *bollettini*) provided I knew fluent Italian. And I could attend press conferences provided I knew about when they would be held.

As for any help setting up interviews or answering any questions, forget it. The Sala Stampa did none of that. I was on my own.

I was to learn later that the Vatican harbors a special distrust of authors, precisely because they are more difficult to control. Journalists working for newspapers or magazines can be *punished* if they are too frank in their reports about the Holy See. Irish Bob, for example—who now publishes a magazine dedicated to the Vatican—was banned from the Sala Stampa for an entire year. And one of the first things Navarro-Valls did, upon being named chief of the Sala Stampa, was to ban Domenico Del Rio, the religious affairs writer for *La Repubblica,* from flying on the papal plane with the rest of the Vatican press corps. Del Rio had written one too many articles critical of the pope, even going so far as to call him a "showman."

Authors, in contrast, unless they plan an entire series of books on the papacy, are less vulnerable to such vengeful tactics.

My application for press credentials taken care of, I decided to go meet some journalist friends I knew who worked at a French press agency in Rome. I had known these people for years; they used to buy some of my articles and translate them for use in Europe. One of the reporters who rented an office there, a good-natured, boyish-looking former UPI staffer named Greg Burke, was all that was left of the dwindling Rome bureau of *Time* magazine.

I found the office only after driving all over the city, with an Italian friend of mine, the rest of the morning. The agency's secretary, who had a thick French accent, had told me over the telephone that the office was on "Forza" Pallavicini. In fact, it was on Sforza Pallavicini—the difference of that single "S" being roughly the distance between a piazza a few miles south of my apartment and an office next door to Castel Sant'Angelo. A distance, in other words, of ten miles or more.

We finally figured out the error and my friend dropped me off on the banks of the Tiber, near the Vittorio Emanuele bridge. I walked across, staring up at the fortress of Castel Sant'Angelo, and found the correct address.

Greg, friendly and buoyant as ever, was in good spirits despite the recent cutbacks among American news organizations. All the big news groups were slashing their overseas budgets like so much salami. "You see that phone," Greg told me when I arrived, pointing to an old-fashioned Italian phone sitting on his cluttered desk. "That's the Rome bureau of *Time* magazine." *Newsweek* had downgraded its Rome bureau to nothing more than a single stringer, paid by the word, working out of his apartment. And while we were chatting, Greg got a call about a major layoff at one of the TV networks.

I knew that Greg was quickly gaining a reputation as a veteran Vatican correspondent, at least for the English-speaking world. He'd been in Rome seven years, spoke fluent Italian. We'd last met in Princeton, New Jersey, shortly before he left for Rome.

Greg told me that covering the Vatican was actually *worse* than you might expect. Reporters are trained to expect politicians to lie to them; but even politicians will tell you *something,* if only so they don't look as if they're covering things up. But the Vatican has no such scruples.

The Sala Stampa office tells you absolutely nothing, merely handing out press releases (*bollettini*) prepared by other offices and expecting everyone to be satisfied with that. With a little patience you can eventually make some contacts with people who actually do work in the Vatican, but when you sit them down to discuss something, even something utterly trivial—say, for example, whether the pope prefers to write encyclicals in longhand or with a computer—they immediately insist that they can't speak on the record.

When you point out to them that you are, after all, talking about writing implements, not state secrets, the carefully cultivated contacts wring their hands and look as though they're about to pass out from the stress of being interrogated in such an aggressive manner.

Then, of course, the higher-ranking people in the Vatican, Greg said, had mastered the art of the un-interview. He put his cigarette lighter on the table. That, he said, pointing to the lighter, is the topic at hand—say, church finances or declining vocations to the priesthood.

Then Greg traced an imaginary line all around the lighter that kept winding back and around and below and above the lighter, but never actually got around to the lighter.

That's how Vatican officials operate. They chitchat, never talk. "Oh, so you're from Los Angeles, are you?" they'll say. "Yes, yes. Marvelous city, that. Been there twice myself. Were you born there?"

It took me only a week to discover what Greg was talking about. The Vatican puts on a friendly face to all the souvenir-buying, alms-paying tourists; but once you move beyond Bernini's columns into the inner offices of the Curia, the smiling face all too often turns into a snarl.

The first person to snarl at me was an old lady named Marjorie, the all-powerful doyenne of the Pontifical Council for Social Communications. An American woman from Whittier, California, Marjorie had worked in the Vatican since the days of Pope John XXIII in the early 1960s, slowly climbing her way up the Vatican bureaucracy. Despite her position as de facto head of the Vatican's public relations office, Marjorie had a reputation for being utterly obstructionist. "Anything you want to do in the Vatican, you have to figure out a way to go around Marjorie," one woman journalist had told me. "She won't lift a finger to help anyone."

But I had been told, in a memo from the Sala Stampa, that Marjorie "is the person responsible for arranging filming and photography accreditation and who on longer-term projects such as these [books] facilitates interviews and curial introductions."

Not only that, everyone I spoke to in the Vatican said they wouldn't talk to me until and unless Marjorie said it was okay.

So, naturally, I called her up.

"How did you get this number," she shrieked as soon as she answered the phone. "This is my private number! You're not supposed to call here! I could have been in a meeting!"

"I found this number in the *Elenco Telefonico,* the Vatican phone book," I replied.

"Oh, you must have an old phone book!" she said. "That number was changed last year. Don't call here again. What do you want?"

Somewhat startled by her hostility, I explained that I was in Rome seeing the sights and working on a book, and that I had been told by the Sala Stampa that she was the person to help arrange interviews for book-length projects.

"Absolutely not!" Marjorie replied, now nearly in a rage. "Absolutely not! All I handle is photography. You have to find someone else to help you. The Sala Stampa is supposed to help you. Go talk to them. Now, if you'll excuse me . . ."

I quickly explained that the people at the Sala Stampa had said they *don't* help set up interviews, that I have to arrange for them myself, on my own, but that everyone I called, in every department, insisted that she, Marjorie, had to give her approval before they could speak with me.

"Well, they're wrong!" she snapped. "I don't have time for people like you! You just have to call people up and see if they're interested in wasting their time with you. People are tired. They don't want to be bothered. I'm sorry, but I gotta go."

And then she hung up on me.

I quickly discovered that this is a popular game Vatican (and, to be fair, Roman) bureaucrats play, setting up elaborate Catch-22 situations—Department A saying you must talk to Department B, and Department B saying you must talk to Department A—in the hope that the annoying petitioner or journalist will eventually be worn down and simply go away.

A few days later, I called up the Pontifical Institute for Christian Archaeology. I was researching a particular point about St. Peter's Basilica and wanted to set up an interview with the institute's president, a French monsignor. His assistant, a priest, answered the phone, and gruffly told me that his boss was away on a trip to Moscow. I asked if there were any other experts at the Pontifical Institute to whom I could turn for information. The priest replied, and this is a quote, "No, no, no, no, no, no, no, no, no," and then hung up the phone.

Later that morning I called the Centro Elaborazione Dati, the Vatican's central computer office, to ask about the then-brand-new Vatican Internet site. The priest who answered the phone nearly flipped out. "How did you get this number?" he screamed. "If you're a journalist, you know I can't talk to you! I can't even give you my name! You have to talk to Marjorie!"

And then he, too, hung up.

Astute investigative journalist that I am, I was beginning to notice a pattern. I called up a friendly priest I knew who worked in one of the

Vatican congregations and asked to meet him for lunch. He agreed. We met at a small, out-of-the-way place in the Borgo.

He let me rant for five minutes, chuckling into his cannelloni. "My God, you really don't have a clue, do you?" he finally said.

And then he explained to me about the Vatican's Omertà, the Code of Silence.

The Omertà is the Mafia's famous Code of Silence, in which made members of the Italian underworld are forced to swear a blood oath that if they reveal any secrets of the Mafia they will sacrifice their lives.

Like the Mafia, the Vatican imposes the same Omertà on its employees—in some cases, almost literally. Staff members of many dicasteries, such as the Secretariat of State or the Sacred Congregation for the Doctrine of the Faith, must take special oaths in which they promise total secrecy or face excommunication. There is actually a special office in the Curia, the Disciplinary Commission of the Roman Curia, that, as one writer put it, "handles matters arising from a breach of confidentiality in Curia affairs." Everyone who works in the Vatican—from the Swiss Guards to the staff editors of *L'Osservatore Romano*—knows that speaking to anyone without permission, especially a reporter, is to invite the death penalty . . . banishment back home to Indiana.

There are some exceptions to this, as you'll see throughout this book, brave souls who are either too valuable or too senior in rank to worry about the Code of Silence. But they are rare. As a result, Vatican reporters jealously guard their handful of contacts who will speak freely (off the record, of course); they will even trade them, like poker chips. "I'll tell you what," a reporter might say, "I'll give you my guy in the Secretariat of State if you can get my photographer into the Swiss Guards' barracks."

All of this is incredibly damaging to the Church's reputation. Vatican officials, in their oh-so-ancient wisdom, believe they should carefully select and give access to the five percent of reporters whom they judge to be harmless to the interests of the Holy See—in other words, those pious journalists who won't let a critical word pass their lips. Like the old Kremlin, the Vatican wants to see only good news written about it, and its strategy to make sure only good news is written is to allow only reporters it can "trust" into its hallowed halls. One bishop told me that I should never write anything critical about the Holy See, because, after all, it's "beaten up enough" by the pagan secular media and so a good Catholic like myself should write only positive things.

Beyond the self-serving nature of such a suggestion lies the inescapable fact that the Vatican's media relations policy *doesn't work*. It would be one thing if the world's newspapers, magazines, and television shows were wrapped around the papacy's write-gloved finger; but in point of fact the Vatican faces a media establishment that is, with a few exceptions, often hostile.

Having spoken with Marjorie, I now know why.

From a purely public relations point of view, what the Vatican does in order to select its five percent of "trustworthy" reporters is to alienate and make implacable enemies out of the ninety-five percent who don't pass the Holy See's litmus tests.

Early on, I managed to meet a high-level official in a congregation because I was acquainted with an Italian journalist who knew him well. The official agreed to meet with me only because I knew this Italian journalist and because I promised I would not mention his name.

This official was an extremely genial, even expansive host, and he shared with me a number of fascinating insider perspectives on the Apostolic Palace. But after a while he started telling me about another journalist who had called him the same day I did, a religion reporter from a major East Coast daily who was in Rome doing some background stories on the Vatican. The reporter had called him up because they happened to be from the same city in America, the official said, "and that immediately set off a warning signal for me." He continued: "That means this guy was checking up on me, he knew where I was from."

He said it as though this were something nefarious, like a CIA plot or something.

"So what?" I asked, genuinely perplexed. "*Of course* this reporter asked around to find out which prelate in the Vatican was from his hometown. He figured that would give him some kind of in, some shared area of interest. He thought you'd see him because you might be loyal to your hometown newspaper."

The prelate just nodded his head, pretending to understand my point. But he confided that he had refused to see this reporter and even chuckled that the reporter would almost certainly be shut out of almost every Vatican office, because he didn't have the proper connections.

I was appalled. I knew if that happened, all these smarmy Vatican bureaucrats were doing was ensuring that in every story this reporter would ever write about the Vatican, for the rest of his life probably, he'd go out of his way to make a little dig. And sure enough, six months later I happened upon a wire story written by this very reporter, datelined "from Vatican City" with the title, "Rumblings of the Papacy in Decline." The reporter quoted primarily other journalists, the *vaticanisti*—always a sign of limited access—and his conclusions, while balanced and certainly defensible, had a distinctly negative, even gloomy tinge.

That Friday night I had dinner with a delightful, witty, urbane priest who calls himself Friar Tuck, which is the pen name he uses when writing restaurant reviews for a local magazine.

Friar Tuck looked for all the world like the American country singer Lyle Lovett: Very tall, very thin, with a long, tight face topped by this outrageously vertical mass of brown hair. It looked as if he just stuck his tongue into one of those round European 220-volt electrical outlets.

He was actually a forty-year-old British academic, doctor of sacred theology, professor at various pontifical universities in Rome, fluent in six languages (the usual: English, French, German, Italian, Latin, and Greek). He was dressed, not in Roman collar, but in a fashionable collarless shirt, three-piece suit, no tie. His passion was mystery novels—and American movies. I asked him to be my guide to Italian cuisine, and he threw himself into his assignment with gusto.

After a quick drink at a pub, the good friar (he's actually a diocesan priest) took me to what he assured me was an "authentic Roman" restaurant, Il Matriciano, located on Via dei Gracchi in the upscale Prati district next to the Borgo—about ten minutes' walk from St. Peter's Square. We arrived around eight o'clock, early for Italians, and found we were the first ones there.

"Now, there are many different types of Italian food, you must understand," Friar Tuck began in his soft, very posh BBC voice. "There's Ambrosian, Milanese. But this is the *cucina romanesca,* what the Romans eat."

I saw the framed photographs of World War II fighter aircraft on the walls—and then noticed the color of the flags painted on the planes: orange, green, and white. It dawned on me that these were the planes of Fascist Italy they were celebrating. I wondered if in a good restaurant in Munich you'd find similar photos of the Luftwaffe hanging proudly over steaming plates of sauerbraten and schnitzel.

Friar Tuck started off with a soup, while I dove right in and ordered the *tagliolini alla baccorola,* little round tubes of pasta stuffed with bacon and cheese and served in a hot, spicy chicken broth. It was *delizioso,* I told the waiter suavely, only to be told that Italians usually say *squisito.*

While we both slurped our soups, we discussed the frustrations my fellow writers have when covering the Vatican.

Friar Tuck, who once worked inside the Apostolic Palace and had spent twenty years in Rome, said he entirely sympathized. But you have to understand, he added quickly, that the Vatican has been around a very long time; it's quite literally seen empires come and go, witnessed the rise and fall of entire dynasties, philosophies, and nations. *The New York Times* may feel that when it asks a question, by God it deserves an answer by the close of business that day, but the Vatican simply doesn't share that view.

I looked around us. The place was now packed with locals, not a tourist among them. Sitting next to us were two young Italian women in their late twenties wearing plunging, tight black dresses and covered in gold jewelry. They were laughing loudly and drinking red wine. I noticed the girls; my new friend the priest-gourmet noticed the social status of the other patrons. "There must be some sort of VIPs here tonight," he commented. "Look at all the hired help waiting outside." And indeed, there appeared to be a number of drivers or other assistants waiting outside the restaurant, smoking.

After polishing off my *tagliolini,* I ordered *straccetti di pezza,* which turned out to be shredded beef strips with little pieces of rogeta mixed in. The herbs gave the dish a light, zesty taste. I poured myself another glass of the house red wine we'd ordered and returned to our topic.

"I understand all about how old and venerable the Vatican is," I said, "but my colleagues complain that the Vatican is secretive about the most trivial things. If you ask some official whether the pope writes encyclicals with a ballpoint pen or a computer, you're likely to be told that this information is confidential. Or to be asked why you want to know? This is not an important state secret."

Friar Tuck merely sighed. He thought for a moment.

"You see, in many ways the Vatican is like an aging woman who is long past her prime and knows it," he said finally. "She's desperately attempting to maintain her dignity and what little allure she has left. As a result, when some pushy journalist starts asking all these seemingly trivial but sometimes very personal questions, the Vatican can be very testy. She feels, in a sense, that it's an inappropriate invasion of her privacy . . . but she'll answer your question if she's in a good mood and if you ask respectfully and at the right time."

It was then my turn to sigh.

Friar Tuck gave me a look as if to say "Chin up, old boy," and suggested we order dessert. I had crème brûlée, Italian style—all chopped up on a plate—and the noble friar had fruit.

It was going to be an interesting trip.

IV

An Evening Out
with the Pope

The famous Miserere was sung this afternoon in the Sistine Chapel.
The saying at Rome is, that it cannot be imitated, not only by any other
choir, but in any other chapel in the world. The Emperor of Austria
sent Mozart to Rome on purpose to have it sung at Vienna with like effect,
but it failed.

RALPH WALDO EMERSON, *Journals*, April 3, 1833

A week or so went by, and then one morning Glenn and I picked up
the phone and heard this recording of an Italian woman. She used
words like *bolletta* and Telecom Italia and *per contratto*. Fluent in Italian
as we were, we quickly deduced that our phone had been disconnected
. . . and assumed that Massimo and Franca, the owners of the apartment,
had not paid their phone bill.

As it turned out, they hadn't paid *any* of their bills.

Rather than asking for some kind of utilities deposit, their strategy was not to pay their bills for six months, have everything eventually be turned off, and thus force their tenants into paying all of the utility bills in advance. That way, they didn't have to worry about tenants skipping out on unpaid bills—or at least I think that was their strategy. It could be they just didn't feel like paying the bills for an apartment in which they didn't live.

Like everything else in Rome, getting the phone turned back on was a major undertaking. First of all, since we no longer had a phone, we couldn't call anyone—let alone anyone who spoke English—to find out how to fix it. We had Anne call the phone company when she got home that first night, and she reported back the next day that, yes, the phone was indeed disconnected. We had to go down to the nearest post office with a copy of our bill (which we found buried in a drawer) and pay it.

As a result, the next day Glenn, Anne, and our three kids walked up to the post office, located about two miles away on the other side of San Giovanni di Dio. They paid the rather sizable bill, in cash of course, and came home. Four, five days went by—and still no phone. Finally Glenn went back up to the post office. They said, well, you paid the most *recent* bill, but there was still an outstanding bill from the last cycle—which, of course, they hadn't mentioned the first time. The owners, we then discovered, had not paid the phone bill for six months. We paid the second bill and waited.

It was a serious inconvenience, because I had written letters to and called many Vatican officials asking for interviews, and now it appeared that they couldn't call me back. I worried that they might assume I had left Rome. More trips to the post office ensued, more calls by Anne when she went home at night.

All this time, if I wanted to call anyone, I had to walk two blocks down Via Francesco Catel to Via Ozanam, where there was a public phone. In those days, and probably still today, the public phones in Italy used these special cardboard debit cards that you bought at tobacco shops in denominations of 5,000 lire. I always lost mine. Whenever I went to use the phone, I'd paw my pockets, looking for a phone card, and then have to go over to the tobacco store and buy a new one.

I finally found it easier to use a phone in the Sala Stampa.

It was during one of these marathon telephone sessions that Suor Giovanna came up to me and asked if I'd like to attend a special concert for the pope.

"You want to see the pope, yes?" she declared in her no-argument way. The birdlike eyes glittered behind her glasses. There was to be a special command performance of Handel's *Messiah* by the Austrian National Symphony and Choir in two weeks. Because I was . . . drumroll, please . . . an official Vatican correspondent, I was able to get tickets; but I had to sign up right then.

I replied that my wife enjoys Handel's *Messiah* immensely and would surely love to go. The plump nun walked me over to the main desk by the door, fished around for a clipboard, and put me down for two tickets. I noticed that various other members of the cynical Vatican press corps were going—Catholic News Service had two tickets, RAI had a couple, even *The New York Times* was showing up. Most of these people preferred to watch papal events on Telepace, the Vatican's version of C-SPAN, from the warmth and comfort of their Sala Stampa cubbyholes.

I had yet to see the pope at this point, except as a dim white blob on TV, and was looking forward to the evening. I wondered where we'd sit.

Finally, the night of the concert arrived.

Anne had agreed to baby-sit, and Glenn and I piled into a taxi around five o'clock. We told the driver to let us off at the Sant'Ufficio, the Holy Office, which was close to the courtyard entrance to the Audience Hall. Glenn and I climbed out of the taxi, only to see a long line of people, most dressed in suits or evening gowns, proceeding through a police barricade. We got into line and waited. After fifteen minutes or so we came to the barricade and an Italian policeman waved a metal detector over my body—but not, I noticed, over Glenn, who was wearing a rather tight dark blue dress. I quickly thought that were I a terrorist out to assassinate the pope, I'd plant the bomb on a sexy blonde and count on Italian chivalry to get it through security.

The Paul VI Audience Hall—or *Áula,* as it is known around the Vatican—was built in 1970 by the Italian architect Pier Luigi Nervi. It's just the sort of ultra-mod, curvy concrete structure you see on college campuses and which today, like most things from the 1970s, looks about as silly as bell-bottom pants on a U.S. senator. The inside has high curved ceilings that appear to be made out of panels of light. On the sides are large oval windows of colored glass.

Down in front, on the main stage, lies what looks for all the world like a gigantic piece of orange coral—with hundreds of thick rocky tendrils seeming to grow out of a central honeycomb—but which is, in fact, some kind of weird modern sculpture. It turns out the thing was made out of bronze by the artist Pericle Fazzini, allegedly a favorite of Jackie Onassis's. In the center of this orange mass is a large piece of coral that is supposed to be, I think, the Risen Christ. Modern art has never been my thing. When I look at a Jackson Pollock painting, I just see a ground cloth some house painters left behind after a job. Glenn, on the other hand, was raised by parents who love and appreciate modern art, and she was impressed.

The *Áula* normally seats 6,500 people but can accommodate twice that number without the seats. The auditorium curves downward toward a central "stage" in front. The stage is actually just two blocks of steps—a first set made of white marble leading up to a second set covered in red carpet. Normally, as during weekly Wednesday audiences in the winter, the papal throne is positioned in the center of the red-carpeted platform. Behind that lies the coral reef.

This evening, though, as Glenn and I walked through the main doors, we could see that the *sampietrini* had set up some risers from which the Austrian National Choir would sing.

Swiss Guards, sporting their black berets, directed us this way and that. We figured that as writers and journalists or whatever, the Vatican would have us sit back in the cloakroom, with all the other riffraff.

Much to our astonishment, however, when we came in some Swiss Guards led us over to the far left wall, and then down the side aisle to a row about one third of the way up from the central stage. We walked in the row all the way back to the central aisle and sat down. Great seats!

In front of us was another aisle that cut across the auditorium from left to right. It divided a block of seats in front—plainly occupied by VIPs, diplomats, and visiting celebrities—from the rest of the seats. You could tell the occupants were diplomats and VIPs because the men wore white tails and sashes and the women wore sequined gowns. We sat in the first row of the cheap seats with assorted grubby journalists and "junior diplomats."

A young priest behind us, with a dark black beard and wild eyes, introduced himself. His name was Father Juan Daniel Alcorlo San José. He was a reporter for a Spanish newspaper, *Vida Nueva,* but spoke only Spanish, Italian, and German. We had some mutual friends. He was very friendly and kept trying to communicate with us. I kept trying French, he kept trying German, and we ended up not understanding a single word either of us was saying. Glenn had better luck with a young Chilean consular official next to her, who was stationed, he said, at Chile's embassy in Cairo. He was impeccably dressed in a light brown gabardine suit. I had spent a few weeks in Cairo, so we quickly struck up a conversation, trading stories about Tahrir Square and the crazy Egyptian buses.

Eventually, Glenn nudged me and pointed to an old yellow chair that was standing in the center aisle directly next to us and which we hadn't noticed before. It looked like a comfortable but worn living room chair, something you might flop down in to watch a little TV. The back needed to be reupholstered.

Glenn and I traded looks, then both shook our heads, dismissing the idea outright.

"Nah, that couldn't be what I think it is, could it?" I said.

"Definitely not."

The German-speaking Spanish priest was less sure. He said something in German that I thought meant, "Maybe."

Suddenly, the entire auditorium erupted into what can be described only as pandemonium. Everyone leapt to their feet, yelling and screaming. The pope came shuffling down the center aisle above us, shaking hands, photographers walking in front of him (backward), snapping shot after shot. Only two or three priests accompanied him.

The distinguished white-tie and bejeweled crowd was acting like teenage girls at a rock concert, squealing and lunging out to touch the pope. I had never seen anything like this. The nuns were the worst, chanting these strange rhythmic chants in Spanish and pushing and shoving their way to the center aisle. "*El Papa! El Papa!*" they screamed. "*Viva el Papa!*"

Glenn and I were straining our necks to catch a brief glimpse of the man, when, much to our astonishment, he proceeded to walk right over to us and stand in front of the old yellow chair.

We couldn't believe it! Suor Giovanna had given us the seats right next to the pope. He was literally five feet away.

The three priests who walked down the aisle with the pope sat on folding chairs placed directly in front of us and across from, it turned out, the papal throne. Two of the priests had gray hair. One I recognized as the papal secretary, but the one in the middle was about twenty-five years old, with a thick neck and close-cropped crew cut. He looked like a U.S. marine, not a priest. "Bodyguard," I whispered to Glenn, nodding my head toward the young priest.

I also noticed dispersed throughout the crowd, in our area, heavy-set men in suits with what looked like hearing aids in their ears. Either there was an epidemic of deafness in the Vatican or those were under-cover Swiss Guards.

The noise was deafening. The crowd just kept clapping and clapping. There were a few whistles and howls as well.

Down in front, and on the other side of the pope, sat the cardinals, dressed in their crimson-fringed black cassocks and skullcaps. *They* didn't clap.

After waving with that palms-up wave that only popes use—described by my pagan friends as the same gesture a man would use to pantomime a woman with really large breasts—the pope sat down in his yellow TV chair. The crowd calmed down and eventually sat as well.

Then the concert began.

Handel's *Messiah* is an oratorio, which my dictionary says is sort of like an opera only without the stage props, costumes, or colorful scenery that make an opera tolerable. Basically, it's a very long collection of hymns sung by people with either very deep or very high voices. I try my best to be a cultured guy—I mean, I read books and all—but I was soon bored senseless. I assumed the same was true of many of the cardinals, because I saw more than one red-capped white head bobbing up and down, a sure sign that there was some cardinalatial snoozing going on.

The pope, much to my astonishment, remained entirely focused throughout the entire evening, never once dozing off. I know this because I spent most of the time, as did everyone else around me, watching him. It occurred to me that part of his special training as pope was to develop a preternatural capacity to endure boredom—such as hour after hour of tedious ceremonies, year in and year out, without letup.

I tried not to stare, looking sideways until I thought my eyes might get stuck in that position; but we all were so close, we could see the white hair in his ears, the broken capillaries on his cheeks. I'd never been within a football-stadium length of a pope before, and here I was within spitting distance.

The pope's secretary, I saw, also spent most of his time closely watching his boss, whether for fear of his health or fear that he might doze off, I'm not sure. But he never took his eyes off the pope.

The concert dragged on for what seemed like an eternity with no break. I had forgotten that *The Messiah* is actually in English, and so at least I could understand the words. Finally, after the only part I really knew—the rousing HALL . . . *lay-lou-yah!* HALL . . . *lay-lou-yah!*—the concert came to an end.

The pope stood up promptly and a microphone appeared out of nowhere in front of his yellow chair. He read a speech, in Italian and German, thanking the Austrian National Symphony and Choir for their magnificent performance. (I know what he said only because Suor Giovanna helpfully provided me with a *bollettino* about the evening the next day.)

When the pope finished, he next shuffled down to shake hands with the folks in the VIP seats right in front of us.

That's when every crazed nun in Rome decided my wife and I were expendable and literally pushed us out of our seats. A vast throng of veiled figures—many Italian, some Mexican or Filipino—pushed their way to the front where we were standing, elbows flying. The Spanish priest, who had a camera, stood up on a chair to get out of the way and, in a quite magnanimous gesture, I thought, did his best to get a picture of my wife and me with the pope. Soon everyone else around us was also standing on their chairs, towering above us. It was crazy.

The pope walked over to a strange man with a green bow tie—probably an ambassador—and shook hands with him, a woman who appeared to be his wife, and their son, about ten years old. He then made a circuit around two rows of seats and ended up right back in front of us. Then the nuns went really nuts and simply shoved Glenn and me to the back. For a moment I forgot that we were in the *Áula* and thought we had been magically transported to some kind of early seventies London punk rock club, and these screaming women in black robes were really Sex Pistols groupies in disguise.

By that time we were quite willing to relinquish our prime seats, having had quite enough of the whole scene.

The pope looked tired and sick, but stuck through the entire two-hour ordeal like a trooper. Glenn was ecstatic to see him, although a little sad. Everyone present obviously felt sorry for the pope, who had just had a major operation, whose left hand shook from some neurological disease, who plainly would have rather been back in bed watching reruns of *The Beverly Hillbillies* on TV . . . but who was instead dragged out in front of this huge crowd, all straining to touch him, and then forced to listen to a boring oratorio for two hours.

After another ten minutes or so, the pope left. The crowd dispersed. We chatted with the junior-level Chilean diplomat as we walked out. The Spanish priest promised to send us his pictures of us with the pope and he did eventually (the backs of our two heads in front of the pope). The following week, I happened to pass a photography shop on Borgo Vittorio, a block from Porta Sant'Anna, and saw rows of color contact sheets from the event. Apparently, *L'Osservatore Romano* photographers who attend these events give their negatives to the owners of this shop, who display the contact sheets. If you happen to see a shot of yourself with the pope, you can go in and have it developed for a fee. I saw a really good one of the pope, without us in it, and bought it.

Glenn and I strolled through the *Áula* courtyard, through Bernini's columns and into St. Peter's Square. It was a warm Roman evening and the fashionably dressed crowd was now fanning out in search of food. We walked down the Via di Porta Angelica through the Piazza del Risorgimento toward the Prati district. Eventually we found a nice restaurant and had a delightful dinner, seated next to a German couple from Frankfurt who kept ordering plate after plate of pasta.

Glenn and I both had mixed emotions about the whole event. On the one hand, it was fun to sit that close to the pope. On the other hand, we felt sorry for him—this poor, brilliant old man trapped in such a dead-end job.

What non-Catholics sometimes don't understand is that most ordinary Catholics usually have a kind of familial concern for the pope, as though he were a grandfather. Theology is beside the point. You might disagree with the pope on some issue but still worry about his health, enjoy his company, listen respectfully to what he has to say—as you would to your own grandfather. You also might ignore your grandfather's advice, of course, but that doesn't mean you want him to stop giving it. You understand that he's telling it to you for your own good and that even when you ignore the advice, he's probably right.

Anyway, after my second Limoncello I was feeling very relaxed. It had been a marvelous evening, a romantic date in the Eternal City. After the usual scurrying around, we finally found a taxi and headed up the Viale delle Mura Aurelie for home.

I kept thinking I was going to have to thank Suor Giovanna for the great tickets.

V

The Apostolic Camera Is Out of Focus

He who travels in the barque of Peter had better not look
too close into the engine-room.

MONSIGNOR RONALD KNOX

The truly unsettling thing about the Vatican, at least for me, is its size.
Even though it is the center of a worldwide church with one billion
members, the Vatican itself is smaller—in terms of personnel and financial resources—than many Catholic dioceses and most corporations.

Of the 1,300 or so employees who work inside the Vatican itself,
maybe 150, or less, make any decisions. One bishop I spoke to, who
works in the Apostolic Palace, told me that only about twenty people run
the Catholic Church. The rest do various types of clerical work, man

the telephones, answer letters, clean up after the tourists, make sure the generators run, and so on.

Over the years, various systems analysts and business consultants have studied the Vatican's organizational structure and concluded that it is one of the most efficiently run operations on earth—a conclusion that only causes incredulity, if not hysterical shrieks of laughter, from the jaded Vatican press corps and anyone else who has spent any time at all in curial offices.

From the point of view of contemporary business standards, at least, the Vatican still operates quite literally in the Dark Ages. Despite all the talk about the Vatican and the Internet, one cardinal complained to me that many curial offices still didn't have computers and almost literally use quill pens and large ledger books. The mentality, rampant throughout Italy, is pretty much: *Why get a fax machine when carrier pigeons have done such a magnificent job all these centuries?*

Despite impressive titles and often substantial history, many Vatican offices and departments are little more than weathered facades staffed with a handful of personnel. The Pontifical Academy of Sciences, for example, meets once a year in an abandoned (albeit beautiful) building in the Vatican Gardens and has only one regular employee. The much-vaunted "Biblicum," or Pontifical Biblical Institute, is housed in a crumbling tenement across the street (actually across the *alley*) from the Gregorian University, on Via della Pilotta. The Vatican Observatory, with its handful of Jesuit astronomers, long ago moved away from the outdated equipment at Castel Gandolfo to more modern facilities in Tucson, Arizona.

I realize, of course, that the quality of institutions is measured more by their people than by their physical structures; but nevertheless it's a bit dispiriting when you walk into a Vatican office and see just how few people work there, just how little substance lies behind the grandiloquent name. More than once in Rome, I had the sinking feeling I experienced in the past when, doing stories for *The Hollywood Reporter,* I visited film and TV sets. You see the cheap construction, the fake jewelry, the painted and artificially enhanced actresses, the leading men in elevator shoes and Hair Club for Men toupees, and you think to yourself: *My God, this is what has held me riveted to the TV screen week after week?*

Of course, the mystique of the papacy endures partly because the pope, and his tiny band of black- and scarlet-robed minions in the Vatican, oversee a fairly vast empire by anyone's standards.

As I said earlier, the Catholic Church worldwide has an estimated one *billion* communicants spread throughout 2,571 dioceses found in almost every nation on earth, although as few as ten to twenty-five percent in many countries attend weekly Mass and can be considered active, practicing members. Most of the world's Catholics are still concentrated in Europe and the Americas, with half found in just ten countries—Brazil (135 million), Mexico (83 million), the United States (56 million), Italy (55 million), France (47 million), Spain (37 million), Poland (36 million), Columbia (31 million), Argentina (29 million), and Germany (28 million). Two countries in Asia have large numbers of Catholics, the Philippines (52 million) and India (14 million); and two in Africa, Zaire (18 million) and Nigeria (10 million).

Caring for—the theologically correct term would be "ministering to"—this community are 4,200 bishops, 403,000 priests, and 900,000 religious sisters. In addition, the Church controls or influences a vast, loosely connected network of hospitals, schools, orphanages, and universities, and, in some countries, political parties. More than 164 nations have diplomatic relations with the Holy See, and the Vatican, precisely because it represents so many people and institutions worldwide, still packs a substantial wallop in international bodies such as the United Nations.

And overseeing or at least attempting to oversee this vast empire—

appointing key personnel, directing policy, and setting standards, as it were—are the pope and the permanent Vatican bureaucracy known as the Curia. How they are able to do it all—given the work habits of Italian bureaucrats and the limited amount of resources at their disposal—is a testimony to just how decentralized this allegedly centralized organization really is.

The political and spiritual center for this vast international network is, of course, the State of Vatican City, which is merely the visible civic arm of the more ethereal Holy See. Today, Vatican City is the world's smallest country, a walled-off enclave of churches, palaces, office buildings, stores, museums, satellite dishes, dirty monuments, a cemetery, a heliport, tennis courts, gardens, and a gas station spread out over 108.7 acres in the northwestern part of Rome. (The Vatican also has sovereign control over some "extraterritorial" properties, such as the papal summer residence of Castel Gandolfo, south of Rome; the large, historically important basilicas of St. John Lateran and St. Mary Major; and some office and apartment buildings in the nearby neighborhood of Trastevere.)

The center of the complex, St. Peter's Basilica, has stood on the same spot for more than 1,600 years, since the Emperor Constantine began building the first basilica in the year A.D. 324. There are only five entrances to the main Vatican City complex, all of them closely watched by Swiss Guards and Vatican police (the Vigilanza): The Arch of the Bells, located directly to the left of St. Peter's; St. Anne's Gate, located to the immediate right; the entrance to the Vatican Museums, found along the outside wall to the right of St. Peter's; the entrance to the Paul VI Audience Hall near the palace of the Holy Office; and the Bronze Portal, the official access for dignitaries found at the end of the right-side colonnade.

Officially, most of Vatican City is off limits to tourists, who are only allowed into St. Peter's Basilica, the Vatican Museums, and, with specially arranged tours, the Vatican Gardens. In practice, more than

8,000 people have access to the Vatican's low-cost store, pharmacy, gas tanks, and so on; and many more are allowed in if they have a good reason (such as an appointment with a specific official). The only part of the Vatican that is really and truly off limits is the Apostolic Palace, which is where the pope has his private apartments and many of the Church's most important administrative offices are located. To see it requires connections with a high church official who actually works in the building and is willing to show you around.

As an independent sovereign nation, the Vatican City-State is an absolute monarchy ruled directly by the pope: He exercises supreme legislative, executive, and judicial authority through an intricate, maze-like structure of overlapping commissions and tribunals. The papacy may have strongly supported democracy in recent decades as the best form of government for secular states, but it definitely does not practice what it preaches. In Catholic theology there is no authority on earth higher than the pope, not even an ecumenical council (because none of its decrees has binding force until approved by the reigning pope).

On an organizational chart—which of course means as little in the Vatican as it does anywhere else—the pope, the Sommo Pontefice, is at the top. Directly beneath him are two bodies of bishops—the College of Cardinals, whose primary function is to elect the next pope but which has been taking on more of an advisory role in recent decades, and the Synod of Bishops. The synod, which was officially inaugurated in 1967, is a creation of Vatican II, when bishops decided they liked having a say in the governing of the universal Church. The "ordinary" synod, which is made up of about 250 bishops worldwide, meets every four years or so to discuss an agenda set and presided over by the pope. Its role is purely advisory and it does not function, as many people imagine and some would like, as a kind of Vatican parliament.

The real power in the Vatican lies in the Secretariat of State, which controls the offices of the vicariate of Rome, the nine congregations, three tribunals, twelve pontifical councils, five Holy See offices, and twenty-one curial agencies that, collectively, make up the Vatican. The Secretariat of State oversees basically everything (including both the Government of Vatican City and the Papal Diplomatic Corps) with one big exception—the Vatican Bank, which reports directly to the pope.

It also is above the Apostolic Camera, one of the oldest of Vatican departments, which is charged with governing the Church during the *sede vacante,* the period between the death of one pope and the election of another. *Camera* is the Italian (and Latin) word for room, but the term Apostolic Camera actually stems from the title of the medieval Church's finance minister, the *camerarius.* This important department is run by a cardinal known as the *camerlengo,* who supervises the burial of the dead pope and organizes the conclave to elect the new one. In former times, when the interregnum could be quite lengthy, the position of *camerlengo* was extremely powerful because he basically ran the Church until a new pope was elected.

Unlike the Apostolic Camera, most of the various Vatican departments—which are all called "dicasteries" in the official language of the Holy See—are actually quite new, part of the explosion of ecclesiastical bureaucracy, both at the Vatican and in the dioceses, that followed the various mandates of Vatican II.

As a practical matter, the day-to-day running of Vatican City is overseen by the Pontifical Commission for the State of Vatican City, located in a large five-story office building, the Government Palace, found directly behind St. Peter's. At this writing, Vatican City itself has officially 1,339 employees, 471 citizens, and only 314 residents, most of them cardinals and high-ranking prelates, as well as some nuns and the Swiss Guards. Only about ten children can be found playing behind the Vatican's medieval walls, the children of the handful of married Swiss Guards.

The irony of worldwide Catholicism, though, is that this tiny, all-powerful, highly centralized monarchy is able to maintain such great influence over the worldwide Catholic community. It is able to do so precisely because, contrary to popular belief, it exercises very little actual control over the day-to-day business of the Church.

While the Vatican itself may be a monarchy, the organizational model the Catholic Church as a whole resembles the most is actually Amway. It's a vast multilevel, multinational, worldwide organization in which all of the component parts—while selling the same products in the same manner—are largely but not completely autonomous.

In the popular imagination, the pope runs everything, inside and outside of Rome; but in fact all of the thousands of dioceses, religious orders, schools, and hospitals are largely independent, with their own organizational structures, their own policies, and, most important of all, their own money. When the Vatican does exercise power, it does so only where it can be most effective—in the appointments of bishops, for example, or in setting what might be termed global policy—and that power is, in fact if not in theory, strictly limited.

Prior to 1870, Rome and the Vatican had been the capital of the Papal States—vast lands in central Italy, the so-called *Patrimonium Petri,* which had been bequeathed to the Church over centuries. By 1870 the Papal States consisted of more than 16,000 square miles of central Italy (roughly the size of Denmark). What is now Italy was nothing more than a series of tiny fiefdoms. But during the 1850s and 1860s, a national movement to unify all of the Italian peninsula, known as the *Risorgimento,* gathered steam under patriots such as Giuseppe Garibaldi. The duke of Savoy, Vittorio Emanuele II, was declared the first king of Italy in 1861.

During this period, the pope and Rome itself were protected by foreign powers, primarily by the French, who were able to keep the nationalist Italian forces at bay. But in 1870, following the outbreak of the Franco-Prussian War, this shield collapsed. The French pulled their forces out of Italy and the Italian nationalists promptly attacked Rome. After a brief skirmish at Porta Pia, Italian forces finally broke through the Aurelian Wall on September 20, 1870. About a dozen Italian and three papal soldiers were killed until finally, recognizing defeat when he saw it, Pope Pius IX (1846–1878) told his forces not to resist and declared himself a "prisoner in the Vatican." Supposedly, the pope was not entirely displeased with the loss of his enormous territories, telling the French ambassador that "all I want is a small corner of earth where I am master."

The political status of the Vatican and its historic territories thus remained an open question in international law until February 11, 1929. That was when the Holy See signed a controversial concordat with the Fascist government of Mussolini which, among other things, resolved the Vatican's long-disputed legal status and gave to the Holy See a large sum of money (750 million lire in cash and one billion lire in bonds) in compensation for the annexation of the Papal States and other properties, such as the magnificent Quirinal Palace (now home to the president of Italy). A second concordat was signed in 1985, which fine-tuned the original agreement—for example, by eliminating the provision that the Italian state pay the salaries of all priests in Italy.

By the way, this history explains much of the weird schizoid quality of the relationship Italians have with the papacy—and with their religion. On the one hand, most Italians—with the exception of journalists, some politicians, and the Mafia—pledge at least nominal loyalty to the pope and to Catholicism. At the same time, they openly and quite understandably celebrate their military victory over the papacy and the conquest of the historic Italian capital.

I came to appreciate the depth of feeling over this victory because, almost every day, I used to go by the Garibaldi monument on the top of the Janiculum. It is a magnificent monument with a truly gigantic bronze statue of the great man astride his horse, and the view over the rooftops of Rome is simply stunning.

At the base of the monument is inscribed Garibaldi's famous cry, *Roma o Morte,* "Rome or death." And every day at noon the government fires off a cannon salute to commemorate the Italian victory over the pope.

VI

When in Rome,
Do as the Romans

REPORTER: How many people work in the Vatican?
POPE JOHN XXIII: About half.

O ne of the hardest things for a stranger to get used to when visiting the Vatican is the relentless, even obstinate Italianness of the place.

Given that the Catholic Church claims to be the universal church of all nations—in which Italians (most of whom never darken a church door anyway) account for perhaps six percent of the total Catholic population—the stranglehold that Italians have over the Vatican's central administration seems anachronistic to say the least. This stranglehold has nothing to do with devotion and everything to do, like most things in Italy, with money and jobs and making sure that both stay in the family.

Most Americans and northern Europeans are unaware of just how absurdly nationalistic Italians really are. The Italian way of doing things is not merely the best way; it's the *only* way, quite literally. It doesn't even occur to the typical Italian that people in other countries might do things differently from the way they do them in Italy. Telling an Italian that you don't *like* grappa is like telling him you don't like air—an absurdity that isn't even worth considering.

In other words, Italians are in fact what Americans are always accused of being in theory: utterly uninterested in, and even unaware of, events and points of view outside of their own admittedly picturesque piece of turf.

This jingoistic myopia extends, of course, to the language. Before I first came to Italy, I believed the lie that Americans are the most linguistically illiterate people on earth, that we alone of all peoples arrogantly refuse to learn other languages and expect all visitors to America to speak our language and only our language.

That may well be true, but I've discovered a group of people who make Americans seem like polyglot virtuosos: the Italians.

You need to know Italian in Italy like you need your liver. When I tell people that Italians do not speak a single word of any other language except Italian, I don't mean they know only a few simple phrases or studied English a little in high school.

I mean they don't know a single word. Not one.

In France or Germany, Holland or Denmark, even Israel, you can get by using the hundreds of cognates modern languages share—words that sound similar in the various languages, like television and bank, taxi and American Express.

But such a strategy is utterly ineffective in Italy. In Italy there are no cognates. There is only Italian.

When I first arrived in Rome, I was looking for a bank to get some money out of a cash machine. Just past Porta Sant'Anna, where the Swiss Guards have their barracks, I walked up to a newspaper stand and asked for directions.

"*Scusi, signora, dov'è un* bank," I said cheerfully, struggling, I thought heroically, with my few Italian words.

The newspaper lady squinted up her face in a look of complete and utter disgust, as though I had just tossed a paper bag full of cow manure into her stand. She puckered up her mouth until I thought she was about to hack out a wad of chewing tobacco straight in my face.

"Ehhhhhh?" she grunted back.

I tried again.

"*Mi dispiace, non parlo Italiano . . . ma dov'è un* bank?" Roughly: I'm sorry, I don't speak Italian. But where is a bank?

The Italian lady now looked pissed off. I could just as well have been speaking Czech. She just shook her head . . . and turned away.

I couldn't believe it! She was turning her back on me!

I wasn't about to give up. I stepped closer and said, loudly this time, "*Scusi, dov'è un* bank?!"

The woman whirled around, faced me, and let loose a torrent of what I could only imagine was abusive Italian that I did not, of course, understand. But I'm stubborn when I feel oppressed or insulted and so, like a typical tourist, I pressed on to the point of belligerency: "*Dov'è . . .* bank. *Banca. Bancarista. Bankenheimer. Banco.*"

I was stammering, but figured something had to click eventually.

Suddenly, miraculously, her face perked up. "*Banco?*" she asked tentatively, now sweet as honey.

I nodded my head up and down like a puppy. "*Sì, sì, sì,*" I said. "*Banco.* Yes, *banco. Dov'è banco?*"

And that solved it. The lady smiled, pointed to the end of the block, and made a gesture to go "*a destra,*" to the right.

But the point is this: Saying "bank" or even "bahnk" wasn't good enough. Until I said it precisely as the Italians say it—with the "oh" sound on the end—she was utterly clueless. The mental leap was too great.

And that's how it is everywhere in Italy, even in the allegedly high-tourist areas such as Rome, even in the Vatican.

For the first three weeks I was in Rome, I had to repeat street names ten, twenty, thirty times before I'd give up, get out a map, and show the taxi driver precisely where I wanted to go. And when I went into the official Vatican bookshop, to look for a good guidebook to St. Peter's, I was astonished that ninety-eight percent of the books were written only in Italian.

The moral of the story is: When in Rome, do as the Romans. And the Romans, nowadays at least, speak Italian.

Naturally, then, I quickly realized that I needed an assistant to deal with Vatican officials—an *Italian* assistant. Not only was my grasp of the language woefully inadequate (actually nonexistent), I needed that local connection, that common fraternal bond that smoothes the way when two countrymen are dealing with each other.

And I found it, luckily enough, close at home.

Anne's boyfriend was the son of an Italian diplomat who had lived all over the world. His name was Luca. He was a short, good-looking young man with curly brown hair and a bright smile. He had lived in Iran, Holland, the United States, and Guatemala. He had attended the American school in Amsterdam and gone to high school in, of all places, Houston, Texas. As a result, Luca was one of those rare creatures—a truly bilingual person. He spoke absolutely fluent English without a trace of an accent (even using such unlikely idioms as "I'll be back in a jiff") and had a passionate fondness for steak and onion rings.

And he was unemployed, like too many young Italians. At age twenty-six, Luca was just finishing up his "license" in economics at the Jesuit-run Gregorian University, across town, but didn't have a clue what he wanted to do when he grew up. He talked about becoming a writer . . . or a wood refinisher . . . or maybe a hotelier. He and Anne lived in a tiny apartment owned by his parents, who were, at that time, stationed in Guatemala.

Luca was also a very angry young man, boiling over with rage about the corruption of the "pigs" who ran Italian politics. Refreshingly, he didn't blame the United States for most of Italy's troubles—like many of his fellow students—and had the good sense to realize that Italy was in the state it was in largely because it's full of Italians. I hired Luca at 12,000 lire an hour (about $8) to be my translator, research assistant, and occasional driver. He was and is wholly responsible for the skewed and utterly one-sided view I have of Italy.

Luca was fairly Americanized, but he was still Italian. This was evident from two things he spent most of his time doing: lecturing me . . . and complaining.

"This is not really a republic," Luca explained to me one day in a typical hour-long rant about his native country. "People's votes don't matter. The politicians think they're running the country, but most of them are corrupt and taking bribes. The ones who are really running the country meet in secret associations for their own private profit. If that's not a dictatorship, I don't know what is. That's why we've got to kill the free masonry that we've got here. We've got one in particular, the *pee-duay* (P2), the grand master masons, that counts 420 military officials that have secret meetings. Talk about a Fascist state! You've got people who are indicted for being in the Mafia, people who were indicted for business fraud, meeting regularly with the same top military leaders as part of the *pee-duay* group. The guy that's the leader of it was an ex-Fascist who passed to the Nazi S.S. at the end of the war. He was friends with the CIA and at the same time gave bombs to the Communist rebels, just to show you what a piece of shit he is."

Being Italian, Luca naturally had the answer for everything, and he would launch himself into lengthy disquisitions on the slightest provocation. He would do this even when he knew that I was more knowledgeable on a particular subject—the alarming increase in the price of Mexican beer, say—than he.

To be fair, this hubris wasn't limited to Luca. Whenever I struck up a conversation with a Roman, eventually I found myself in the position of listening quietly, like a dutiful student, while *il professore* lectured me, at length, about whatever it was we were discussing. If the dominant "voice" of Israelis (as Paul Theroux so accurately says) is the barked command, the dominant voice of Romans is that of a bored, slightly condescending *professore*.

Luca may have been long-winded, even a bit cocky, but he was basically a good kid who helped me find my way through the morass of Italian bureaucracy. I discovered just how useful this could be when I lost my Vatican press pass.

Suor Giovanna was not amused. I'd had it for only one month.

I called her on the phone. I thanked her for the great tickets to the papal concert, explaining our proximity to the pope. I said my wife was thrilled.

And, oh, by the way, one other little thing. I lost my press pass.

Silence.

"You lost it?"

Yes, Sister, I lost it. It's been two years, at least, since my last confession.

"Where? Where did you lose it?"

I quickly explained what I believed happened, how I thought the clip had come off the plastic cover.

She told me that I had to go to the police and report the lost card.

The police?

"Yes, yes, the police."

The next day I had to meet Greg, the *Time* bureau chief, at the Sala Stampa. I told him my plight. He laughed out loud. He, too, had once lost his press pass.

"I'll tell you exactly what they'll tell you," he said. "They'll tell you that you have to go out to a drugstore or someplace and buy this *carta di cazzo*—literally, this piece of prick, *cazzo* means prick and the Italians just throw it into phrases when they want to give them emphasis—you have to buy this *carta di cazzo,* a special kind of paper, two pieces stuck together, for them to use to make their report. They'll write their report up on that, stamp and sign it, and then give you one to give to the press office."

Italians love stamps, the more the better. Every document, every piece of paper, must be properly stamped and signed by the right official—and then that official's signature must be in turn witnessed, itself stamped, and then dated and signed by the witness. Sometimes it's necessary to have your stamps stamped. I was warned about this before I came to Italy, but it still surprised me.

I sighed. Greg laughed. "No, no, no, this will be great for your book," he said. "This is what it's like dealing with the Vatican."

I went outside. It was a warm afternoon, around two-thirty. I walked around the side of the Piazza Pio, through the gate in the Passetto and into the area where a line of number 64 buses stood, waiting for tourists eager to have their pockets picked. I quickly spied the police office between a photo developer and another shop. It was a simple door.

I went upstairs, looking for the office where you report lost stuff. On the second-floor landing I saw what looked like some kind of squad room. Suddenly, a short, fat Italian man walked up to me with no uniform on, his belly button (literally) showing, and barked, "Stranger! Stranger! You talk to me!"

He said this in a nonthreatening but authoritative way. "Pardon me?" I said.

"Stranger, what you want?"

I explained my plight as best I could. I told him I was told to report my lost press card here.

"No," he said. "You stranger. You must go to central police office, Stranger Office. Termini. Take bus sixty-four outside."

Huh?

He repeated himself. As near as I could determine, he said I had to go to the main police office, near the central bus station. Via Genova. I had to make my report there. Stranger Office.

But, I said, I was told to make my report *here*.

Well, yeah, he smiled, sure. But now he was telling me to go *there*. How could I argue with that logic?

I said okay, figuring, well, I deserved some sort of punishment for being such an idiot.

So I walked six blocks or so down the street to the Ottaviano metro station, went down the steps, and crowbarred myself into one of the baking metro cars. A little old lady carrying *La Repubblica* under her arm elbowed me in the rib cage with a professionalism and precision I found unsettling. I got off at Termini, only to discover, outside, that the main police station was located at Piazza della Repubblica, one metro stop back, and so had to go down into the metro again and backtrack.

Once I finally found the police station, on Via Genova just off Via Nazionale, I had to look around for the right office. I found a sign that said, sure enough, STRANGER OFFICE. THIS WAY. I followed the arrows up the street, turned right, and was stopped dead in my tracks. There in front of me was a crowd of angry, hot "strangers"—about sixty or so— waiting in line. Most of them appeared to be Arabs. They were pushing and shoving in the traditional Islamic manner. A single policeman, standing at the entrance, was calling out numbers. "*Duecento tre?*" he was saying. "Two hundred three?"

It was then three-thirty. There was no way I was going to get into that melee this late in the afternoon. Once, on a ferry from Algeciras to

Tangier, I saw a similar mob of Moroccans storm the passport control table set up on the deck. They made the same semicircle of screaming, shoving hysteria, with the passport officials occasionally rising from their seats and literally pushing and shoving the crowd back two or three feet from the tables. The European tourists on board took one look at this minor riot and did the only reasonable thing. We headed for the bar. After two or three drinks the mob had abated. We then proceeded to "queue up"—with lots of "You first" and "Oh no, after you," and felt very smug and superior.

There was no way in hell, in other words, that I was going to get in that line outside the Stranger Office. I decided this would be a good time to test Luca's mettle with Italian bureaucracy.

The next day I had Luca call the Italian police and speak to them, in Italian, of course. After about fifteen minutes of chuckling, he got off the phone and told me the situation.

As I suspected, the police had sent me to the Stranger Office only because they didn't speak any English; they send all strangers there, regardless of the situation.

Now, Luca said, you and I know that the cops are *not* going to go look for your lost press card, yet you're supposed to report it lost in the local police district where you think you lost it. However, if you don't know exactly where you lost it, then you can simply go into any local neighborhood police station, report the loss, and have them give you the official report. Luca happened to know that there was a small police office a mile or so away in Monte Verde. He'd drive me over right now.

So we jumped in the car and dashed on over. The office was located on the ground floor of what looked like an apartment building. Everything went smoothly. The local police were friendly, sympathetic, even helpful. I did not, as Greg had predicted, have to go out and buy a *carta bollata,* which is what the legal paper Greg described is actually called. They had some on hand.

I did, however, have to fill out two identical police reports, because Italians would much rather hand-copy documents than resort to such absurd modern inventions as copy machines or even, God forbid, carbon paper. And we did have to wait while each of these hand-copied documents was duly notarized, stamped, signed, stamped again, and then witnessed by Luca.

But all in all it only took about an hour. Luca had to produce his official police identity papers—which made him very nervous—and swear that I was who I said I was. But I had my official police report, which I took the next day to Suor Giovanna—and then collected a pool from journalist friends for how long it would take the irate nun to give me a replacement press card.

I had learned my lesson though.

When in Rome, hire yourself an Italian research assistant.

VII

Reggae in St. Peter's Square

As a mere promenade, St. Peter's is unequalled. It is better than the Boulevards, than Piccadilly or Broadway, and if it were not the most beautiful place in the world, it would be the most entertaining.

HENRY JAMES, *Transatlantic Sketches,* 1873

The sacred and the profane, the sublime and the ridiculous, comingle in the Vatican, as in Catholicism itself, in a startling way.

You see that as soon as you take one look at the outside of St. Peter's Basilica. Plastered right on the front of the greatest, most magnificent church in Christendom, literally centered over the main door, lies the most absurd act of ecclesiastical self-promotion in the entire history of the papacy.

In chiseled letters fifteen feet high are the words: IN HONOREM PRINCIPIS APOST. PAVLVS V BVRGHESIVS ROMANVS PONT. MAX AN. MDCXII PONT. VII— which, roughly translated, means, "In honor of the Prince of the

Apostles, Paul V Borghese, Roman, Supreme Pontiff, in the year 1612, the seventh year of his pontificate." The family name "Burghesius" is dead center over the main door.

Talk about chutzpah! Paul V, who also made sure his name was prominently displayed over each door in the portico and on everything else he could think of, was merely the pope who happened to be around when a century's work on St. Peter's rebuilding was coming to a close and the architects and builders were walking around picking up leftover nails.

This is a bit of an exaggeration, I admit—Paul V actually oversaw the construction of the nave, portico, and facade—but that didn't mean he should take credit for the whole project, indeed making it appear that St. Peter's is a temple to his own exalted self. It would be as if Richard Nixon, upon his election as U.S. president, had had the words "Nixon's Place" chiseled above the main door of the White House.

I was thinking these irreverent thoughts at ten o'clock in the morning on a beautiful, sunny, somewhat cool Sunday in St. Peter's Square, a couple months after we had arrived in Rome. By then I had my bearings a little and was eager to see the pope in action.

The last person I expected to meet there, as the crowds gathered to hear the pope's weekly Angelus talk, was Randraanantoandro Clement.

With chocolate-brown skin and Rastafarian dreadlocks flying in the wind, Clement looked as if he'd stepped right off one of my old Bob Marley albums. He was wearing pants made out of a quilt of a dozen different fabrics, Japanese zori slippers, and a black ski parka. As he and some friends pranced around the square, enthusiastically videotaping everything in sight, I went up and introduced myself.

Clement, who was thirty-six and had a smile as warm as a cup of hot buttered rum, was from the island of Madagascar, just off the southern tip of Africa. He was in Rome, he said, to perform at the Colosseum with the Justin Vali Trio for the World Food Day Concert. By coincidence, I had heard him rehearse the day before and was entranced by the music, a lively, thumping ska-sound that reminded me of UB40. He played the kabosy, a traditional wind instrument from his native island.

When I asked him why a Rastafarian would want to visit St. Peter's, he laughed and said he was not Rastafarian. He just dressed that way because he was a musician. He had come to St. Peter's because he'd felt drawn to it. "It's a very old place, and it dates back to the beginnings of Christianity," he said in French. He wasn't Catholic but followed the traditional ways of the people in Madagascar: "We believe in God, in Christ, but also in the spirits of our ancestors, who live on after they die and help people left in this world."

Randraanantoandro, the faux-Rasta musician, waved good-bye, and then an Asian man asked me to take his picture. His name was Song Toon Hung, twenty-two, from Taegu, South Korea. He'd been in Rome a month, but he came to St. Peter's every Sunday to hear the pope. We struck up a conversation with Phillip Molle, a Belgian Knight of the Holy Sepulcher. Originally from Zaire, he was wearing the distinctive white cape with blood-red Jerusalem Cross that is the mark of this ancient order of warrior-priests, which dates back to the First Crusade in the eleventh century. Behind us, as we were chatting, we all heard the sing-song cadence of some Scandinavian language and noticed a small group of about a dozen well-dressed middle-aged couples, in expensive blazers and turtlenecks, listening to a tour guide lecture about the Vatican.

Standing around St. Peter's Square for an hour or two before a Sunday papal Angelus is like being in a United Nations exposition, only more so. Theologians will tell you that the word "catholic" comes from the Greek for "universal," but that is a mere platitude until you encounter the mind-boggling assortment of weird characters you see in St. Peter's, from every country on earth, who have come to hear the pope speak or just to hang out. If you visit the basilica on a weekday, or merely as a tourist, you miss this aspect of contemporary Catholicism, the way in which the papacy still is able to unite a worldwide community that has very little else in common.

Italian carabinieri, in their somewhat chilling all-black uniforms with the red stripe running down the pants legs, strutted around the square in their black boots and gloves, the distinctive silver flame insignia of their caps gleaming in the sun. Many European Catholic youth groups, who wore yellow papal caps and neck kerchiefs along with their "Maui and Sons" T-shirts, flocked around young priests dressed in full-length Roman-style cassocks. German girls, noses and exposed belly buttons pierced, wearing tight black miniskirts, stood next to Muslims from central Africa, dressed in billowing white muslin garments and colorful headdresses. I noticed what looked like a small troupe of Tibetan monks in their burgundy robes, but it turned out to be a half-dozen members of the Handmaids of the Precious Blood, a contemplative Catholic religious order based in Jemez Springs, New Mexico.

I asked a member of the group behind me what language I was hearing, and she smiled and said it was Norwegian. I added that to my list. I had personally overheard more than a dozen languages, including English, Spanish, Arabic, French, German, Swedish, Korean, Chinese, Hungarian, Polish, Japanese, Hebrew, Dutch, what I think may have been Thai, some Indian dialect (perhaps Hindi), and Russian or maybe Ukrainian.

The atmosphere of St. Peter's Square is unlike anything else in the world, a reminder of the sheer spectacle that is still the papacy. It is part religious extravaganza, part block party, and part circus.

Crowds of pilgrims and tourists walk single-file down the wide avenue that is the Via della Conciliazione, built by Mussolini in honor of the Concordat signed with the Vatican in 1929, and into the welcoming arms of Bernini's double colonnade. The effect of the colonnade, topped by one hundred forty statues each ten feet tall, is intriguing: The famous basilica rises majestically in the distance, a squat mass of travertine blocks and Baroque ego, but the keyhole-shaped piazza in front, with the two arms of the colonnade forming half circles around the people, suggests a singular openness, as though the crowds are being welcomed by the saints on top of the colonnade and funneled quite literally into the doors of the church.

In the front of the colonnade there were six *carrozza* horse-cabs, with bright orange steel wheels, waiting for tourists willing to pay 200,000 lire for a tour of the city center. A squad of about a dozen itinerant trinket salesmen carrying their supplies of rosaries and small crucifixes walked around, working the crowd.

One of the vendors, Antonio Padruzzi, sixty-five, his face wizened and cracked from the weather, had been selling rosaries and other trinkets in St. Peter's Square for more than forty years. He had had to change his stock of papal key chains five different times. Antonio told me that 20,000 people come through the square on an ordinary day, 50,000 on a typical Sunday. Special events and major holy days, of course, can easily attract more than 250,000. As for his livelihood, he made, on average, about 100,000 lire a day (about $66 at this writing). The most popular items were the rose-scented wooden rosaries and Vatican coins. "So, my friend," he said, "what do you want to buy?"

The Apostolic Palace, where the pope lives, stands off to the right of the square, rising above the colonnade. It is a rather ordinary, even somewhat tacky-looking building made of light gray bricks. The roof is flat, the clear glass windows look as if they need washing. You know which window the pope speaks from because there is a burgundy banner, about twenty feet long and with the papal seal on it, hanging from it.

Immediately below the window, through the colonnade, you can still see the medieval turrets of what looks like a castle wall but which is actually the Passetto, the long walkway, built in 1277 on top of a city wall originally constructed in 850, which was meant as an emergency escape route for the pope in case of attack. Popes have quite literally run for their lives along this imposing corridor, fleeing crowds of impious

Romans (or maybe journalists); it still exists and goes all the way to the former papal fortress of Castel Sant'Angelo, a mile or so away on the Tiber.

Suddenly, the pope appeared in the window, the second one from the right on the top floor. He was a distant figure in white. He greeted the crowd, read part of a prepared text in four modern languages (but not English), and then recited the Angelus, the daily prayer in honor of the Blessed Virgin Mary, in Latin. The crowds cheered. They interrupted his talk intermittently with applause.

I was standing directly below, right next to one of the fountains. I turned around to take a look at the crowd and was suddenly a bit alarmed. The square, which was perhaps a fifth full the last time I looked, was now jam-packed with people standing shoulder to shoulder.

Somehow I had slipped into a rock concert and didn't even know it. Behind me, a youth group had raised a large banner that read WE LOVE THE POPE in French.

After a few more remarks, the pope said *Arrivederci* and disappeared from the window. The crowd flowed out of the square as though someone had pulled a plug somewhere. A few groups of pilgrims lingered to chat, but the square was virtually empty within ten minutes.

VIII

A Tour of St. Peter's Basilica with the *Sampietrini*

I love St. Peter's church. It grieves me to think that after a few days I shall see it no more. It has a peculiar smell from the quantity of incense burned in it. The music that is heard in it is always good and the eye is always charmed. It is an ornament of the earth.

RALPH WALDO EMERSON, *Journals*, April 7, 1833

The interior of the basilica, of course, is stunning. Your jaw really does drop when you see it for the first time. Even if you think the pope is the Antichrist in disguise, the implacable enemy of scientific progress and full frontal nudity on television, you can't help but feel, passing through Filarete's ancient bronze doors or standing under Michelangelo's sublime dome, a primordial astonishment, even pride, that human beings are capable of such an awesome artistic achievement.

Coming from the United States as I did—where the primary model of church architecture in the decades after Vatican II has been the high school auditorium—I felt a genuine awe well up inside of me when I stepped into St. Peter's again.

This is how my guide to Rome, Henry James, put it in 1873:

> *When you are weary of the swarming democracy of your fellow-tourists,*
> *of the unremunerative aspects of human nature on Corso and Pincio, of*
> *the oppressively frequent combination of coronets on carriage panels*
> *and stupid faces in carriages, of addled brains and lacquered boots, of*
> *ruin and dirt and decay, of priests and beggars and takers of advantage,*
> *of the myriad tokens of a halting civilization, the image of the great*
> *temple depresses the balance of your doubts, seems to rise above even*
> *the highest tide of vulgarity and make you still believe in the heroic will*
> *and the heroic act. It's a relief, in other words to feel that there's nothing*
> *but a cab-fare between your pessimism and one of the greatest of human*
> *achievements.*

It's a huge building, as Mark Twain noted, a bit sarcastically, in *The Innocents Abroad.* "Of course we have been to the monster Church of St. Peter frequently," he wrote. "I knew its dimensions. I knew it was a prodigious structure. I knew it was just about the length of the Capitol in Washington—say 730 feet. I knew it was 364 feet wide, and consequently wider than the Capitol. I knew that the cross on the top of the dome of the church was 438 feet above the ground, and therefore about 100 or maybe 125 feet higher than the dome of the Capitol."

Twain didn't tell the half of it though, because work was still going on when he visited in 1868. St. Peter's today has no less than 44 altars, 27 chapels, 11 domes, 800 chandeliers, 778 columns, 395 statues, 290 windows, and 135 mosaics. The whole thing covers 25,000 square yards and is still not finished. If you put bleachers up in the side aisles, two NFL football teams could easily play a game in the central nave.

Everyone has an opinion, of course, about whether the building is larger or smaller than they were led to believe. To make sure you know for certain, the Vatican has helpfully installed weird competitive markers in the marble on the floor of the nave, to show the length of other, *lesser* churches. One marks Winchester Cathedral, another the Shrine of the Immaculate Conception in Washington, D.C., and so on.

And yet, standing in the back of the nave—with the statue of St. Peter Alcantras on my left and that of St. Teresa of Avila gazing sweetly down at me from my right—all I could think of was: *Who dusts all of this stuff?*

Unlike the massive, lofty Gothic cathedrals of France and England—which, for all their great beauty, now have the dark, musty emptiness of mausoleums—St. Peter's positively *glows* with warm light. The sun streams in through high windows in rays of soft yellow, full of dust motes. The intricate red and green marble floor, the massive columns, are polished until they glisten. Everything is so clean, freshly painted and in tip-top repair, it must take an army, I think, to maintain it all.

But as it turns out, it doesn't. A relatively small corps of men called the *sampietrini* are charged with maintaining the great temple, setting up the elaborate decorations and wooden partitions used for most major liturgical celebrations, and cleaning up after the millions of pilgrims and tourists who flock through St. Peter's doors each and every year.

I decided that the best way to really find out about St. Peter's was to spend some time with the people who have to clean it up.

Three days later I set out to meet the *sampietrini,* who usually gather in the outer portico of the basilica around seven A.M., when it opens. To get to the church by seven, I had to get up at five-thirty, take a quick shower, get dressed, and be outside at Piazza Ceresi by six in order to catch the 144 bus down the Janiculum hill.

It's a marvelous time to see Rome, in the early dawn. St. Peter's Square is mostly empty, but the basilica itself is quietly humming with activity. At all of the four dozen side altars, you see priests celebrating Mass, often alone or with just a lone altar boy or tourist to assist them. Later in the day the side altars are usually empty. Thousands of priests come to Rome each year, leading pilgrimages or on their own, and most try to say Mass in the great basilica if they get a chance. It is a poignant reminder just how much this one ritual act, the eucharistic liturgy, is the center and focus of Catholic life on a daily basis.

By the way, *basilica* is the name given to a type of building in ancient Rome, basically just a long rectangular hall with two rows of pillars on the interior supporting a flat ceiling. The flat or slightly rounded ceiling is usually a dead giveaway for a basilica. This type of architecture was taken over by Roman Christians in the fourth century, when they were finally allowed to build churches, and eventually became a technical term for a church of great historical importance. It was also the dominant form of ecclesiastical architecture, with a few variations, until the Middle Ages.

That's when a bunch of avant-garde French architects, tired of building the same old boring basilicas, started experimenting with radical new designs. In many ways, the medieval French were just like contemporary people today. The dull, practical Romans had low, flat ceilings, and the French wanted high, vaulted ceilings. The Romans placed small windows high above the pillars. The French wanted entire walls of glass that let the light flood the interior.

You can just hear the French bishop's architect: "Oh, Excellency, we just *have* to do something about this horrid dark church of yours! We'll tear down these nasty walls, put up some glorious stained-glass windows—I know *just* the contractor who can do it!—and every bishop from here to Rome will just be dying with envy. Trust me."

Eventually, these radical new designs created what became known as the Gothic cathedral. A *cathedral* (from the Latin word for chair, *cathe-*

dra) is merely the "home church" of the diocesan bishop. It's possible, therefore, for a cathedral also to be a basilica—for example, the Archbasilica of St. John Lateran, and not St. Peter's, is the cathedral of the bishop of Rome (the pope), his "home church." But it is also a basilica in style, with a flat ceiling, two rows of pillars on both sides, and small windows located high above.

St. Peter's, on the other hand, is a basilica but not a cathedral. It is actually the second basilica on the site, as we'll see in a later chapter. The first—called Old St. Peter's—was built by the Emperor Constantine in A.D. 324 and lasted for more than 1,100 years. Eventually it began to fall down, so in 1506 the warrior-pope Julius II—Rex Harrison in the film *The Agony and the Ecstasy*—began rebuilding it section by section. The work took 120 years to complete and was planned by some of the greatest artists in Europe, including Michelangelo (1475–1564), Bramante (1444–1514), Raphael (1483–1520), Fontana (1543–1607), Della Porta (1537–1602), Bernini (1598–1680), Maderno (1556–1629), and others. The men who did the actual work, however, who hauled the travertine blocks three hundred feet in the air and actually built the building, and who *continue* to maintain the building today, were the *sampietrini,* perhaps one of the oldest contracting unions in existence. The origin of the name is obscure, and today, in ordinary Italian, *sampietrini* is the name for the omnipresent cobblestones that line Italian streets. In fact, when I asked various Italian *vaticanisti* if they had ever heard of the *sampietrini,* they said of course they had: They're the little rocks that Italians, wisely, use to make their streets, unlike the horrid asphalt that uncouth Americans prefer.

The human *sampietrini* are usually easy to recognize: When they're not cleaning or repairing something, they wear knee-length gray overcoats with an unusual crimson collar with gold fringe. The other two categories of personnel you are likely to encounter in St. Peter's are young men in dark suits with Vatican name badges on them, usually college students, who act as voluntary ushers; and blue-suited men who are members of the Vigilanza, the Vatican's official police force.

After I entered the basilica that morning, I walked up the central nave to where a small group of *sampietrini* were standing near Bernini's gilded bronze *baldacchino*. They all had their heads cranked back, staring at the top of the *baldacchino* where two or three men were walking around. An elaborate temporary scaffolding was erected at the side, and the men used this to climb up on top. Right about then Luca came running up. I had arranged to meet him at seven, by the *Pietà*, but he was, as usual, late, and so had to search all over the basilica to find me.

Just as he arrived, a *sampietrino* on top of the *baldacchino* was being lowered down on what looked like a wooden swing—they called it a "horse"—from the top along the side of one of the bronze columns. All of this was part of an elaborate twice-yearly cleaning operation.

The *baldacchino,* built in 1624, is a curious structure, rarely seen in the United States or even in many European countries but common in Italy (in such churches as St. John Lateran and Santa Maria in Cosmedin). It is basically an elaborate fixed canopy over a main altar, also called a civory or ciborium. The Vatican's is the largest and most famous in the world, built by Bernini. It is a hundred feet high (roughly the height of an eight-story building), made up of four massive bronze columns that are twisted around like huge pieces of black licorice, each decorated with swirls of gold olive and laurel branches. On top of the four columns is a bronze canopy structure, festooned with statues, papal symbols, and a large golden globe with a cross on top. Through the columns of the *baldacchino* you can see, in the very back center of the basilica, the brilliant golden window in which an image of a dove, symbol of the Holy Spirit, can be seen, and below that the gigantic bronze Chair that symbolizes St. Peter's authority as the first bishop of Rome. It's enough to make any Protestant quiver in indignation . . . and it has. "The huge, uncouth structure, reared over the high altar, awakens, both from its ugliness and inappropriateness, a double effusion of iconoclastic zeal," wrote the nineteenth-century New England Puritan George Stillman Hillard, of the *baldacchino*. "It has neither beauty nor grandeur; and resembles nothing so much as a colossal four-post bedstead without the curtains."

A common but unfounded myth has it that Bernini cannibalized bronze from the Pantheon to build the *baldacchino,* and it led to the famous snide remark, referring to the Barberini popes, that "what the barbarians didn't destroy, the Barberini did." In any event, the whole thing weighs nearly two hundred thousand pounds, which is why the builders had to excavate below the basilica to build a special foundation just for the *baldacchino.* When they did so, they accidentally discovered the ancient Roman cemetery that lies beneath St. Peter's, which dates back to the first century, and the jittery workers had to be given huge bonuses just to complete the work. The seventeenth-century builders faced protest marches calling for them to cease desecrating the holy shrine of the apostles, and they hurriedly finished their foundation work and didn't dig further. It wasn't until 1939 that this ancient Roman cemetery was rediscovered and partially excavated, but that's another chapter.

Luca and I were standing near the statue of St. Andrew the Apostle, brother of St. Peter, near the left front corner of the *baldacchino.* This was one of what are called the Four Relics—four massive statues twenty feet high (St. Veronica, St. Helena, St. Longinus, and St. Andrew) that stand in special niches at the four corners of the central square beneath the dome. The *baldacchino* is in the center of the square. Built into the wall above each of the four statues is a small chapel, with a balcony in front of it, which contains relics of each saint. The chapel above St. Veronica's statue also contains St. Peter's Passion Relics (such as a piece of the True Cross, the lance used to pierce Christ's side, and so on).

Luca and I stood there, watching the man on the swing. The men on top appeared to be holding on to the ropes and letting him down slowly. There didn't appear to be any safety harness. In fact, the *sampietrini* are known for their acrobatic derring-do, sort of like Quasimodo flying around the bell towers of Notre Dame. In the old days they used to use ropes and swing around the outside of Michelangelo's dome, placing candles in special holders that were visible for miles.

I and Luca, acting as a translator, approached a couple of the *sampietrini* to ask them questions, but they, like most of the lower-level staff in the Vatican, ran off like terrified rabbits as soon as they spotted my tape recorder. Finally, we found one old guy, who looked as though he was of retirement age and therefore was no longer afraid of the cardinal rector of the basilica, and he agreed to show us the ropes, quite literally. His name was Antonio. He was short and bald, talked out of the side of his mouth, and had a wry sense of humor. He didn't even mind when I followed him around with a tape recorder.

Antonio had been working as a *sampietrino* for twenty-seven years, back when the corps was really made of something. There were at least eighty of them then, but today there are only fifty or so working *sampietrini* and another ten in the office. They are almost all Italian, although an Albanian was recently hired. They do everything it takes to keep St. Peter's spotless—carpentry, masonry, plumbing, polishing, and cleaning—as well as serving as guides and docents at certain places in the basilica (such as the elevator to the dome).

"Ah, the old *sampietrini,* they were real men," Antonio said wistfully. "They were awesome." I asked him if there are any accidents, given the heights at which they work, but Antonio said no, never. The guys smash their shins into steps all the time, but no one ever falls.

I expressed a little skepticism. Antonio smiled. "What can I say?" he asked. "St. Peter protects us."

"I hope so," I replied, glancing up at the fellow swinging back and forth a hundred feet above the marble.

While they polish the marble floor every single day, they clean the

390 statues only twice a year—but it's an arduous job, considering that many of them are high above the pavement. They usually get to these by being lowered down on the "horses," merely a wooden swing we saw the guy using on the *baldacchino*.

Antonio started to walk around and Luca and I tagged along. Like most people, once you get them talking about their work, Antonio was now expansive.

It's a pretty good job, he said. The *sampietrini* work six hours per day in two different shifts—from seven A.M. to one P.M. and from one to seven P.M.—alternating every other day. The pay is okay, but that is not why most of them are there. In the old days, the jobs were handed down from father to son—just like everything else in Italy—but that is less true today. And in the last twenty years or so, the Vatican began hiring student volunteers—the young men in suits with badges—who deal with the public so the *sampietrini* can concentrate on maintenance.

The cardinal rector of the basilica is a hard-ass, Antonio said, but that was okay with him. "In general, people here are very square, very professional," he said. "The cardinal is very outright. If there's something he doesn't like, he says it right to your face. I like that kind of sincerity."

We were standing near the bizarre monument to the intellectual Pope Alexander VII, which is also a monument to death. The pope who took in the freethinking (and bisexual) Queen Christina of Sweden, when she converted to Catholicism and abdicated her throne—putting her up in the Tower of the Winds—had a thing about death. He had his good friend Bernini build a small coffin for his bedroom so that every morning, upon arising, he would think of his final end. And his monument, which is an artistic if gruesome marvel, reflects this same spiritual obsession. In front of a statue of the kneeling pope there are folds upon folds of red Sicilian jasper, representing a funeral draping, and beneath these folds, rising up from the ground, is a life-size golden skeleton (death) holding an hourglass. It's a creepy sculpture that nevertheless is almost mesmerizing. The golden skeleton and folds of jasper hang down, partially blocking a doorway. I stood beneath the skeleton, admiring the anatomical detail.

Antonio and Luca were chatting away in Italian and I was momentarily distracted. But then I pointed to a group of tourists who were just approaching us and I asked Antonio what he thought about the tourists. They must drive the *sampietrini* nuts, I said.

He chuckled. "Millions of people come here," he agreed. "And there's always some nut. We have to tell them to calm down but be very friendly and polite about it. This is a house of God, open to all, and so everyone has a right to come here, even lunatics."

Antonio winked at me. "We even let writers in," he added.

IX

Rendering unto Caesar

Recognizing their craftiness, he said to them, "Show me a *denarius*; whose image and name does it bear?" They replied, "Caesar's." So he said to them, "Then render unto Caesar what belongs to Caesar, and unto God what belongs to God."

Luke 20:20–25

The line outside the Ufficio Filatelico e Numismatico was longer than usual. A new issue of Vatican stamps had just been released, and knowledgeable collectors had already begun buying up their sets before they officially went on sale, a few days later, at the satellite Vatican Post Office in St. Peter's Square.

Little known outside of Rome, the Vatican Philatelic and Numismatic Office is located on the ground floor of the Government Palace, just behind St. Peter's Basilica and the ornate garden replica of the papal coat of arms (that is seen from an aerial view in most Vatican guidebooks). To visit the office, you must first stop at the Vigilanza post just inside the Arch of the Bells (to the left of St. Peter's and guarded by two Swiss Guards) and pick up a special visitor's pass.

Though small, with just seventeen regular employees, the office nevertheless is responsible for designing and producing all the money and stamps used by the Vatican. The office has the dual responsibility of showcasing the mission and culture of the Holy See, with designs that reflect the highest artistic standards, as well as making a profit. It succeeds at both. Collectors agree that the Vatican's stamps and coins are among the world's most beautiful.

During my first months in Rome, I kept trying to check out the story of the Vatican's money and stamps. Both of these items make big money for the Holy See, and it always fascinated me that this tiny little enclave had its own monetary system, sort of. The stamps and coins are very popular with tourists and are sold all over Rome.

But naturally, no one in the Vatican knew anything about them— neither the *vaticanisti* nor the ordinary Vatican officials. The few who might have known something didn't want to talk about it.

I had Luca working the phones for days trying to get me an appointment. He even called up the Zekka, the Italian mint, and found out all about how the money is minted. Everyone in the Vatican, as usual, gave him the runaround. The minting of coins was a big secret.

Actually, like everything else with the Holy See, it was merely a question of finding the one bureaucrat who knew something. If a bureaucrat didn't know anything, he or she told you it was all top secret.

Finally, I managed to contact a young marketing official at the Philatelic and Numismatic Office named Dr. Mauro Olivieri and made an appointment with him. A young man in his late thirties, with short black hair and oval, gold-rimmed glasses, Olivieri spoke fluent English and was only too happy to discuss the stamps and coins of the Vatican. They were his passion.

I made an appointment and, after getting a security pass from the Vigilanza, climbed up the hill behind St. Peter's Basilica and walked into the Government Palace. There I waited with the large crowd of stamp collectors for the new issue. After a while I was called from the foyer and admitted into the inner offices.

Olivieri was a charming fellow. He shook my hand warmly and told me he'd be delighted to answer any questions I might have. On the walls of his simple office were proudly hung large full-color reproductions of recent stamps by the Italian artist David Vangelli.

After months of dealing with snotty Italian priests, Olivieri was a breath of fresh air—and gave me hope that, with time, I might be able to dig up some stories inside the Vatican.

I asked Olivieri how such a conservative organization as the Vatican was able to produce such colorful, artistically daring stamps.

"We obviously have very strict guidelines concerning both the themes we may use as well as the artistic standards we expect," Dr. Olivieri told me. The office tries to pick various aspects of the Vatican to highlight each year—from the Vatican Observatory or Radio to the pope's collection of automobiles—as well as such standard themes as the pope's travels.

In the early years of the city-state, from 1929 on, the stamps were small and fairly straightforward, usually just silhouette designs of the reigning pope (Pius XI or Pius XII) or of various well-known saints. Just three designers—Carrado Mezzana, Edmondo Pizzi, and Casimira Dabrowska—were responsible for nearly all of the stamp designs for more than thirty years.

But beginning with the pontificate of Pope John XXIII and the exciting years of the Second Vatican Council, the Vatican began using a greater variety of artists and designers and allowing more innovative, stylized approaches. One issue in 1962, designed by Marcus Topno, featured the Holy Family in the likeness of pastoral Indians, with dark skin. An issue designed for Expo '70 in Osaka depicted the Blessed Virgin and Christ Child with Asian features.

Throughout the 1970s, the stamp office began to draw upon the cultural treasures of the Vatican, featuring designs based on both classic and modern works of art—from the frescoes of Michelangelo and the famous Gallery of Geographical Maps to works by such contemporary artists as Patrizia Ghione, Carole Manadili, Asami Tsuboi, and Thala Ntobu.

In Pope John Paul II's pontificate, the stamps became larger, more colorful, and more artistically daring. Designers such as David Vangelli, Patrizia Gabriele, Tullio Mele, Renato Cristiano, and Giovanni Hajnal used bright colors and abstract designs to illustrate such religious themes as the Redemption or the Eucharist. Nudity, in the form of classical statues from the Vatican Museums, was permitted for the first time, in 1983.

There is good economic sense behind the Vatican's commitment to artistic excellence. Approximately two thirds of all Vatican stamps are bought, not for use in the mail, but by collectors. The Philatelic and Numismatic Office markets its stamps (and to a lesser extent its coins) at approximately a dozen exhibitions a year, half of which are outside Italy. Four employees in the office will travel to such cities as Singapore, New York, Paris, even Beijing, to sell the Vatican's stamps to collectors there. And collectors want to buy beautiful, artistically elegant stamps.

"Up until twenty years ago, we sold stamps only in Italy and didn't even try to sell them in other countries," Olivieri explained. But then there was a "crisis" in the world of stamp collecting and the whole philatelic marked changed. There was a catastrophic decline in sales—and so the Vatican had to look for new markets outside Italy.

You may laugh, but stamps and coins are big business. Unlike many offices within the Vatican, the Philatelic and Numismatic Office makes a profit for the Holy See.

The reason, Dr. Olivieri explained, is obvious: The cost of producing stamps, particularly, is very low—at high volume, the printing costs are negligible—yet the Vatican sells the stamps at face value. In effect, printing stamps is just like printing money. A half million stamps sold for, say, 1,250 Italian lire each will therefore gross 625 million lire, or $417,000. And that is merely one stamp from one issue.

In the past, Olivieri added, the Vatican would print as many stamps as the market wanted—two or three million at a time—but now it keeps its supply lower, by printing only 500,000, and therefore demand is higher. "It's a very difficult business," Olivieri said with a wry smile. "Very complicated."

The coins are simpler—and less profitable. Each year, the Vatican issues a set of eight coins—in denominations of 10, 20, 50, 100, 200, 500, and 1,000 lire (with the 1,000-lira coins made out of silver). It also produces a set of two commemorative 500-lira coins each year, made out of silver. A typical commemorative coin will feature World Youth Day in Paris as its theme. No paper money is produced.

In the late 1990s, the Vatican once again began issuing gold coins, in 50,000-lira and 100,000-lira denominations. The coins feature external and internal views of Rome's four major basilicas, St. Peter, St. John Lateran, St. Paul, and St. Mary Major. Prior to that, the last time the Vatican minted gold coins was in 1959.

The Vatican's agreement with Italy, updated annually, allows it to mint one billion lire worth of circulating coins with the same denominations and specifications as those of Italy. Vatican and Italian coins are legal tender in both countries as well as in San Marino.

The circulating coins cost about half of their face value to mint, so a 500-lira coin costs the Vatican only 250 lire to produce. In addition, the Vatican sells the commemorative coins at more than five times their face value. A set of two 10,000-lira silver commemorative coins, for example, retails for 118,000 lire.

Neither the stamps nor the Vatican's coins are produced within the city-state but are "outsourced." The stamps are manufactured by various specialty printers in France, Germany, Holland, and Canada and then shipped to the Vatican. The coins, under a treaty agreement with Italy in effect since 1929, are produced solely by the Italian mint, or Zekka.

According to Olivieri, the office staff typically presents a certain number of ideas or themes to a special committee, the Pontifical Commission for the State of Vatican City, made up of five to seven cardinals, and the committee chooses which ones it likes. Next, the office will commission various artists to produce two or three different versions of each set. The president of the Pontifical Commission, at that time Cardinal Rosalio José Castillo Lara, as well as the commission secretary, Monsignor Gianni Danzi, decide which of the designs they like the best. The artist is then given the go-ahead to produce a final work.

Everything is done outside. The office, according to Olivieri, does not have a production department at all and merely turns over the camera-ready artwork—or sometimes computer disks—to the various printers. Artists are only too happy to have their work showcased as a Vatican stamp and therefore do not charge too much for their designs. Dr. Olivieri estimated a typical design might cost the Holy See around three million lire, or $2,500. Some artists even donate their designs.

The same design process is used in producing the Vatican coins, with the same committee choosing the designs. The difference is that fewer designers (sculptors) and designs are used. Unlike most countries, however—which keep the same coin designs for decades—the Vatican has a new design each year. The designers submit a chalk model, about the size of a Frisbee. Once the design is approved, the Italian mint will produce a final bronze model for approval. The coins are released in stages throughout the year.

At that point, I had learned more about the Vatican's stamps and coins than I had wanted. The indefatigable Olivieri, however, eager to promote his product, wanted to give me a tour. For hard-core stamp and coin enthusiasts, the Vatican has a Philatelic and Numismatic Museum, located on the top floor of the Vatican's old train station, to the left of the Government Palace near the southern wall of the state. The museum, he told me, features a fascinating display of all the Vatican's stamp and coin issues from 1929 to the present, arranged in chronological order. It also features little-known stamps from the Papal States that existed prior to 1870, with philatelic issues from 1852, 1864, 1867, and 1868. There is a lifesize reproduction of an 1837 road map of the old Papal States, showing the mail routes (to Appia, Cassia, Flaminia, Aurelia, etc.), where the Vatican mail coaches used to run.

I begged off. I told Olivieri, however, how refreshing it was to meet a Vatican official who not only answered my questions but offered me more information than I could use! He laughed. He had worked in the Vatican long enough to know how frustrating its bureaucracy was to outsiders.

Olivieri walked me out of the Philatelic and Numismatic Office and then into a marble hallway. I asked him if I could buy a set of coins, for a souvenir, and he quickly disappeared into a doorway. He returned with a complete set in a red velvet case. "Consider this a gift from the Holy See," he said.

I was horrified. Travel writers have a reputation for being moochers and freeloaders, but I hadn't been trying to finagle a free set of coins out of the guy. I insisted on paying for the set, but Olivieri wouldn't let me.

So in the interest of full disclosure, let me be up front about it: The Vatican gave me money for this chapter.

I walked out of the Government Palace full of new hope. All the people who work in the Vatican aren't uncooperative after all. The press officials were a waste of time, it's true, but that was so of almost any organization.

I called Glenn and then headed off for lunch. After a hard morning of interviewing, I was starved. A steaming plate of pasta and a little chicken cutlet sounded good.

How the Vatican Lost St. Peter's Bones

"I can show you the mortal spoils of the Apostles. You will find their remains in the Vatican [Peter], or along the road to Ostia [Paul]."

POPE ZEPHYRINUS (199–217)

"Pope Anacletus built and set in order a memorial shrine to the blessed Peter where the bishops might be buried."

Liber Pontificalis

About a hundred feet inside the Arch of the Bells, on the left side of the basilica, lies the tiny office of what are called, in Italian, the Scavi. This is where you go if you'd like to receive special permission to view the excavations—*scavi*—that have been conducted since the 1940s directly under the basilica.

These excavations were and still are one of the most astonishing finds in twentieth-century archaeology, guaranteed to send a *Raiders of the Lost Ark* thrill racing up your spine.

In a nutshell, not only did archaeologists discover what is almost certainly the first-century burial shrine of the apostle Peter—at least what second- and third-century Christians *believed* was the burial shrine—they may very well have discovered the apostle's actual bones as well.

But the entire project was so badly mucked up by a combination of sloppy archaeology, priestly piety, and bureaucratic arrogance, the Vatican rightly seems almost embarrassed by the whole affair and does little to publicize it.

The way the excavations were handled—bones whisked away in the middle of the night, stuffed in boxes and literally forgotten for more than a decade—there is good reason why most people, even most Catholics, know nothing about the whole story. It ends up sounding like a Hollywood movie all right, but more like a Laurel and Hardy farce than *Raiders of the Lost Ark*.

I had heard tidbits about this story for years. On February 24, 1939, while preparing a tomb for the recently deceased Pope Pius XI, *sampietrini* digging in the basilica's lower level, the so-called grottoes where all the popes are buried, made an amazing discovery: *Below* the grottoes, on a still lower, hitherto unknown level, were a series of ancient mausoleums. The reigning pope, Pius XII, gave cautious permission for excavations to proceed, and within a few years archaeologists were astonished to find an entire necropolis, or city of the dead, that dated all the way back to the first century.

Apparently it had been lying there, perfectly intact and untouched, since the construction of the first St. Peter's Basilica in A.D. 324.

What was more, supposedly the archaeologists also found an inscription that read, in Greek, "Peter is here." It was said—and indeed many guidebooks today still say—that the archaeologists found Peter's grave but, alas, it was empty. One paranoid Italian traditionalist magazine implied that a certain Jesuit had hidden away a key piece of evidence in his room at the Gregorian University out of a misplaced zeal for ecumenical relations. He was allegedly afraid that the discovery of Peter's bones would make efforts to patch things up between Catholics and Protestants more difficult. Catholics, after having had to listen for centuries to Protestant taunts that there was no proof that Peter ever even visited Rome, might be tempted to say, "See, we told you so, you evangelical blockheads!"

It's a great story, one well worth investigating. For nearly two thousand years the papacy has rested on a simple but, from a scientific viewpoint, as yet unverified claim: That the apostle Peter, appointed by Jesus Christ to be the head of his disciples, came to Rome, was martyred there during the persecutions of Nero in A.D. 64, and was succeeded in his office by an unbroken chain of bishops of Rome who act as the representative of Christ on earth.

This central claim of Catholicism is difficult to miss when you visit the basilica. Looking up from the high altar, you see, along the circular base of Michelangelo's glittering dome, written in six-foot-high golden letters, the words TU ES PETRUS, & SUPER HANC PETRAM ÆDIFICABO ECCLESIAM MEAM, & TIBI DABO CLAVES REGNI CÆLORUM.

"You are Peter, and upon this rock I will build my Church . . . and I will give to you the keys of the kingdom of heaven (Matthew 16:18)." This is a famous play on words—the words for "rock" in Latin (*petrus*), Greek (*petros*), and Aramaic (*kepha*) being the same as the name "Peter"—but it is not merely that . . . and perhaps not merely a metaphor. If it somehow turned out also to be literally true—that the center of the Roman Catholic Church was indeed built directly on top of the "rock" of Peter's mortal remains—that would be quite an apologetic coup.

There is no doubt that early Christians believed that both St. Peter and St. Paul came to Rome and perished in the Neronian persecution of the early A.D. 60s, the first organized attempt by Roman authorities to stamp out the new religion. St. Clement of Rome, who died around the year 100, wrote that both Peter and Paul died as part of the "great multitude of the elect" who were martyred by Nero. St. Eusebius of Caesarea (c. 260–339), the church historian, was more precise: He claims that both Peter and Paul died around the same time, the first by crucifixion, the second by beheading, in the fourteenth year of Nero's reign, or A.D. 67.

And there is no doubt that the early Christians venerated sites they believed, rightly or wrongly, were where the apostles were buried. Pope Zephyrinus (199–217) wrote in a letter that "I can show you the mortal spoils of the Apostles. You will find their remains in the Vatican [Peter], or along the road to Ostia [Paul]." In the sixth century *Liber Pontificalis,* a chronicle of the early popes, the location of Peter's burial site is fixed: "Peter was crowned with martyrdom along with Paul in the 38th year after the passion of the Lord. He was buried on the Via Aurelia near the temple of Apollo, alongside the circus of Nero on the Vatican near the area called Trionfale, in the area where he was crucified the 29th of June."

Having seen for myself the bizarre and touching burial shrines people fashion for beloved celebrities—from Elvis to Jim Morrison and John Keats—it is certainly plausible that if Peter had lost his life in Rome his friends and disciples would have carefully guarded the place where he was buried, indeed would have (if they could have) made it into some kind of shrine.

But the problem is this: There was never any corroborating archaeological proof to support the testimony of the early Christian writers. Of course, there is little corroborating archaeological proof for most of the Bible, including the existence of Jesus Christ; that in itself proves little. Nevertheless, some of the early Protestant reformers as well as a few modern historians have doubted that Peter ever set foot in Rome, much less was martyred and buried there. After all, these skeptics point out, the New Testament makes no mention whatsoever of Peter coming to Rome. And when you see some of the dubious relics honored by Catholic tradition in Italy—from Mary's house (which was miraculously transported from Palestine to Loreto, Italy) to Christ's crib, enshrined under the main altar at St. Mary Major—it's not unreasonable to wish there were more archaeological proof.

To see the excavations, you have to ask a Swiss Guard at the Arch of the Bells for permission to go to the Scavi Office and then fill out a questionnaire days, sometimes even weeks, in advance. You are then told to come back at a certain time, on a certain day, and that you may not bring any cameras, video equipment, or even tape recorders. Only authorized guides are allowed to show you the excavations.

I did all that and so, at nine-fifteen one morning, Glenn Ellen and I found ourselves standing outside the Scavi Office door with a small group of academics, clergymen, pilgrims, and journalists. Anne, our baby-sitter, was watching the kids while we took a tour together. It was the first date we'd had in weeks.

Our guide, Paul Halladay, was a ruggedly handsome seminarian from Mobile, Alabama, who was in his third year of theological studies at the North American College. He took us outside, in the archway next to the original site of the obelisk, clearly marked on the ground, and asked us to imagine ourselves back in time. This area is called the Piazza of the Protomartyrs.

In the first century, Paul explained, the area that is now the Vatican was largely unpopulated. Traditionally, Rome was built upon seven hills—the Capitoline, Quirinal, Viminal, Esquiline, Caelian, Aventine, and Palatine, still visible today—and the ancient Romans referred to the hilly, undeveloped region west of the Tiber River as the *Mons Vaticanus,* the Vatican Hill. The hill still exists, rising sharply from the rear of St. Peter's Basilica up to where the Vatican's radio towers are located.

In the year 37, the emperor Caligula decided to build a new circus, or oblong chariot racing track, on a flat plain at the base of the Vatican Hill. The circus, similar to the great Circus Maximus still visible in Rome, was roughly 590 yards long by 95 yards wide, extending from the end of the Bernini's colonnade to a point just fifty yards or so beyond the rear of the basilica. It held 80,000 people. Caligula also ordered the obligatory Egyptian obelisk to be imported and placed in the center of the circus on the *spina,* the raised rectangular platform around which the chariots raced. The obelisk, which was accidentally broken in half during transport, stood where Caligula put it for 1,500 years, until it was moved to its present location in 1586, when St. Peter's Square was completed.

Now, one weird thing about the ancient Romans: They liked to build their burial monuments, not off in some distant cemetery, but in a public place, where everyone could see them, such as along major roads like the Via Appia Antica or right outside theaters or circuses. As a result, right outside the Vatican circus were erected dozens of expensive mausoleums and pagan burial shrines. Most of these looked like miniature temples with a small niche to hold a cremation or cinerary urn.

The circus became a very popular spot for games, but by the year 64 it was actually in need of repair. The emperor Nero, who followed Caligula's successor, Claudius, started repair projects but was interrupted by the greatest tragedy to befall Rome since its founding. On July 19, 64 a great fire broke out in the city that burned for an entire week. When it was all over, three quarters of the city had been burned to the ground. (Contrary to popular belief, ancient Rome was not primarily a city of marble temples but rather one of large brick and wood apartment tenements.)

The people were enraged—and full of suspicions that Nero himself had ordered the fire set to make room for his building projects. To get off the hook, Nero did what any politician might do—he started looking around for a scapegoat and decided the new Jewish sect, called Christians, would do nicely. He blamed the fire on the Christians. That's when Nero decided to use the Vatican circus for a new kind of public spectacle: Feeding Christians to the lions! Even Roman enemies of Christianity, such as the historian Tacitus, found the new "games" distasteful. One of Nero's specialties included dipping Christian leaders in pitch and then using them as human torches at night.

Christian tradition has always held that Peter and Paul, as leaders of the Christian community in Rome, were both killed during this persecution—Peter allegedly by being crucified upside down on the *spina* of Caligula's circus. If that were the case, then it is not unreasonable to assume that his friends and disciples would have taken his body for burial in the large pagan cemetery that existed right outside the circus.

Paul brought our little tour group to a small doorway ten feet or so beyond the Scavi Office and then inside the basement of the basilica. There was an anteroom with two large models encased in plastic. The first was a model of a second-century Roman aedicula, or burial monument. The second was a model of Old St. Peter's Basilica.

The model of the aedicula is a reconstruction of what archaeologists discovered directly underneath the main papal altar. On the lowest level they found a primitive grave covered by thousands of Roman coins and slabs of tile tilted against one another forming a triangle. This was the primitive grave marker used by poor people in ancient Rome. Beneath this marker were found bones of two or three individuals (we'll get to that in a moment). Above the tile grave marker was built, around the year 150, an aedicula. An aedicula was a pagan burial shrine that looks like a two-tiered mini-temple, with two columns in front. Incredibly enough, you can still see these structures all over Rome, and I used to pass one almost every day on the Via delle Mura Aurelie.

What historians now believe happened is this. After Peter was crucified, his disciples took his body and buried it hurriedly, probably at night, in an unmarked grave in the nearest possible place—the pagan cemetery right outside the circus where he was executed. Over the decades, Christians continued to come pay their respects secretly but care was taken to make sure the site looked just like any other pagan gravesite, lest the authorities dig it up. Retaining walls were built to prevent dirt from the Vatican Hill from sliding onto the grave; eventually a formal burial monument, the aedicula, was built, but again according to pagan Roman custom (complete with a fake niche for a cinerary urn).

Such a burial monument is mentioned in extant sources. A Roman priest named Gaius, writing around the year 200, mentions the "tropaion [trophy] of Peter" on Vatican Hill, referring to a shrine. A little hole in the floor of this monument was left so that pilgrims could secretly toss in coins and other personal items as gestures of respect. This custom is still quite common in Italy. When I visited the Church of St. Peter in Chains, where Michelangelo's famous *Moses* is found, I was astonished to see, in a space before the main altar, thousands of coins and 1,000-lira notes.

The next big development occurred a century later, in 312, when two pagan Roman generals vying to be emperor, Constantine and his brother-in-law, Maxentius, faced each other in battle at the Milvian Bridge over the Tiber. According to tradition, before the battle Constantine saw a miraculous vision in the sky of the Christian Chi-Rho symbol for Christ (a P superimposed on an X) under which he saw the Greek words, *touto nike,* "by this victory." Not leaving anything to chance, the pagan Constantine had the Greek symbol placed on all his soldiers' shields along with the Latin translation of *touto nike,* which is *in hoc vinces.*

Despite being outnumbered two to one, Constantine won. As a token of his gratitude, he issued the Edict of Milan in 313, granting legal toleration of all religions in the empire, including the once-outlawed Christianity. He also, in 324, laid the foundation for the creation of a magnificent new church in honor of the apostle Peter, to be built directly on top of Peter's tomb. But strangely enough he did not build the church on the huge flat playing field where Caligula's circus once stood. Instead, he built it on the steep hill that rose behind the circus.

Historians insist this was because of the desire to build St. Peter's church above Peter's actual grave—and there is good evidence that this is true. There are many surviving records and drawings of Old St. Peter's, but we know the basilica had one very unusual characteristic: At the front of the church, directly under the apse, and directly over the spot where these ancient builders believed Peter was originally buried, stood a massive marble cube, a mausoleum. The cube, made out of marble and the rare semiprecious stone porphyry, from Egypt, stood nine feet tall. On a solid gold cross placed on the front of the marble monument were written the words: CONSTANTINE AUGUSTUS AND HELENA AUGUSTA (GIVE TO ST. PETER) THIS REGAL ABODE, SURROUNDED BY A HALL OF EQUAL SPLENDOR. Above the monument was an encompassing pergola made of finely carved marble columns brought by Constantine from Greece.

One of the most hair-raising discoveries of the early excavations occurred when archaeologists realized that the main papal altar of the current St. Peter's covers a whole series of earlier papal altars—stacked one on top of the other, like plastic lawn chairs—but that at the bottom of all these papal altars stood Constantine's marble box! It was still there, completely intact. And inside of *it* was the second-century burial monument.

But we're getting ahead of ourselves.

To build Old St. Peter's Basilica on a steep hill, however, Constantine first had to create a level foundation. To do that, he built a series of massive retaining walls—seven feet thick and thirty-five feet high at the base—down the slope. To the horror of the pagan Roman families, Constantine proceeded to simply fill in the brick foundation thus created with soft, porous dirt. This dirt covered the second- and third-century cemetery and completely preserved it, like Pompeii covered by volcanic ash. It lay there undisturbed for sixteen hundred years, until workers began digging in 1939.

With that introduction, Paul took our group down a steep circular staircase into the Scavi itself. We walked through a narrow door and into . . . a first-century Roman street. Actually, it was a Roman street in a Roman cemetery. The walls were made of ultra-thin bricks, which is typical of first-century Roman construction. There was a series of family mausoleums, most about twenty feet square, and each contained the remains of several prominent Romans. Archaeologists have been able to discover a lot about the people still buried in these tombs. Roman pagans by and large cremated their dead, whereas Christians, following Jewish custom, practiced full-body burials. One of the first bodies discovered was that of a Christian woman, Aemelia Gorgonia, who was only twenty-eight years, two months, and twenty-eight days old when she died. Their families left secret signs that only fellow Christians would recognize.

The whole thing reminded me of the Underground Seattle exhibit I saw as a child. When city planners in Seattle decided to raise the level of the city streets in the early twentieth century, they basically placed the old city—streetlamps and shopwindows—below ground. You can visit these old Wild West streets, which still exist, on a special tour. And this is exactly what the Scavi are like.

When the excavations got really interesting, though, was when Pope Pius XII finally and rather reluctantly gave permission for the archaeologists to dig directly beneath the high papal altar. The work began in the middle of the Second World War, in 1942, and continued until the end of the war. A team of four Vatican archaeologists from the Pontifical Institute for Christian Archaeology, led by a Jesuit, Father Engelbert Kirschbaum, worked with the *sampietrini* under strict orders from the pope not to undermine St. Peter's structural integrity. The archaeologists were supervised by the rector of the basilica, Monsignor Ludwig Kaas, a German scholar with no training in archaeology.

It was Monsignor Kaas who, acting on his own initiative, single-handedly screwed up the excavations. One writer described Kaas's actions as "the most regrettable and egregious blunder in archaeological history."

Once the archaeologists received permission to dig under the high papal altar, they turned their attention to what is called the Niche of the Pallia. In the basilica as it exists today—and as it has existed since the sixteenth century—there is a pair of marble stairways that lead down from the top floor of the basilica, in front of the high papal altar, to a special subterranean shrine area. This is not unique to St. Peter's; other great Roman basilicas, such as St. Mary Major's, have similar lower-level shrines below the high altar. In St. Peter's, though, the lower-level shrine area has always been venerated as the apostle's grave, and it is in this shrine area that is kept a special box in which are placed the *pallia,* the narrow strips of white lamb's wool, marked with six purple crosses, that are worn only by the pope and archbishops.

The archaeologists began to systematically probe around this ancient shrine area beneath the papal altar, prying off marble covers and knocking down brick walls that had been untouched for centuries. They quickly made one discovery after the other. First they found a series of papal altars stacked one on top of the other, from the sixteenth century on top of the sixth century on the bottom. Then, underneath the sixth-century altar of Pope Gregory the Great, they discovered a huge marble and porphyry cube, which they quickly identified as Constantine's original monument.

Until this time no one had known that this monument, described in ancient Vatican records, still existed. Next to the monument, extending out from it, they also found an unusual ancient wall covered with a forest of scratched-on graffiti. Near the bottom of this graffiti wall there was a small ragged opening, covered with plaster, and when they peered in through a tiny crack they could see that it was a large, marble-lined cavity of some kind. The archaeologists decided to explore it later and turned to other, more pressing tasks. Finally, the archaeologists tunneled straight down and underneath the monument, discovering a first-century grave and a large number of human bones.

All along, there was incredible tension between the archaeologists and Monsignor Kaas. The rector felt the archaeologists were being far too casual with the bones and human remains that they discovered and numerous arguments broke out. Finally, the archaeologists, fed up with Kaas's interference, proposed a solution: If he would leave them in peace during the day, Monsignor Kaas could come and inspect their work each night. If he found something that bothered him, then the archaeologists and he could have a meeting to settle the dispute. Kaas agreed.

As a result, each night Monsignor Kaas would descend into the excavations with a flashlight, accompanied by a trusted *sampietrino*, Giovanni Segoni, and do his inspections. Whenever he found bones lying about, he would scoop them up and place them in special wooden boxes for reburial at a later date. The day the archaeologists discovered the graffiti wall, therefore, Kaas and Segoni went down, enlarged the crack at the base of the wall—and carefully scooped out dozens of bones and pieces of cloth they found inside. Kaas placed these bones in a box and marked it OSSA-URNA-GRAF (bones-urn-graffiti), and put the box in a cupboard in his office. It was early 1942, and the box remained in his office, unnoticed, for more than a decade.

Meanwhile, the archaeologists, while aware of Kaas's inspections in general, had no idea that he had done this. When they returned to the graffiti wall a week or so later, they set about exploring the cavity and, much to their surprise, found it was completely empty except for a few splinters of bone. As a result, they began tunneling underneath the monument, where they found the grave and bones up inside of it.

By the end of the war, the archaeologists were ready to begin writing their official report. It took four years, but finally, on Christmas Eve 1949, Pope Pius XII told the world, via radio, that the grave of St. Peter had definitely been discovered. As for the bones that were found in the grave, the pope was more restrained: "It is impossible to prove with certainty that they belong to the body of the apostle," he said. The final report stated that the cavity found in the graffiti wall had been found to be empty except for a few bone splinters.

In 1952, Monsignor Kaas died. A few months later, a woman came into the investigation who single-handedly provoked a complete reevaluation of the evidence and led to the discovery of Peter's bones. Her name was Dr. Margherita Guarducci, a fifty-year-old professor of Greek epigraphy at the University of Rome. She was an expert in ancient writing who had been invited by the Vatican to decode some of the strange markings found in the Scavi. It was Dr. Guarducci who finally figured out the elaborate spiritual cryptography that covered the graffiti wall— the way the early Christians altered letters in ordinary names to create a kind of alphabetical symbolism. The Chi-Rho symbol in particular—the P superimposed on an X, forming the first two letters of the word *Christ* in Greek—was altered by turning the bottom part of the P into a small E. This had the effect of making the P look like a key, which was also a symbol of Peter (as in the "keys of the kingdom"). But the most amazing discovery of all occurred when Guarducci was able to translate words written on a small chunk of red plaster that had been found, a decade earlier, inside the graffiti wall cavity. There were two Greek words, one on top of the other—ΠΕΤΡ and ΕΝΙ. Other scholars had instantly recognized this as saying *Petros eni*, which is ordinary Greek for "Peter is here." But Guarducci saw that *eni* could also be a poetic contraction of the Greek verb *eneoti*, meaning "is within." Either way, it was a tantalizing piece of evidence that this spot was indeed Peter's grave.

One day, during a break in her work, Dr. Guarducci accidentally bumped into the *sampietrino* Giovanni Segoni, now promoted to head foreman. The two stood in front of the graffiti wall, and Dr. Guarducci remarked casually that she couldn't believe the Vatican archaeologists hadn't found anything inside the wall cavity, given all the symbols on the wall. "Oh, but we *did* find things, a lot of bones," Segoni replied, genuinely surprised. "I emptied the hole myself."

Guarducci was astonished. The official report clearly indicated that the graffiti wall cavity had been found empty. Segoni took the scholar to a dusty storeroom upstairs in the basilica and showed her dozens and dozens of small wooden and metal boxes, all containing bones discovered early in the excavations. He explained that Monsignor Kaas had collected them for reburial one day, and he, Segoni, still didn't know what to do with them all. He finally located one box in particular, the one in which he had placed all the bones found in the graffiti wall cavity. It was marked, in faded pencil, OSSA-URNA-GRAF.

Guarducci couldn't believe her eyes. Inside the wooden box was found, not the few "splinters" described in the official report, but a large pile of 135 bones, some six to ten inches in length. Also found in the box were shreds of a decaying purple fabric that also had flashes of what looked like gold threads. This incredible discovery, for a variety of reasons, took more than a decade to fully investigate, but eventually, in 1963, anthropologists began to examine the bones scooped out by Monsignor Kaas and Segoni from the graffiti wall cavity. Unlike the bones found in Peter's actual grave—which were from three individuals, two men and one woman—the bones found in the cavity were proven to be all from the same individual, an elderly male of heavy build, about five feet seven inches tall.

What's more, the encrusted soil on the bones matched exactly the soil found in Peter's grave, dating from the first century; and the purple cloth with solid gold threads was found to have been dyed with the same rare purple pigment (made from the Mediterranean shellfish *murex brandaris*) reserved by Roman law for the emperor. A closer examination of the wall cavity also found that it had not been disturbed for at least sixteen hundred years, from the late third century until Segoni and

Monsignor Kaas had widened the small opening and scooped out the bones.

The evidence was substantial that the early Christian community—still fiercely persecuted off and on in the years before Constantine—had dug up Peter's bones in the shallow grave, wrapped them in an expensive cloak of royal purple and gold, and had hidden them in a makeshift cavity in the graffiti wall. Later, a pagan burial monument had been built over the actual gravesite, next to the graffiti wall. When Constantine announced his intention of building a magnificent basilica over Peter's grave, Sylvester I, the reigning pope, had revealed to him the general location of the grave but had kept the actual location of the wall niche a secret. As a result, when Constantine built his fabulous marble and porphyry cube, he had enclosed the whole structure—the pagan *aedicula* monument, the graffiti wall, even a portion of the red wall behind it. Everything was enclosed in the marble box, where it had remained, untouched, until 1942, when Monsignor Kaas and Giovanni Segoni had scooped out the bones found in the graffiti wall niche.

It all made a pretty good case. As a result, on June 27, 1968, Pope Paul VI announced to the world that the bones of St. Peter, the first pope and prince of the apostles, had in fact been found. In a special ceremony, the bones were placed in a series of nineteen clear plastic boxes—provided by the United States Department of Defense—and reinterred in the graffiti wall cavity, where they remain to this day.

Our guide, Paul, took our group up a stairway onto a metal platform. There was a large rectangular window, and through the window he flashed a red laser beam. About ten feet away, through an opening in a wall, we could see one of the plastic boxes with a large white lump inside. "If you look inside this hole right here," Paul said, "what you're going to see is a clear plastic box, and inside that box you'll see a white mass, and that white mass is part of the bones of blessed St. Peter."

Leaning over Glenn's shoulder, I took a good look. Peter's bones looked like a lump of gray clay.

Scholarly reaction to the Vatican's 1968 announcement of the discovery of Peter's bones was somewhat skeptical, to say the least. The absurd lost-and-found aspect of the discovery—the many breaks in what lawyers call the chain of evidence—clearly undermined scholarly confidence in the discovery. The Vatican archaeologists ended up looking like amateurs . . . and Monsignor Kaas like a—well, like a typical Vatican bureaucrat, a bit too sure of his methods.

Still, the whole story was and is pretty eerie. Whether or not the bones resting in the plastic boxes are Peter's actual bones, what has been established beyond a reasonable doubt is that the area now located directly beneath the high papal altar was a Christian grave shrine from the earliest years of Christianity and was carefully preserved, hidden under one altar after another, for two millennia. It definitely gives you a strange thrill to walk around in the Scavi. The very antiquity of the place—the fact that you're clomping around a first-century Roman cemetery, for one thing—is yet another reminder of just how far back in time the Vatican's reach extends.

XI

Survival Strategies in the Roman Curia

The Italians owe a great debt to the Roman church and its clergy. Through their example, we have lost all true religion and become complete unbelievers. Take it as a rule, the nearer a nation dwells to the Roman Curia, the less religion it has.

NICCOLÒ MACHIAVELLI

I t is a sad fact of nature that priests and bishops are early risers and so, if I wanted to talk to any of them, I had to get up, like a monk, before dawn.

The good news, however, was that the early morning is a magical time to see St. Peter's, particularly in the spring or fall. The air is crystal-clear, and features of the great basilica become far more apparent without the harsh glare of direct sunlight glancing off all that porous travertine.

For one thing, I saw better just how dirty parts of the facade have become from pollution. It looked as though someone tipped a large vat of mud over the top and let it slide down the front, missing most of the columns and thinning out toward the bottom.

And there were weird, quirky things to see that early. The square was almost always deserted, but on one particular morning when I arrived, there was a middle-aged man, dressed in a suit and standing in front of the obelisk, singing a song about Mary (I think) at the top of his lungs. He was dancing a sort of jig and pointing up at the central window of the basilica, where the pope appears at big events. I had seen him in the identical spot a month earlier at the same time, singing the same song.

As I mentioned before, the Vatican draws all sorts of weird, psychologically disturbed characters. Many of them are found in what is known as the Curia, the Vatican's central government or bureaucracy.

The word *curia* comes, naturally, from ancient Rome, where it meant pretty much what it does in the Vatican—the emperor's court or central administration. (In the Roman Forum, you can still see the ruins of the ancient Roman Curia building.)

In the early days of the papacy, from about the fourth century onward, the pope's immediate administrative offices were called the Apostolic Chancery. But in 1588, following the Council of Trent, Pope Sixtus V (1585–1590) organized what became the modern Curia—although some of its major departments, such as that in charge of the papal navy, no longer exist. (Yes, the pope once had a naval fleet of sorts.) It is a vast, interwoven bureaucracy of about 1,500 people who make up numerous congregations, offices, commissions, councils, tribunals, and service departments, all called dicasteries, that assist the pope in running the worldwide Church. In the past century there have been three efforts to reform, streamline, and reorganize the Curia—by Pope St. Pius X in 1908, Pope Paul VI in 1967, and Pope John Paul II in 1988—none of them fully successful.

On an organizational chart the College of Cardinals (all the cardinals) and the worldwide Synod of Bishops (all the bishops) come under the pope, followed by the Vatican Secretariat of State, the vicariate of Rome, the nine congregations (each headed by a cardinal), the three tribunals, the twelve pontifical councils, the five Holy See offices, and the twenty-one curial agencies. In actual practice, however, about two thirds of the cardinals and most of the bishops live in other countries and come together only for annual meetings. And as for all of the various agencies in the Vatican, only a handful have any real power—the Secretariat of State above all, the various financial agencies, the Congregation for the Doctrine of the Faith (the Holy Office), and the Prefecture of the Papal Household. While cardinals and archbishops hold the top positions in many Vatican agencies, the real power, as in any bureaucracy, is often wielded by small groups of middle-level bureaucrats, almost always priests.

These bureaucrats have always been viewed with suspicion, if not outright contempt, by ordinary Catholics and even many bishops. During Vatican II, it became obvious that even many high churchmen, found in dioceses all over the world, were seething with resentment over what they believed were the insolence, stupidity, and Italian chauvinism of the Roman Curia.

This is not a new attitude. In Boccaccio's *Decameron,* written in the mid-fourteenth century, there is a story about a Jewish merchant in Paris, Abraam, who was considering converting to Catholicism. But first, he says, he has to visit Rome and see the pope for himself. The merchant's Italian friends are horrified. They realize that if he goes to Rome and sees the debauched and ignominious behavior of the clergy there, he will never convert. In fact, if a Christian went there, he would end up converting to Judaism. The Jewish merchant presses ahead, though, and makes the journey. Upon his return, Abraam announces to his friends that Rome convinced him that Christianity must be the true religion after all.

His Italian friends can't believe it. Has the Curia reformed?

Quite the contrary, the Jewish merchant replies. While visiting the Vatican, he saw more avarice, gluttony, and lust than he ever imagined possible. As a result, he is now convinced that God must be guiding the Church, because otherwise it would never have survived for so long.

Speaking with any high-level curial official is extremely difficult because of the universal Code of Silence discussed earlier. Journalistic credentials are not enough. During my time in Rome, the religion or political writers for a dozen different major U.S. daily newspapers would come to Rome and try to get an appointment to see various curial officials. To the journalists' complete and total astonishment, and increasing anger, no one would talk to them.

They had never encountered such bald-faced stonewalling in their entire careers or, if they had, it was almost always to cover up some known crime.

What many journalists fail to realize, however, is that the Curia does not discriminate. It treats everyone that way—including the world's 2,400 active diocesan bishops. More than one U.S. bishop, accustomed to being treated like a celebrity or CEO back home—in other words, as an all-powerful autocrat in charge of hundreds of millions of dollars—has cooled his heels for days in Rome, waiting for some snotty curial monsignor to make room in his busy schedule to see him.

Every five years a bishop is supposed to make what is called an *ad limina* (literally, "to the thresholds") visit to Rome—to personally report to the pope on the state of his diocese. This is an ancient custom, dating back at least to the ninth century. The bishop makes a pilgrimage to the tombs of St. Peter and St. Paul and then gives an oral summary of the detailed written report, or *relatio,* sent to the pope months earlier. As the Jesuit social scientist Thomas Reese has pointed out, however, new bishops are frequently shocked by the perfunctory treatment they receive in Rome. For one thing, they often find no one has read their report. Their meeting with the pope lasts all of fifteen minutes, during which time the bishop presents the pope with a little envelope containing a fat check. The pope usually asks the most mundane of questions—how many priests are in your diocese? How many people?

The bishop was expecting a serious heart-to-heart discussion with the big guy himself—to let him know how he really feels the Church is faring in his neck of the woods—and he finds, instead, he's treated pretty much the way any visiting Catholic big shot is treated, patted on the head, told to keep up the good work . . . and thanked for his donation.

The mathematics of the situation partly explains all this, of course. With 2,400 active bishops in the world, the pope has to see ten per week to get around to all of them in five years. It's no wonder that in the 1980s, when John Paul II would have lunch with a dozen or so bishops at a time during their *ad limina* visits, he would simply refer to them by the name of their diocese. "So, tell me, Detroit, what do you think of L.A.'s proposal?"

To get in to see members of the Curia you need contacts . . . and, preferably, the ability to speak one or two foreign languages. I finally found some officials who spoke French. And with Luca, my Italian translator, I was able to speak to a few more. The English-speaking Curia officials are very reluctant to talk with journalists because they know their comments are easily traced back to them. In a given Vatican congregation, there may only be one or two monsignors who happen to speak English, so if "unnamed sources" in the Congregation for the Clergy are quoted in, say, *The Times* of London, you'd better believe that the Curia's gestapo chief will be hauling in these two English-speaking prelates and pulling out their fingernails until one of them confesses to the crime.

That's why I had to get up so early. I had an interview with a top curial official and we had to talk before the cardinal, his boss, got to his desk. It was an important congregation, with a large (by the Vatican's standards) staff, but only a few people were around this early. A guard led me up to a spacious office covered with tapestries and a large marble bust of a pope standing on a pedestal. I'll call my contact this day Bishop Arnauld.

A tall, thin man with gray hair and bright green eyes, dressed in a simple black suit (no cassock), Bishop Arnauld received me only because I know a good friend of his—and speak a little French. He insisted that I may not quote him directly by name nor may I refer to the name of his congregation, even as a "high Vatican official" in it. He explained what I said earlier. With so few people working in each congregation, it's easy to track people down by language group.

Once I agreed to these rules, however, Bishop Arnauld relaxed. He offered me a cup of coffee. Curial officials love to gossip—indeed, in some ways it's their stock-in-trade, the ammunition they need to survive—and he was more than willing to name names. But he is, he said, basically a decent enough fellow and doesn't want to attack people without provocation.

In a nutshell, Bishop Arnauld said that the exaggerated stereotypes about the Curia—that it's a vast bureaucracy where power-mad prelates plot small coups d'état without regard for the laws of God or man—are sadly but absolutely true.

At the same time, however, the Curia is somehow able to get a tremendous amount of work done while keeping the innumerable antagonistic forces in the Roman Catholic Church at least somewhat mollified. Bishop Arnauld repeated a thought I've heard elsewhere, that the Curia's icy aloofness, its very Italian love of all things petty and bureaucratic, actually keeps the Church on an even keel, preventing disorienting lurches to the left or the right. Its lumbering inefficiency, in other words, makes for slow but sound judgments.

The problem with the Curia is not on the level of the worldwide Church; it's with the price individuals who work in it have to pay, he said.

Like all entrenched bureaucracies, the Curia is essentially based on a patronage system. You get your job by knowing someone, a friend of a friend of a bishop; and you advance, oftentimes, by carefully and systematically eliminating all rivals for the position you want, including the person currently holding it. You eliminate people either through direct character assassination (hints about their sexual orientation, perhaps) or, more typically, by getting them transferred.

"Oh, it's very easy to get rid of someone if he's a religious," the bishop told me with a chuckle. "It's more difficult with ordinary (secular) priests. All you have to do is have someone you know make a call to that person's provincial, the head of his order, and he'll be gone in a week. You know, they'll tell him, 'You are very much needed at our high school in Dakar.' And he's gone."

The bishop insisted he's not a "player," ("*je ne joue pas*," he said flatly) although he knows the rules of the game only too well. He says that in the Curia there are those who play hardball and those who don't, who just do their jobs and try to survive.

The ones playing the game are aiming high, to be an archbishop or cardinal . . . or even pope. He said he knows of one top Vatican official who, once he was made bishop, actually brought down a white *zucchetto* (the papal skullcap) given to him by a previous pope. "I'll be wearing this one day," the official said.

"Quite honestly, when you look at the ruthlessness of some of these people, you have to wonder if they even believe in God," Bishop Arnauld said.

A particularly dicey time in the Curia is toward the end of a pontificate, when everyone begins maneuvering for more secure jobs, paying off old debts, and, most important of all, settling scores. Although there is a permanent civil service–like quality to the Curia, many top Vatican officials do serve solely at the pleasure of the pope. This means not only do they lose their *jobs* when he dies, but also their ability to fix things for their friends and patrons. As a result, everyone begins scrambling long before a pope actually dies. And ambitious prelates will use the transition periods for pure vengeance.

A widely known event occurred during the year of the three popes, 1978. The then–second in command of the Secretary of State, the powerful *sostituto* ("substitute," or deputy), had a particular loathing for Father John Magee, the burly Irish bodyguard and confidant to Paul VI. When Pope Paul died, the bishop took Magee aside and told him flat out that he wanted his ugly face out of the Apostolic Palace by the following Saturday. In the meantime, the Venetian patriarch Albino Luciani, was elected Pope John Paul I. When the new pope saw Magee packing his bags and preparing to leave, he asked him what was going on. "Well, the *sostituto* told me to be gone by Saturday," Magee replied. "Nonsense," the pope told him. So Magee went back and unpacked his bags.

The bishop saw him and demanded to know why he was still lurking inside the Vatican's walls. Magee told him that he'd have to take the matter up with the pope, because the pope said he should stay.

The bishop fumed. One month later, of course, John Paul I keeled over dead from a heart attack, and the first thing the *sostituto* did was to march into Magee's office and tell him to get lost—*now*! But then John Paul II was elected, and once again Magee got a reprieve. John Paul knew and respected Magee and quickly insisted he wanted him on his team. Eventually, it was the *sostituto* who went packing, exiled to some distant administrative post far from the avenues of power and privilege.

Bishop Arnauld attempted to summarize for me the mentality that lies behind Pope Paul VI's detailed *Regolamento Generale della Curia Romana* (General Rules of the Roman Curia), issued in 1968. The dominant character trait, above all, is circumspection—the ability to avoid expressing an opinion about any person, place, or thing, unless absolutely necessary to further one's own interests. This hypertimidity breeds an atmosphere of secrecy and paranoia that outsiders find pathological but which curial insiders believe to be the noblest kind of discretion.

The avoidance of a declarative statement of any kind, the lawyerly insistence on linguistic precision, extends to the most ordinary kinds of things. If you write a letter to the Vatican about anything, the Vatican agency that receives it does not respond, as most ordinary people would, "Thank you for your letter of August 22." Vatican officials fear that such a response might someday be used against the Holy See, as though by thanking the letter writer the Church might be seen as endorsing whatever cockeyed project or criticism is contained in his letter. As a result, Vatican correspondence always uses the more diplomatic phrase, "We acknowledge receipt of your communication of August 22."

Toward the end of our conversation, Bishop Arnauld resorted to one of the worst clichés any reporter hears in the Vatican. Almost without exception, every Vatican bureaucrat I ever met would eventually fall back on the same expression, "After all, we're just human beings." Some of these bureaucrats indulge in plots and acts of character assassination that would get them instantly *fired* in any large corporation or secular government; yet they routinely seek to excuse or downplay such behavior by appealing, in an allegedly worldly, boys-will-be-boys sort of way, to basic human weakness.

Unlike the puritanical and simplistic Americans, these bureaucrats will say, we worldly Italians understand how life really works—and how fallible human beings *really* are.

I finally heard one American journalist work up the nerve to counter this self-serving position. "I'm certainly not *surprised* that Vatican bureaucrats might ruin someone's life just to advance their own petty little careers . . . but, in any well-run organization, they'd be fired anyway."

Obviously, the higher up the food chain a Vatican bureaucrat happens to be, the less crude his (or, rarely, her) power plays tend to be. Cardinals seem to be far more cordial and smooth than lowly bishops; and bishops are usually easier to deal with than priests. The worst by far are the lay Italians who work inside the Vatican and consider it a sign of their innate superiority to all other forms of life. The Code of Silence—and the vulnerability of their positions—make them almost uniformly hostile, evasive, and rude to anyone not wearing scarlet. (There are exceptions to this, of course, and you will occasionally run into a lay Italian office worker who is actually friendly and helpful.)

My time with Bishop Arnauld was up very quickly. Although we chatted for an hour and a half, it seemed like ten minutes. For a curial official, he was actually amazingly forthright, even downright talkative. I could see that if you were patient—were willing to carefully cultivate friendships over, say, a couple of decades—an enterprising journalist could eventually penetrate at least the outer layers of the Vatican.

But my overwhelming feeling leaving his office was: *Who would want to?*

XII

Inside the Secret Archives

I was frustrated. The Code of Silence was beginning to get on my nerves. One American monsignor, when I told him I found it easier to just interview people informally—as a curious tourist and not as a journalist—told me I had to be very careful I didn't get someone fired. "The rector of St. Peter's is a son of a bitch," he said matter-of-factly. "He'll hunt down whomever you talk to and fire him on the spot. If it's a layperson, he might have a family to support."

This was a cardinal he was talking about, a man, theoretically at least, who could be the next pope. These were the people to whom I was entrusting the care of my soul?

So it was a pleasant surprise when, one warm, sunny afternoon, I came home to find a letter waiting for me in my mailbox at the bottom of the stairs. It was from the Archivio Segreto Vaticano, the Vatican Secret Archives, addressed to the Illustrious Sir "Doctor" Hutchinson. (Italians award themselves the title of "doctor" merely by graduating from a four-year college, a bit of grade inflation that while allowing for impressive titles, makes it very difficult for them to study outside Italy.) I had written to the archives months earlier (in Italian) and had assumed they had, like some other Vatican offices, merely ignored my letters.

I opened the letter and read it . . . or at least tried to. At first my hopes sank. It said *"le visite all'Archivio sono sospese per l'anno in corso e per il anno 19—."* All visits to the archives are suspended for the rest of this year and next year. But then the letter went on, because my visit was "cultural" and necessary for my "volume," they were going to make an exception in my case—if I could visit early in the morning. Please contact the *vice prefetto* at such and such a telephone number.

Yippee! The Vatican Secret Archives!

I danced a little jig around my office. I knew that they allowed in only two hundred scholars a year, and they made them sit at special desks in the Study Room while attendants brought them whatever documents they requested. When I asked Antonio, a veteran Vatican reporter who worked in Irish Bob's office, where he could *never* go in the Vatican, he said only two places—the papal apartments and the Secret Archives.

The next day I had Luca call the telephone numbers and make sure I really did have an invitation. The *vice prefetto* was as friendly as could be, and explained that he would conduct the tour himself personally, if my Italian was up to the task, or he would assign an English- or French-speaking archivist if I preferred that. I replied, through Luca, that I would accept whatever was most convenient to them and we would make do with whatever languages were available. The vice prefect told us to arrive the next day at ten o'clock, through Porta Sant'Anna.

For the rest of the afternoon I reread everything I could about the archives. They were the subject of enormous mystery and scholarly curiosity.

Supposedly, they contain some of the greatest secrets of history—

behind-the-scenes reports of the various papal conclaves; intimate sexual details of illicit affairs conducted by kings and queens, bishops, and even a few popes; the records of annulment proceedings of the Holy Roman Rota; accusations of witchcraft and Masonic occultism in high places; eyewitness accounts of wars, assassinations and coups d'état; the records of the Spanish Inquisition.

There were supposedly more than thirty miles of shelves, all lined with books and files, boxes and boxes of uncatalogued records. There were said to be tens of thousands of documents, gathered by the Vatican's secret agents in top government posts, many still in a special ecclesiastical code, reporting on political intrigues spanning a thousand years.

And much more: boxes and boxes of handwritten letters describing conflicts involving the greatest names of history, from Luther and Calvin to Napoleon and Lenin. One *armadio* contains the handwritten records of the trial of Galileo; another the letters of Joan of Arc, written in the fifteenth century. Still another holds top secret Vatican communiqués about most of the world's leaders, including the reigning monarch of England and the United States president. One special vault, about the size of a large walk-in closet, contains the most precious of the secret documents. In one drawer is the final letter to Pope Paul IV from the deposed English Catholic queen, Mary Tudor, written moments before she was beheaded on orders from Queen Elizabeth I. There is a drawer containing the love letters, allegedly quite spicy, between King Henry VIII and Anne Boleyn. There are ancient parchments that date back to the twelfth century, letters between emperors and popes, documents pertaining to the Crusades, the official texts promulgating the dogma of the Immaculate Conception of Mary in 1854, letters from the Khan of Persia written in Mongolian.

There are incredible handwritten documents that would make any scholar's hands tremble with excitement—such as a letter, in Chinese, from the Empress Helena to Pope Innocent X . . . or a vellum scroll, written in Greek, from the Byzantine emperor.

Most of these documents still remain off limits even to renowned scholars, and the Vatican has declared that no documents more recent than seventy-five years may be examined.

One special locked metal box, kept in the special vault, is said to contain the so-called Third Secret of Fatima, the handwritten record by a nun, Sister Lucia dos Santos, of visions she alleged to have had in Fatima, Portugal, that concern World War III and the end of the world.

The next morning I got up early. It was one of those magical Rome mornings, cool and clear, when the Eternal City seems like the center of the world it once was. The streets glistened with dew. The fresh scent of pine trees and azaleas drifted in the windows. From the balcony of the kitchen I could see the owners of the Enoteca, across the Piazza Ceresi, bringing fresh bread into the store.

Anne, our mother's helper, arrived and helped get the kids breakfast. I took a shower, got dressed, and kissed Glenn and the kids goodbye. I wanted to get an early start.

I took my usual bus down the hill, transferring on the Via Giacinto Carini, and made it to the Vatican in just twenty minutes. I had time for a quick brioche and cappuccino at the little café next to the Secretariat of the Synod, a few doors down from the Sala Stampa.

I had arranged to meet Luca at nine forty-five at Porta Sant'Anna, but he was late. I went in to get our visitor's passes at the Vigilanza office, quickly filling in the special forms they require before issuing a visitor's pass. The Vigilanza guard behind the glass partition looked blankly at me. His only question was the date when my California driver's license had been issued. I had no idea. No one had ever asked me for that before.

But by then I realized that for Italians it is of the utmost importance that every bureaucratic T be crossed, every form filled in and properly stamped, dated, and stamped again, so I quickly searched for the date on the license. Finally, I found at the bottom, in tiny letters, what appeared to be an issue date. The Vigilanza guard, having been duly vigilant, was satisfied. He stamped my pass with two different stamps, signed the circular stamp, and waved me out.

I found Luca outside by the gate, looking for me, and so he had to go through the same procedure. In due course, we both had our visitor's pass and went in search of the Secret Archives.

The entrance, on the northern side of the Cortile del Belvedere, is just fifty feet or so to the left of the entrance to the Vatican Library, so that was easy. As we walked through the gate into the courtyard, we had to dash for the entrance because it had begun to rain lightly.

In the entryway of the Secret Archives, there was what looked like a hotel desk and two Italian doormen, both of whom were very friendly and apparently had been expecting us. On the left wall, as we came in, was a glass case in which were displayed various learned publications about some of the contents of the archives.

A young Italian restorer named Flavian soon appeared, dressed in a white lab coat. He was a short man, with a wispy mustache and light brown hair slightly covering his ears, who had been given the onerous task of showing us around. The vice prefect was tied up in meetings, he said, and didn't speak very good English at any rate.

Flavian had been working at the Secret Archives for only three months. It was clear that Luca and I were not exactly VIPs, but that was true enough and, besides, it turned out we were able to finagle more information out of this young guy than we ever could have out of the cardinal.

Flavian first showed us the ground floor library and *sala di studio,* where the scholars work. As noted before, the Vatican allows only about two hundred scholars a year to use the Secret Archives, and they have to stay seated in this room, or the nearby Index Room, to use the materials. It contains two rows of ancient desks, each about six feet long, now fitted with electrical outlets for the scholars' laptop computers along with the traditional book stands. Flavian took us silently through this room, around the desk where the scholars request their materials, and back up a little series of steps into the Index Room.

The Index Room contains well over a thousand different indexes, many themselves very old, to all of the catalogued material in the archives. The problem, of course, is that much of the material is still uncatalogued. Flavian pointed to two different volumes sitting on a little stand near the front. That, of course, was the Index to the Indexes, so you'd know where to begin looking, at least.

The next stop was what Flavian kept calling the bunker—the Manuscript Depository built in 1980 below the vast Cortile della Pigna (the Courtyard of the Pine Cone). To reach it, he walked us over to one of those tiny European-style elevators that hold only three people and in which, when you step into them, you can actually feel the cables begin to stretch and bounce. We were going underground. Luca, who sheepishly admitted to being claustrophobic, begged off. "I'll just wait for you up here, by the Index Room," he said.

The bunker actually turned out to be nothing more than an underground library—two stories, made up of steel mesh flooring and stairs, with more than 30,000 cubic feet of storage space. It is where the main "deposit," as Flavian called it, is kept. There are actually three "deposits," the main one underground in the bunker and two smaller ones in the old *piani nobili,* the "noble floors."

Down, down, we went. We walked out of the elevator, down a concrete-lined corridor. To my astonishment, there were little library carts on which were casually stacked a few ancient parchments with papal seals still attached. In the Vatican Archives, centuries-old documents that would be proudly on display in any American university library, in the central entryway, are just stacked out of the way.

"It's just like in any other archive," Flavian said, seeing the incredulity on my face. "Things stack up and get pushed to the side."

Flavian then led me into the bunker proper. There was nothing but miles of steel-gray shelves on which were neatly stacked the various *regestra,* thick volumes of bound papers that make up the bulk of the Vatican Secret Archives. Along one wall there was a series of wire cages, their doors locked tight with padlocks, in which were kept more sensitive materials. We went up a metal flight of stairs to the second floor of the bunker and walked through row after row of empty metal shelves.

"I thought I read that the Vatican Archives were full to the point of bursting?" I said. "I see an awful lot of empty shelves."

"Well, empty is a relative word," Flavian replied. "Each year we receive a massive amount of new material, and all of that must find a place here."

Flavian explained that in addition to preserving all the papers of the Vatican's internal organizations, the Secret Archives is also responsible for the Vatican's overseas diplomatic missions as well as the staggering amount of material that is received directly from the 2,700 metropolitan sees, 212,000 individual parishes, heads of states, scientific organizations, non-Catholic religious bodies, cultural leaders, and so on. The sheer amount of paper that washes over the Vatican, Flavian said, boggles the mind.

Flavian then took me into the Parchment Room, where many of the most ancient documents were kept. There were twenty-four glass display cases, each about waist high and approximately five feet by three feet in size. Each was covered by a plain white felt cloth. The top item in the display case could be seen simply by removing the white cloth, but below the topmost display there was also a series of about ten glass drawers, in each of which was also displayed another document or two.

That meant that in this room alone there were approximately 240 to 400 rare documents. There didn't appear to be any special temperature or humidity controls fitted to these display cases, however, and the Vatican apparently doesn't take extraordinary measures for preservation. (Although the pungent odor of insecticide and fungicide could be smelled throughout the buildings, some of the most ancient records were still kept in unlocked wooden cupboards apparently vulnerable to insect attack.)

One by one Flavian began to remove the white cloths, pull open the drawers, and show me the Secret Archives' (less sensitive) treasures. They were stunning, no doubt about it. Most of the parchments were covered by an elegant, cursive Latin script, with large red seals attached at the bottom. Some were illuminated, with beautiful color drawings and initial letters. I kept looking for the celebrated abdication letter of Queen Christina of Sweden, with literally hundreds of seals attached, but couldn't find it. The solid gold seals of Spain were also kept locked up somewhere else.

The tour of the bunker finished, we took the elevator up to the *piani nobili,* the rooms that originally housed the Secret Archives.

The history of the archives is actually somewhat sketchy. Prior to the Renaissance, the papacy's official documents had been preserved in a rather haphazard manner—if only because the pope kept moving around so much and various rampaging armies (most particularly Napoleon's) would occasionally steal everything they could lay their hands on. As we've seen, from A.D. 324 to the thirteenth century, the pope's official residence was not even in the Vatican, but at St. John Lateran. Still, most popes took some measures to preserve their most important papers. Documents were stored at various times in St. Peter's Basilica, the Byzantine *chartularium,* the Palatine cliffs, and Castel Sant'Angelo, the impregnable fortress built by the Roman emperor Hadrian across the Tiber. Finally, Pope Paul V Borghese (1605–1621), who chiseled his name for posterity above the main entrance to St. Peter's Basilica, founded the current Secret Archives in 1610. He set aside the residence, next door to the Vatican Library, used by cardinals who worked there.

Flavian, Luca, and I got off the elevator and walked through a narrow door into the first of the *piani nobili.* There was a series of relatively small rooms with high ceilings, each covered by bright murals of various papal events and containing dark brown *armadi,* or cabinets. There was a large painting of the Secret Archives founder, Paul V, resplendent in a goatee and the camauro, the strange papal earmuffs popes occasionally wear.

Above each of the *armadi* was a Roman numeral. Flavian walked over to one with the number LXI above it, and opened the two doors. "These," he said proudly, "are the official records of the Council of Trent." It was obviously a highlight of the tour. There were shelf after shelf of thick bound *regestra,* yellowing with age, with the handwritten accounts of the various Council debates and canons. I was duly impressed—although somewhat surprised that these irreplaceable documents would be kept in a room like this, apparently without smoke detectors and antifire measures.

We walked into a much larger room with a vaulted ceiling covered, as noted in an earlier chapter, with lifelike paintings of topless women side by side with various popes. In the middle of the room was a bronze bust of Father Denifle, the official archivist of the Holy See in the nineteenth century.

Then it was just more of the same, on and on. We went upstairs to the *secondo piano.* Here there were the same dark *armadi,* but the rooms were sparer, with blank white walls and none of the erotic murals. Here were kept the archives concerning various nations, with each cabinet having the name of a country above it in Italian.

Flavian kept going. He showed us more than we had hoped for—including a rarely seen but fascinating place, part of the Secret Archives known as the Torre dei Venti (the Tower of the Winds).

In 1576, Pope Gregory XIII (1572–1585) commissioned an architect to build a 250-foot-high high tower to be used for astronomical observations. It was from this tower, in the 1620s, that the founder of modern astronomy, Galileo, attempted to prove to curial critics why the heliocentric universe should not be dismissed out of hand. The top room in the tower, known as the Meridian Room, was covered with elaborate murals by the artist Nicolo Circignani. It was in the Meridian Room that the world's calendar was recalculated.

Most people don't realize it, but the calendar now used throughout almost the entire world (with the exception of some Islamic nations) was created by an Egyptian astronomer named Sosigenes for Julius Caesar. Sosigenes actually modified an earlier Roman calendar, keeping the names of the months but changing it from one based on the lunar cycle to one based on the sun.

Sosigenes's calendar worked fine for sixteen centuries. But soon a problem was noticed. The solar year, the time it takes for the earth to revolve around the sun, is not really 365.25 days, as Sosigenes calculated, but actually 365.242199 days. Sosigenes was off by eleven minutes and fourteen seconds per year—an error for which we might be inclined to forgive Sosigenes but which, after sixteen centuries, added up to ten full days. The vernal equinox was not falling on March 21, as it should. In was in the Meridian Room of the Tower of the Winds that the astronomical calculations were made to fix the calendar.

As is true with many things in the Vatican, stepping into the Meridian Room is like stepping back in time. It has remained virtually untouched since the sixteenth century. The frescoes depicting the scenes of Christ calming the seas and the shipwreck of St. Paul on Malta are in excellent condition. On the ceiling there is a large mural of naked cherubs and old men, one holding up a papal triple crown, others holding garlands of roses. In the center of this mural is a large open space, painted dark blue, with six concentric circles painted in gold. Around one of the outer circles are written the names of the major winds in Greek capital letters (Zephyrus and Boreas). In the middle of all the circles is a large black metal arrow, once attached to an aerometer on the roof, that would show where the winds were blowing.

The purpose of this room, though, could be seen high up on the mural of Christ calming the seas. In the top right-hand corner, in the middle of a portrait of an old man puffing his cheeks and looking over a cloud (one of the winds, I think), there is a small hole, about the size of a quarter, through which the sun shines and projects a small circle of light onto the floor. In the center of the floor there is a marble block with the signs of the zodiac etched out and a meridian line cutting it in half.

This elaborate solar observatory was designed by one of the Vatican's first official astronomers, Father Ignazio Danti (c. 1536–1586). Danti showed Pope Gregory XIII that the bright light of the sun, which on March 21 was supposed to fall on the vernal equinox line cut into the floor, was in fact off by a distance of sixty centimeters. This convinced the pope that action had to be taken quickly to reform the Julian calendar.

After discussing the situation with numerous experts, including the Jesuit astronomer Christopher Clavius (1537–1612), Gregory issued a bull in 1582 that declared a solution. In order to bring the vernal equinox back to its proper location on March 21, the pope simply decided to cut ten days out of the calendar. He ordered that the day after October 5 would be officially October 15. In addition, he declared officially that a year would be 365.2422 days long, which meant that the calendar would be off only 3.12 days every 400 years. The solution to *that* problem was to say that three out of every four centennial (100) years would be common (that is, not leap) years. Finally, the pope declared that January 1 would be the start of the new year, not December 25 or March 25, as it had been in some countries.

Despite ongoing wars between Catholic and Protestant countries, one by one the world's nations adopted the pope's new system—now called the Gregorian calendar. But for centuries the world was divided between those following the Old Style (Julian) and New Style (Gregorian) calendars. Gradually, non-Catholic countries accepted the "Catholic" calendar, beginning with Britain (in 1752), Japan (in 1873), Egypt (1875), and China (1912). Among the last countries to accept it were the new Soviet Union (1918) and Greece (1923). The people of Alaska, under Russian control, followed the old Julian calendar until 1867.

One interesting piece of trivia in the Meridian Room, pointed out to me by Flavian, is a partially scratched off Latin proverb that says "All bad things come from the north." When Queen Christina of Sweden converted to Catholicism and renounced her throne, she came to the Vatican and was temporarily put up by Pope Alexander VII (1655–1667) in the Tower of the Winds. Attendants hurriedly attempted to erase this slogan, considered, naturally enough, to be insulting to someone from Sweden.

After we saw the Meridian Room, Flavian took us to see the suite of rooms in the tower that the pope had built for the wild Swedish queen, as far from the papal residence as you can get. They, too, looked untouched, and they've never been used since Queen Christina's time. From here I went up the metal staircase to the roof and then climbed up a metal ladder to the very top of the tower.

It's the second highest point in the Vatican, second only to the top of St. Peter's dome. The view of Rome is phenomenal—but I could enjoy it only for a moment, because the winds are so strong I was almost blown over the edge. There is a metal fence around the perimeter of the tower, but the winds are fierce and very cold. Tower of the Winds, indeed.

I quickly climbed down.

It was quite a tour. Flavian took us down the stairs to a small elevator, in which we descended to the first floor of the Secret Archives. We walked out together to the Court of the Belvedere.

It took me a moment to catch my breath. I suddenly realized that I had been standing on the same windy platform as Galileo, looking over the Vatican gardens as he had.

The Vatican does that to you. No matter how unimpressed you might be, suddenly a piece of history winds up, punches you playfully in the stomach, and you're left standing there, dazed and a little out of breath.

I asked Flavian to thank the vice prefect for his gracious hospitality, and both Luca and I thanked Flavian for putting up with us.

I could tell that Luca enjoyed himself. Despite his youthful cynicism, he realized he'd just taken a tour that even visiting Oxford dons rarely enjoy.

For once, he was grateful. And I was a little more hopeful that with patience and persistence, some of the locked doors of the Vatican might be opened to us. In good spirits, we walked out of Porta Sant'-Anna and into the Borgo in search of lunch.

XIII

A Day at Castel Gandolfo

The Jesuit astronomers at the Vatican are somewhat obsessed with Galileo, the founder of modern science and the inventor (or at least perfecter) of the telescope. His portrait now hangs prominently in the Vatican Observatory complex. After all, it was a Jesuit, the brilliant if somewhat unimaginative Cardinal Robert Bellarmine, who led the Curia's bungled handling of the entire Galileo affair—yet another example of the Vatican's singular talent for public relations blunders.

The entire episode gave the Church an undeserved reputation for being antiscience that it has still, four centuries later, not quite lived down. (The Secret Archives released the entire file on Galileo, at Pope John Paul II's insistence, in 1984.)

The truth of the entire sordid business was, of course, much more complex than the Church's enemies have portrayed it; but as we have seen before, the fine nuances and complex philosophical distinctions, of which cardinals and theologians are so proud, are lost in the bold print of newspaper headlines or the simplistic polemics of history.

The facts of the matter were these: (1) Galileo was an arrogant polemicist who openly mocked the papacy (his book, *Dialogues Concern-*

ing the Two New Sciences, had the pope portrayed as "Simplicio" and virtually invited his own condemnation); and (2) he just happened to be correct.

The whole embarrassing spectacle that resulted—Galileo quickly recanting under the ignominious threat of torture—could have been prevented with a little more finesse on both sides. But the Vatican's Italian bureaucrats displayed the same legalistic myopia for which they continue to be justly famous. On June 22, 1633, a panel of seven Italian cardinals (three more cardinals, including a Spaniard, refused to sign the document) gave their final sentence: Galileo was guilty of heresy. "That the sun is the center of the world and motionless is a proposition which is philosophically absurd and false, and formally heretical, for being explicitly contrary to Holy Scripture," they wrote.

The irony was that many churchmen, including Galileo's friend Pope Urban VIII, actually were in sympathy with the new cosmology—or at least not opposed to its discussion. In fact, Urban was a great admirer of Galileo's and had been instrumental, before his election as pope, in preventing him from being condemned by the Inquisition seventeen years earlier, in 1616. Just as Catholic theology has never opposed the scientific theory of evolution per se—but only its extrapolation into grander philosophical conclusions that leave God entirely out of the picture—so, too, Church theologians weren't all that interested in saving the geocentric universe as such. The Church was concerned, not so much to refute a heliocentric view of the universe, as is so often supposed, but to prevent careless philosophical conclusions from being drawn that would undermine the authority of the Bible and therefore of Christian Faith.

But no matter how much spin theologians give to the whole affair, the fact of the matter is that Vatican bureaucrats screwed up big-time. The affirmation that the heliocentric universe was "heretical" and "contrary to Scripture" never became part of Catholic doctrine, but it did cast a pall over the Church's relationship with scientists that would last for several centuries.

As if in a kind of institutional penance for its sins during the Galileo controversy, the Vatican has taken great pains, over the centuries, to portray itself as being engaged in and supporting serious scientific research. The hallmark of this public relations effort is the Pontifical Academy of Sciences, now housed in an abandoned summerhouse in the Vatican gardens, which gathers together eminent scientists from all over the world for annual symposia on subjects where science and religion intersect. Recent popes, such as Pius XII and John Paul II, have had a keen interest in scientific research. And the Vatican has spent considerable money, in recent years, buying telescopes for the Vatican Observatory.

I wanted to see the Vatican Observatory—or Specola, as it's known—more than I wanted to see the papal summer residence at Castel Gandolfo, but considering that the one is located inside the other, I figured I could hit two birds with one stone. I knew that the Jesuit astronomers had long ago packed up their astrolabes and antique slide rules and moved to the high mountains of Arizona, where the air is free both of pollution and the ambient light of metropolitan Rome that makes viewing so difficult. But I also knew that the old observatory complex was still at Castel Gandolfo along with the five large telescopes that for more than a century helped the Church keep its eyes on the heavens.

I made an appointment with Father Sabino Maffeo, a Jesuit physicist in charge of the Castel Gandolfo complex, who agreed to show me around. Previously, Father Maffeo was for thirty years the technical director of Vatican Radio.

Luca and I decided to drive out to Castel Gandolfo rather than take a train.

We left on a Tuesday at seven-thirty in the morning, in a pounding rainstorm. I thought it was a return of the biblical flood or perhaps a sign that the Jesuits didn't want us poking around their old stuff. The rain came down in gallon buckets. I squeezed myself into Luca's Fiat 127, maps and umbrella in hand, and we set off across the narrow cobblestone streets of Rome in search of the Via Appia Nuova, which is the road out to Lake Albano, where the papal summer residence is located.

Driving in Rome—full, as it is, with Romans—is not easy under the best of circumstances. But driving there in a rainstorm, in a tiny, broken-down old Fiat with no heat, is positively suicidal. Also, Luca, despite being Italian, didn't really know Rome very well, and so we had to stop every other block to ask for directions. Finally, though, through sheer dogged persistence, we somehow made it onto the Via Appia Nuova, which is a straight shot, past the autostrada, out and up to Lake Albano.

The drive through the suburban countryside would have been gorgeous if we could have seen it. But I was reaching over constantly to wipe the windshield with a dirty rag so that Luca could see enough to drive. Thankfully, though, by the time we reached the used-Fiat dealership (LA CITTÀ DELLA AUTOMOBILE the sign proclaimed) that marked the turnoff point up into the hills of Albano, the rain finally began to let up. We wound our way up a lush, ivy-covered corridor of trees and a large field of sheep ("Wave at the sheep!" Luca screamed. "The Sardinians say it will bring you money!") until we reached a flat plateau that marked the development surrounding Castel Gandolfo.

All I knew about the castle was that it was built in the twelfth century by the Gandolfi dukes and later transferred to the Savelli family, who, after many ups and downs in their fortunes, finally sold it to Pope Clement VII. Later, Prince Maffeo Barberini (Pope Urban VIII) enlarged the castle—taking over the nearby family-owned Villa Barberini, originally built by the Roman Emperor Domitian—and, each year, moved there with the entire papal court to get out of Rome's summer heat. The popes came every year until 1870, when Italy was unified under the king and the pope became a "prisoner in the Vatican." The place was allowed to fall into ruin until the 1929 Lateran Pact, when Pope Pius XI restored it.

Luca and I weren't sure if there would be parking in the actual castle complex, so we parked the by-now-smoking Fiat across the street from the Antico Ristorante Pagnanelli and next to a small bar, where we grabbed a quick brioche. We walked uphill the remaining two blocks, next to a thick, high wall, to the main entryway, a large arch, of the castle.

Castel Gandolfo is not exactly a castle in the medieval sense—with towers and a moat—but more of a walled village with three arched entrances. We went in through the main entrance, noting the shell marks on the walls—left from a famous gun battle, between Allied forces and retreating German soldiers, following the landing at Anzio. Inside the archway we saw a central square with a small fountain (built by Bernini, we were proudly told later) in the center, and numerous shops, restaurants, banks, the small parish Church of St. Thomas of Villanova, and so on. "We have everything we need here," Father Maffeo would tell us later. "Restaurant, bank, store, parish priest"—he pointed to the church—"even the police."

The view was astonishing. Lake Albano, the site of rowing competitions during the 1960 Olympics, is found in the middle of a volcanic crater and looks a bit like a miniature version of Crater Lake or Lake Tahoe, with green, tree-covered hillsides rising up steeply from the deep blue water. Castel Gandolfo is built on the western edge of one hillside near the middle of the two-square-mile lake. It's a lovely little village of about three thousand people. The popes have found its picturesque charms impossible to resist, especially during the stifling Roman summers. Two recent popes, Pius XII and Paul VI, died there.

I didn't know where exactly the papal residence or Vatican Observatory were located—although we could see one of the astronomical domes looming above us—so I asked a *carabiniere* who was standing, machine gun cradled in his arm, near the entrance. Chuckling, he pointed to the large yellow palazzo located twenty feet directly in front of us.

I assumed that this building must be the observatory, because that is what we asked for and because it had a large dome. From the outside, the building didn't look like much. It was a three-story palazzo painted a garish mustard yellow, its front facade facing the square and covered with windows, most of which were closed tight with white shutters. A large wooden door, about eighteen feet high, was located in the center, surrounded by a stone archway. A little ramp led up steeply to the door. Above the door was a sculpture of the papal coat of arms, and above that, on the edge of the flat roof, a large clock. It turned out that this relatively small building not only housed the Vatican Observatory but served as the papal residence as well!

Luca and I walked up to the door and rang the doorbell. "Yes, excuse me, is the pope in?" I thought about saying. A white-haired man dressed in a business suit opened the door, grimaced when he saw us— oh, God, journalists!—and asked us what we wanted. We explained that we had an appointment with Father Maffeo, and, his reluctance visible, the man let us in. Like many *palazzi,* this particular building was, in essence, a large square box with the center cut out. In the center was a stark cobblestone courtyard, again with all the windows, on all four sides, shut up tight with white shutters.

On each side of the entryway into the courtyard there was a large statue, one of St. Peter and the other of St. Paul, and, from in here, you could plainly see the twin domes on the roof.

Father Maffeo appeared shortly, a large, handsome, solid-looking man of about sixty-five, with thick white hair and square-rimmed glasses. He wore a blue cardigan and had a friendly manner. His English, while a bit rough around the edges, was clearly better than my Italian.

As no one was around, and it was still drizzling, he gave us a tour of the complex. The papal residence, as such, is merely a few rooms in the palazzo as well as a nicely decorated, very modern papal chapel. In the summer the pope gives his weekly Angelus talk from the balcony, under yet another clock located on the interior of the courtyard. Sometimes, when the crowds are larger, he'll speak from one of the central windows facing the square.

Father Maffeo took us up the brick circular stairway, designed by Bernini so donkeys could climb it, to the flat roof. From the roof we had a magnificent view of the entire area. The lake loomed below us and we saw, farther off in the distance, flat plains covered with small villas. Off to the right, as we looked at the lake, we could see the Villa Barberini, which is where the papal gardens are located and where Pope John Paul II built his famous swimming pool.

When popes come to Castel Gandolfo, they usually fly by helicopter to a landing pad located at the far end of the gardens, and then take a papal limousine along a private, tree-lined road—another "*Passetto*"—to a building just outside the arched entryway. There, behind a tall, locked metal gate, the pope takes an elevator up to the level of the papal apartments and crosses over via a covered walkway to the actual residence. Later, Father Maffeo unlocked the gate for me so I could see the long, tree-covered road leading to the Villa Barberini.

I was eager to see the observatories though. On the wall below one of the domes, carved in stone, were the words DEVM CREATOREM VENITE ADOREMVS ("Creator God, come let us adore you"). Below, in a small classroom on the ground floor, Father Maffeo had shown me proudly the Vatican Observatory's collection of meteorites, which includes the famous l'Aigle meteorite—a small brown rock discovered in 1803 by Jean-Baptiste Biot that eventually convinced scientists that meteorites are "masses foreign to our planet." In the same display case is a copy of the papal flag carried to the moon on Apollo 17 as well as a piece of moon rock, taken from the Taurus Littrow Valley, given to the "people of the Vatican City-State" by Richard Nixon. On the walls are photographs of purple nebulae and a somber-looking Albert Einstein.

Father Maffeo took Luca and me up to the first dome, where a small (forty-centimeter) refractor telescope is mounted on an old English-style observation platform. The telescope looks just like your average backyard telescope, only larger, about twenty feet long and maybe two feet in diameter. Father Maffeo opened the old wooden dome, the slats of the boards covered by resin, by pulling on a thick white rope. He then proudly mounted the observation platform, a metal cagelike structure that is attached by thick steel girders to what looks to me like a large oil-pumping rig. He pushed little black buttons on the platform, a deafening noise ensued, and the giant metal arms lifted the platform up so he could position the telescope out of the narrow slit in the wooden dome.

Father Maffeo gave Luca a brief lecture on how telescopes work while I nosed around. The whole observatory looked like it dates from the 1930s, which it did. The white paint on the telescope was peeling off. On one wall was what looked to be a kind of rickety grandfather clock, complete with a pendulum, but which was actually an old chronometer used for determining the precise time necessary for astronomical observations. On top of the cabinet was a small, cheap plastic statue of Mary.

I kind of felt sorry for the Vatican, trying to keep up scientific appearances with this antiquated equipment. But in fact there are four other telescopes at Castel Gandolfo—including a much more modern Schmidt reflector telescope. Nevertheless, in the early 1980s the University of Arizona made the Jesuit astronomers at Castel Gandolfo an offer they couldn't refuse (although the Vatican could).

Engineers had discovered a brand-new way to "spin-cast" the large mirrors used for making reflector telescopes. Rather than taking decades and costing millions of dollars in materials, the new process took hardly any time at all and made possible the development of much larger, single-piece mirrors. The U of A people asked the Jesuit astronomers if they'd be interested in having one of the mirror prototypes—free. All they'd have to do was come up with the $2.5 million it would take to mount the mirror and turn it into an actual telescope. The Jesuits went to the Vatican Secretariat of State, told them about the offer, but were told flat-out that the Holy See didn't have an extra $2.5 million to spend on mirrors. As a result, the Jesuits set out raising the money on their own, through private donations, and succeeded.

The announcement that the Jesuits, and the Vatican, were building their new telescope on Mt. Graham, near Tucson, caused a flurry of controversy in the late 1980s. It was a delicious irony that the politically correct Jesuits—always eager to be on the progressive side in any political conflict—found themselves at odds with environmentalists and alleged Apache religious activists over the building of the observatory complex. The environmentalists claimed that building astronomical observatories—surely one of the cleanest activities around—would prove fatal to the hapless red squirrel. When the environmentalists failed to make their case in court, losing hearing after hearing, suddenly a "coalition" of Apaches appeared out of nowhere, claiming that Mt. Graham was a sacred religious sanctuary and that building observatories there would constitute a "desecration." The Jesuits insisted that there was no evidence whatsoever that Mr. Graham had ever been a sacred shrine of any kind. The Jesuits won.

Father Maffeo took Luca and me downstairs to a kind of living room area and showed us a movie about the new facilities in Arizona. I kept wondering if the pope, after a hard day of pontificating, would slip down here in the summer, kick back on one of these very couches, and watch a video. I couldn't resist checking out the videotapes the Jesuits had stored on a shelf, but alas there was nothing racy to report—the film *Thelma & Louise* was about as wild as it got.

Father Maffeo recommended a wonderful restaurant for lunch that overlooked the lake, just a quarter of a mile from the papal residence. He told us to tell the owners that he had sent us.

We thanked him and decided to take him up on the suggestion. We walked out the main doors, past the fountain in the center of the square and the small church, and down a cobblestone street lined with small boutiques and bank machines. The sun had come out, and, after the rain, the air was clear and fresh. This small village is a popular resort, and it was easy to see why. I was still reading Goethe's journals around this time, and he described Castel Gandolfo as being full of "hustle and bustle."

At one small lane we turned left and headed toward the lake. We found the restaurant, Bucci's, and went inside. The view was as astonishing as Father Maffeo had promised. Our waitress, Monica, the daughter of the owner, was a cute, pixielike girl with short brown hair, bright white teeth, and a teasing, playful manner. She openly flirted with Luca, who seemed embarrassed. I promised to tell Anne about it.

I decided, looking out at the sapphire waters of Lake Albano, that I had to figure out a way to keep this job. I ordered some *bruschetta*—open pieces of toasted bread brushed with garlic, olive oil, and fresh tomatoes—and then the *lombata alla pizzaiola* and a carafe of white wine. Luca was driving and skipped the wine. He was halfway through the cannelloni he had ordered, when Monica brought us a new dish, *pappardella con salsa di lepre*, on the house. It was some kind of rabbit stew served on wide noodles, and she insisted that it would be the most delicious food I had ever eaten. I politely nibbled a few bites and then gave it to Luca, who laughed at my American squeamishness and devoured it.

We stayed at this delightful restaurant for two hours, gazing dreamily out at the lake. Luca chatted with Monica—in Italian half the time. Finally, as it was getting to be late afternoon, we decided we had to get home.

We bid the alluring Monica *arrivederci*—Luca somewhat reluctantly—and walked back to the main gate, down the side of the castle wall, and back to the car. I found a pay phone and called Glenn so she wouldn't worry, and we headed back down the highway. At a central intersection, in the meridian, I saw a large shrine with a statue of the

Blessed Virgin Mary inside—another forceful reminder that this was Italy and not America. These roadside shrines are everywhere in Italy.

I had enjoyed our tour of Castel Gandolfo. The views are incredible, the air breathable, and the telescopes interesting. It's easy to see why the popes—baking in the fetid air of a Roman summer—were eager to spend as much time as possible by the lake. I wanted to come back, maybe bring Glenn and the kids.

But for now I had a lot of work to do. It was time for me to start investigating the seamier side of the Vatican.

XIV

Flunking Out of the College of Cardinals

Had I but served my God with half the zeal as I have served
my King, He would not at my age have left me naked to my enemies.

THOMAS CARDINAL WOLSEY

The headlines in Paris got right to the point. A Roman Catholic cardinal, the eminent Jesuit theologian Jean Daniélou, was found dead in the home of a famous nightclub stripper, Mimi Santoni, in May 1974.

The anticlerical French press was in ecstasy. Daniélou, while a conservative and a member of the Academie Française, was known for his willingness to wear ordinary street clothes and hobnob with the French intelligentsia. As is true with most stories involving Church scandals—from theft of diocesan funds to pedophilia—at first the hierarchy tried to prevaricate. (The doctrine of mental reservation certainly comes in handy sometimes.)

French Church officials said that the sixty-nine-year-old cardinal collapsed while visiting "friends." Later, a police source leaked to the press that the cardinal had been with just *one* friend, Santoni, age twenty-four—a leggy ingenue who had a body, as Raymond Chandler put it, that would make a bishop kick a hole in a stained glass window. The cardinal had been carrying a lot of money in cash when he died, apparently of a burst blood vessel.

Naturally, *l'affaire* Daniélou, as it was called, was not the first or the last in which scandal touched the highest levels of the Catholic hierarchy.

The cardinal archbishop of Chicago, the infamous John Patrick Cody, was under a federal investigation for diverting tax exempt church funds to a longtime friend, divorcée Helen Dolan Wilson, when he died, at age seventy-four, in 1982.

Vatican officials had insisted that the cardinal retire early, but, feisty and defiant to the end, he had staunchly refused. Cody's successor, the popular liberal Cardinal Joseph L. Bernardin, brought some stability to the large and affluent Chicago diocese, until he, too, was touched by scandal, albeit unfairly. In the late 1980s, a former seminarian claimed that Bernardin had molested him years earlier, when Bernardin was just a priest, a charge the young man later recanted before he died of AIDS. In 1995, however, Cardinal Hans Hermann Groer of Vienna, then seventy-five, resigned when five former male students at a Catholic school claimed that he had sexually molested them as youths in the 1960s and '70s. The cardinal neither confirmed nor denied the truth of the allegations.

In general, though, sexual scandal is not something you normally would associate with the College of Cardinals, if only for the fact that these are, by and large, very old men. When I visited Rome, the average age of cardinals was sixty-four. If they do keep mistresses off in some apartment in Trastevere, they have more energy and initiative than they are given credit for.

In fact, what you most associate with the princes of the Church is not reckless daring but an almost pathological caution. Cardinals are, by definition, "discreet." They watch and wait. Above all, they listen. But they don't speak, certainly not carelessly and rarely, if at all, with journalists.

In interviews I had with a half dozen cardinals, most off the record, they lived up to their reputation as being living embodiments of curial diplomacy. They follow the old Jesuit dictum to the letter: *Never deny, rarely affirm, always distinguish.*

Getting a declarative sentence out of them, therefore—the sky is blue, for example—requires a prosecutorial persistence.

"So, Eminence, it seems to me that you're saying that the sky is blue," you might begin.

"Not necessarily," the cardinal will reply. "From some points of view, it's clear that the sky does not appear blue."

"Well, yes, I suppose so," you might concede. "But surely, on a sunny day, at least, the sky is blue."

The cardinal will frown. He doesn't like you putting words in his mouth, words that could someday be used against him.

"You have to distinguish carefully," he says, lapsing into philosophy. "The sky may appear to be blue at certain times and to certain people, but it does not necessarily follow, therefore, that the sky really is or is not blue."

Now it's your turn to frown. What exactly is his point?

"So what you're saying is that the blueness of the sky depends entirely on the perception of the person looking at it?"

The cardinal chuckles. It's obvious you're trying to trap him into staking out a philosophical position. But he's not about to fall for it.

"Certainly not," he says. "The issue is not perception as such, but whether the apparent blueness of the sky to some people, at certain times and under certain conditions, reflects what they are actually perceiving or merely what they appear to be perceiving. You can't, on this basis alone, simply make the bare assertion that the sky is blue. It's a very complex question, one on which many experts disagree."

It's at this point that you feel the dull throb of a headache begin at the base of your neck. You have another twenty minutes to go. Maybe you should move on.

There is a reason, of course, for this diplomatic gobbledygook.

The next pope will be selected from among these cautious, white-haired old men, and even though the vast majority are not really *papabile*—likely candidates—no one would deliberately, and unnecessarily, skewer his chances by actually saying anything.

The College of Cardinals is one of those Catholic "traditions of men" that drive Protestants bananas.

Where in the Bible, they'll ask plaintively, *does it say that the government of the Christian church should be determined by a bunch of Italian men wearing red dresses?*

The answer, of course, is nowhere.

There is no rationale, either in Scripture or even in Catholic theology, for cardinals to be the sole electors of the pope. It is, like many things in the Catholic Church, purely a matter of custom.

Although Church historians lamely point to such ancient institutions as the Seventy Elders chosen by Moses, and the "assistants" mentioned in Acts 6, as the basis upon which the College of Cardinals arose, in fact cardinals were originally merely the lay counselors who advised the pope in the early centuries of the Church.

It wasn't until 1059 that cardinals earned the right to be the sole papal electors and not until the Third Lateran Council, in A.D. 1179, that the Church declared that only cardinals could assume the papal throne (a requirement that has since, strictly speaking, been abandoned). Until the pontificate of Leo XIII in the mid-nineteenth century, cardinals could be simple unmarried laymen and did not have to be ordained priests to participate in the election of the pope.

Because the status of cardinals as sole papal electors has no basis, strictly speaking, in either Scripture or theology, Vatican officials say the entire college could be theoretically eliminated without undermining the Church's doctrinal foundation. There is also no doctrinal reason why the college could not be expanded to include lay people and women as electors (as liberals demand)—although the person chosen pope would have to be, Pope John Paul II made clear in *Ordinatio Sacerdotalis,* male in order to be ordained priest and consecrated bishop (which liberals do not like).

Curiously, at one time, in the sixteenth and seventeenth centuries, the majority of the cardinals *were* laypeople (albeit all male), and that was precisely when the College gained an international reputation for general debauchery and licentious behavior.

In the early years of the Church, the bishop of Rome was elected first by the entire Roman Christian community and then, when purely political factions contaminated the process, just by the Roman clergy. To give some sort of legitimacy to the College of Cardinals as the sole papal electors, an elaborate fiction was created. Because the pope is, first and foremost, the bishop of Rome, it became necessary to portray the cardinals as representatives of the people and clergy of Rome.

That is why each of the cardinals is named the "titular" (in name only) head of one of the hundreds of churches or hospices (diaconia) in Rome or to a diocese in the Roman area.

There are three basic classes of cardinals. *Cardinal deacons* are top Vatican officials who work in the Curia but do not have an episcopal see of their own. *Cardinal priests* are residential bishops (who don't live in Rome) who have their own diocese or archdiocese somewhere in the world. *Cardinal bishops* are the highest-ranking Vatican officials, cardinals who have been named to one of the traditional six suburbicarian sees surrounding Rome (those of Albano, Ostia, Porto-Santa Rufina, Palestrina, Sabina-Possio Mirteto, Frascati, and Velletri-Segni), as well as patriarchs of the Eastern Churches. The nominal head of the College is what is called the *cardinal dean,* and he is always titular bishop of the See of Ostia in addition to another of the suburbicarian sees.

The pope alone "creates" cardinals, in groups of fifteen to thirty, at public gatherings of the sacred College, called "consistories," held every few years. (In recent years, consistories have also been called as purely advisory meetings to help the pope.)

Outside of a papal coronation, the ceremonies surrounding the creation of cardinals are probably the most elaborate in the Catholic Church—even more elaborate than canonizations. In presenting the new cardinals the "red hat" (nowadays, merely a red biretta and not the sombrerolike *galero*), the pope enjoins them to "show yourself fearless" (*te intrepidum exhibere debeas*) and "defend the Faith with your very blood, if necessary" (*usque ad sanguinis effusionem inclusive*).

This is not necessarily melodramatic rhetoric. A few cardinals and archbishops have paid a high price for their stubborn refusal to obey government orders. Cardinal Josyf Slipyj spent eighteen years in a Soviet concentration camp, for example, and in 1980 Archbishop Oscar A. Romero of El Salvador was gunned down by government assassins while saying Mass. Romero's murder was almost identical to what happened to St. Thomas à Becket 800 years earlier and was done for the same reasons.

In the earliest days of the papacy there were never more than twenty-four cardinals, the same number as the original twenty-four parish churches of Rome, traditionally established by St. Peter's successor, Pope

Cletus. Throughout the Middle Ages, however, the number of cardinals increased.

In 1586 Pope Sixtus V set the number at a maximum of seventy, which was the rule until 1958—when Pope John XXIII simply ignored it (popes can do things like that). Pope Paul VI fixed a new maximum of 120, but, in his still-controversial apostolic letter *Ingravescentem Aetatem,* decreed that cardinals over the age of eighty could no longer vote in a conclave or hold curial office. This means that today there is a limit of 120 cardinals eligible to vote, but no limit on the total number of cardinals.

At this writing there is a record number of cardinals, 154, but only 115 of them are under age eighty and thus eligible to vote in conclave. Most are still from Europe (83) and South America (25), but there are also 16 from Africa, 15 from Asia, 15 from North America, and 4 from Oceania.

The trend in recent years has been, just as in the Curia generally, to "internationalize" the College. In 1978, the conclave that elected Karol Wojtyla as Pope John Paul II consisted of twenty-six Italian cardinals. By 1997 the number of Italian cardinals eligible to vote had fallen to just eighteen.

Most cardinals do not live in Rome. Of the 115 cardinals under the age of eighty, the vast majority are heads of large archdioceses—such as Los Angeles or London, Paris or Manila. Only about twenty-five work in the Vatican congregations, and it is these who control the real power in the Catholic Church.

Curial cardinals live in spacious Vatican-owned apartments near St. Peter's or inside the Vatican itself. Most live either in the Palazzo di San Callisto, facing the ancient Basilica of Santa Maria in Trastevere, or in a large apartment complex in the Piazza della Città Leonina, right in front of the number 64 bus stop outside the Vatican and only a few steps from Porta Sant'Anna. A few others live nearby in buildings on Via Rusticucci or Via di Porta Angelica.

While these free apartments are often spacious, with high ceilings and luxurious appointments, most cardinals are on a somewhat limited budget. Their salaries are lower, in the mid-$30,000 range in the late 1990s, than those of average American office workers. From their meager salaries—often supplemented by personal gifts from wealthy Catholics or dioceses—cardinals must pay for their food, utilities, personal toiletry items, clothes, and the stipends of whatever staff they can cobble together. Most cardinals expect to have a personal secretary, almost always an ambitious priest, and a housekeeper or cook, hopefully provided gratis by an order of women religious.

Of course, a cardinal resident in Rome has diplomatic immunity and Vatican citizenship, so he pays no taxes; and the duty-free Vatican store, the Annona, offers goods (including booze, perfume, and cigarettes) at thirty to fifty percent less than can be found in Roman supermarkets. Plus, a cardinal has free use of a limousine from the Vatican motor pool.

But still, Rome is expensive and the Vatican somewhat niggardly. One cardinal I interviewed said that were it not for the pension he received from the United States, he could not afford to live in Rome. The princes of the Church, it seems, live on a budget like everyone else.

XV

Sex Lives of the Popes

God has given us the papacy. Let us enjoy it.

POPE LEO X

The wonderful thing about Rome is that when you have a little spare time—a few hours before lunch, an open afternoon after a canceled appointment—you can always find something interesting to see. I walked around Rome for months with a list of places I wanted to visit when I got the chance.

One of them, of course, was Castel Sant'Angelo, the mammoth round fortress on the banks of the Tiber, directly down the Via della Conciliazione from St. Peter's. I saw it almost every day, but it took me many months before I actually went inside. Unlike many of the other buildings in Rome that figure prominently in the history of the papacy—most of which date from the Italian Renaissance or later—Castel Sant'-Angelo is almost as old as the papacy itself. Begun in A.D. 139 as the emperor Hadrian's mausoleum, the castle was incorporated into the Aurelian Wall in 271 and fortified. Throughout the centuries, the popes have used it variously as an emergency fortress, an archive, a prison, and a place for amorous *rendez-vous*.

In A.D. 590 Pope Gregory the Great saw a vision of an angel on top of the castle, which is where the castle got its name. In 1277 Pope Nicholas III, the first pope to make the Vatican his home, built a secret passageway along an ancient aqueductlike wall all the way from St. Peter's to Castel Sant'Angelo. This prescient construction project saved the life of Pope Clement VII 250 years later, in 1527, when the original Swiss Guardsmen bundled the pope off to the safety of the castle in the face of marauding German mercenaries sent by the holy Roman emperor.

Despite its name, Castel Sant'Angelo actually has a somewhat checkered past. It has figured prominently in a number of unsavory Vatican intrigues—and it was these, of course, that were on my mind as I hiked up the wide, dark circular staircase that takes you from the ground floor up to the top of the castle. The writer H. V. Morton described Castel Sant'Angelo as "one of the most frightening buildings in the world" and insisted that compared to it, "the Tower of London is almost a happy place." He added:

> One does not need to be psychic, or even unduly sensitive or fanciful, to feel that agony and suffering still cling to the dark corridors. Mounting the stone steps in the dim light, it would not surprise one to hear a fearful scream, or opening a door to come upon some scene of murder or torture. There are beautiful rooms in which a man might sit listening to music, while a few yards off are dungeons; in at least one of the gayest rooms a trapdoor opens on an oubliette.

My ultimate aim was the restaurant that is located on the middle level. It has, from its western ramparts, one of the most stunning views in all Rome, with the dark green waters of the Tiber immediately below and the majestic dome of St. Peter's rising up at the other end of the Via della Conciliazione. It was in this restaurant that I planned to have a long, leisurely lunch and begin my research about the sex lives of the Roman popes.

As I observed in an earlier chapter, the papal apartments in Castel Sant'Angelo are anything but ascetic. They are covered by murals of buxom women, naked from the waist up, holding their breasts in their cupped hands like so many Playmates of the Month. These apartments were the scene for some of the papal promiscuity that gave the Vatican such an unsavory reputation for centuries. It is plain that some of the earlier popes had more on their minds than merely expanding the Papal States.

Before I went up for my lunch, I had done my best to find the papal dungeon in the basement of the castle. The sixteenth century Italian writer Benvenuto Cellini, who was imprisoned in the castle for a less than flattering remark about his papal patron, Paul III, wrote that he was "taken into a gloomy dungeon below the level of a garden, which swam with water, and was full of big spiders and many venomous worms." There were a number of rooms that were candidates, because the entire place looks and feels like a dungeon—the walls are twenty feet thick and have withstood almost every cannon ball ever thrown against them. But none of my guidebooks told me which room was the official dungeon and none of the Italian docents knew either.

My interest in the dungeon was on account of a beautiful Roman aristocrat named Marozia, who was the granddaughter of one pope, mistress of a second, the mother of a third, the aunt of a fourth, and the grandmother of a fifth.

She also had the distinction of spending more time locked up in the papal dungeon in Castel Sant'Angelo, an incredible fifty-four years, than any other person. Marozia and her mother, the promiscuous courtesan Theodora, shaped the papacy for more than a century—but Marozia paid a horrible price.

It all began, when Marozia was only six years old, at one of the most bizarre events in the history of the papacy, the so-called Cadaver Synod. In January 897, Pope Stephen VI (896–897) ordered the body of a predecessor, Pope Formosus (891–896) dug up, his corpse clad in papal vestments, and put on trial for perjury and other crimes.

Stephen hated Formosus's guts, as you might deduce, and was determined to undo everything the former pope had done, including nullifying the priestly ordinations of Formosus's priests and bishops (excluding himself). The trial, conducted in the magnificent Basilica of St. John Lateran, concluded with Formosus being found guilty, all his acts declared null and void, the fingers of his right hand cut off, and his body thrown into the Tiber. When it was all over, a massive earthquake erupted in Rome, nearly destroying the Lateran—which the superstitious Romans took as a sign of divine disapproval. As a result, Pope Stephen VI lasted only eight more months himself. The people of Rome deposed him, threw him in prison, and had him strangled.

Present at the bizarre Cadaver Synod was the lovely aristocrat and senatrix Theodora—wife of the financial administrator of the Holy See—and her beautiful daughter, Marozia, then only six. Theodora, matron of the most powerful family in Rome at the time, was a notorious mistress of popes and helped determine the outcome of more than one papal election. Despite her young age, Marozia caught the eye of a thirty-six-year-old cardinal named Sergius, who became (eight popes and much bloodshed later) Pope Sergius III.

Marozia and her mother, Theodora, spent a lot of time at the Lateran Palace, where Sergius, as a cardinal, worked. Historians believe Sergius forced himself on Marozia, perhaps with her mother's blessing, when she was still just a child. In any event, on January 29, 904, Sergius was elected pope, and two years later—when Marozia was fifteen and he was forty-five—Marozia bore him a son, the future Pope John XI. So powerful was Marozia's family that, as *The Oxford Dictionary of Popes* puts it, Sergius's "and his immediate successors' dependence on the family was complete, and degrading, causing the following decades to be castigated as the pornocracy of the Holy See."

Sergius died four years later, when Marozia was nineteen. She had three more marriages and countless affairs, but still lusted for the papacy. Marozia, then at the height of her beauty, ran a tavern on the Isola Tiberina, the small island in the Tiber that has long been (and still is) home to Rome's Jewish community. During this time, Marozia's mother, the still-formidable Theodora, was up to her old tricks. She plotted to have her new lover, John, the Archbishop of Ravenna and son of Pope Lando I, elected Pope John X (914–928).

Supposedly, Marozia, who had her own papal ambitions for her son, developed a dangerous rivalry with her mother. She convinced her new husband, a prince from Lombardy named Alberic, to attack Rome and attempt to depose the pope. When the coup failed, Alberic was killed and Marozia was forced to view his mutilated corpse. Marozia had a son by Alberic, however, Alberic II, who was to be her ultimate undoing. She spent the next two decades plotting her revenge against the killing of her first husband, allegedly managing to poison two popes, Leo VI and Stephen VII, to make way for her son by Sergius III to be crowned Pope John XI in 931.

It gets weirder—*a lot* weirder. Marozia decided to marry her late husband's brother, Hugo, who was inconveniently married at the time to another woman, so she had her son, then Pope John XI, arrange for an annulment and then preside personally at the wedding. Marozia's other son, Alberic II, and his uncle cordially despised each other and allegedly traded insults at Marozia's wedding. Just a few months later, Alberic II, like his father before him, attacked the city with troops, but, unlike his father, was successful. He ruled Rome like a latter-day emperor for twenty-two years. One of his first acts was to throw his mother, Marozia, then forty-two years old, into the dungeon of Castel Sant' Angelo. She was kept there for fifty-four years.

Alberic appointed the next five popes. When he died, Pope John

XV (985–996) took pity on the ninety-six-year-old woman living in the dungeon of Castel Sant'Angelo. He lifted the sentence of excommunication, had her exorcised of demons, and then promptly executed. The day before her execution, a bishop visited her in the dungeon, finding nothing but a pile of rags and bones, Marozia barely alive, and read the indictment:

> *Inasmuch as you, Marozia, did from the beginning and at the age of fifteen conspire against the rights of the See of Peter in the reign of Holy Father Pope Sergius, following the example of your satanic mother, Theodora . . .*

On and on the indictment went. Marozia was accused of plotting to take over the papacy, and of being responsible for the criminal acts of her grandson, Pope John XII, who "flayed the skin off Bishop Otger, cut off the head of Notary Azzo, and beheaded sixty-three of Rome's clergy and nobility." Moreover, the randy Pope John XII "while having illicit and filthy relations with a Roman matron . . . was surprised in the act of sin by the matron's angry husband who, in just wrath, smashed his skull with a hammer and thus liberated his evil soul into the grasp of Satan . . ."

Marozia was then smothered by an executioner. The old woman's legacy lived on, however, because she was to be the great-grandmother of two more popes, Benedict VIII (1012–1024) and John XIX (1024–1032), and great-great-grandmother of Pope Benedict IX (1032–1044).

Incredible as it may seem, Marozia's tale is hardly unique. I was sitting there, on the terrace of Castel Sant'Angelo, enjoying remarkably good ravioli and a glass of red wine, reading all about the sex lives of the popes. I knew there had been occasional indiscretions, of course, but there was a period for a while when the papacy was *almost* as corrupt as Martin Luther, in his most fevered polemics, alleged.

Pope John XII (955–964), as we have seen, was accused of running a brothel out of St. Peter's and died, still in his twenties, after having suffered a stroke in bed with a married woman (Vatican records also state he had his head bashed in by the irate husband). Pope Benedict IX (1032–1044), the only pope to serve three separate "terms," was an insatiable bisexual whom St. Peter Damian condemned as a wretch who "feasted on immorality." Dante consigned Pope Boniface VIII (1294–1303) to the lowest circles of hell for his notorious sexual adventures, which included keeping a married woman and her daughter simultaneously as his mistresses. The poet Petrarch described Pope Clement VI (1342–1352) as "an ecclesiastical Dionysus" who was "swept along in a flood of the most obscene pleasure, an incredible storm of debauch, the most horrid and unprecedented shipwreck of chastity."

Because of these and other scandals, the High Middle Ages saw various reforms of the Church as well as of the papacy. Just as they do today, people anguished over the problem of clerical celibacy. On the one hand, in theory celibacy allowed priests to be completely dedicated to their apostolates and prevented the practice, not uncommon, of Church property being willed to widows and children. On the other hand, a wife was a good deterrent to unchecked clerical promiscuity or, worse, pederasty. As St. Bernard of Clairvaux put it, "Take from the Church an honorable marriage and an immaculate marriage bed and do you not fill it with concubinage, incest, homosexuality and every kind of uncleanness?"

Under various popes—from St. Damasus I (366–384) to St. Gregory VII (1073–1085)—there was a concerted effort to ban clerical marriage and enforce the Church's sexual discipline. One novel approach was the imposition of the so-called "sex tax," or *cullagium*. This allowed a priest to keep a concubine for a fixed annual fee. All of this met with varying degrees of success. Throughout the Middle Ages there was a pattern of alternating good and bad popes. One pope would attempt to curb clerical licentiousness and episcopal promiscuity and then he would be followed, almost like clockwork, by a pope determined that his ecclesiastical duties would not interfere with his personal appetites.

Things really got out of hand, however, during the Italian Renaissance. The rediscovery of classical art and literature led to a new acceptance of Greek sexual mores as well. The Renaissance began with a string of openly gay popes. Pope Paul II (1464–1471) was such a flamboyant homosexual that he was called by his cardinals "Our Lady of Pity," a reference, one historian notes, "to his tendency to burst into tears at the slightest provocation." Paul's successor, the infamous Sixtus IV (1471–1484), being bisexual, was not as exclusive in his sexual appetites. Sixtus is now best known as the builder of the Sistine Chapel and founder of the Spanish Inquisition, appointing the feared Torquemada as its Grand Inquisitor. Some historians claim that Sixtus even engaged in incest with some of his own illegitimate sons or "nephews," some of whom he made cardinals. One of Sixtus's sons, the handsome Pietro Riario, was even said to have been the offspring of an illicit liaison between the pope and his sister. The next pope, Innocent VIII (1484–1492), was also bisexual, allegedly fathering sixteen illegitimate children and engaging in innumerable homosexual liaisons. To his credit, however, Innocent never abandoned or disowned his children once he was elected pope. He baptized them, married them off, and even found them cushy jobs in the Vatican.

Another good place to contemplate the sex lives of the popes is the Borgia Apartments, now part of the Vatican Museums. After finishing my lunch, I decided to walk down the Via della Conciliazione to the museums. They usually close around one o'clock, but on this particular day, I knew, they'd be open until four-thirty in the afternoon. One of the few perks of having a Vatican press pass is that you are allowed into the museums free, and I spent many days wandering around the long hallways of what is, most people agree, one of the world's greatest museums.

Toward the end of the museums tour, near the Sistine Chapel, lies a series of rooms that form the Borgia Apartments, built and decorated by perhaps the most dissolute man ever to sit on the throne of Peter. He was the hot-blooded and corrupt Spaniard, Rodrigo de Borja y Borja (Borgia in Italian), whom the great historian Edward Gibbon would term "the Tiberius of Christian Rome."

A dissolute young man who was named a cardinal (without ordination) at the age of twenty-six, Rodrigo had literally dozens of children with numerous Spanish women. He had one affair with a Spanish widow of astonishing beauty and then proceeded to have three children with the widow's teenage daughter. Once he was made cardinal, he went on to father, with the almond-eyed Roman aristocrat Vannozza Catanei, several children. Two of these children were notorious—the murderous sadist Cesare, who became a cardinal, and the beautiful Lucrezia, perhaps the most powerful and promiscuous woman ever to live within the Vatican.

Rodrigo openly campaigned for the papacy, losing out to both Sixtus IV and Innocent VIII. But at the conclave following Innocent's death, Rodrigo simply bribed his brother cardinals with promises of lucrative sees and won the election as Alexander VI (1492–1503). He would spend most of his years as pope engaged, along with his son Cesare, his brutal henchman, in a campaign of ruthless assassination and theft. The ultimate aim was to plunder the riches of the papacy and transfer virtually all the Papal States to the Borgia family.

Alexander was simultaneously orthodox in his religious beliefs, profligate in his sexual conduct, and utterly corrupt in his management of Church finances.

His sexual escapades almost defy belief. He had numerous mistresses, indulged in drunken orgies (perhaps with his own daughter participating), and kept a steady stream of lovely Roman prostitutes flowing in and out of the Vatican. As pope, and fifty-eight years old, Alexander took as a mistress the fifteen-year-old Roman beauty Giulia Farnese—nicknamed Julia the Beautiful—even though Giulia had recently been married. The pope eventually had a daughter with Giulia, and Giulia became close friends with Alexander's older daughter, Lucrezia, from his liaison with Vannozza. The pope's passionate, sexually explicit love letters to the beautiful young woman have survived. By the way, Alexander gained the cooperation of Giulia's brother, Alessandro Farnese—who would normally be expected to guard his sister's honor—simply by making him a cardinal. He would later become Pope Paul III (1534–1549) and himself father three sons and a daughter. (You can see why Giulia was called "the beautiful" by visiting the monument to Pope Paul III in St. Peter's: The figure of Justice, originally stark naked but subsequently covered up with a metal dress, is modeled on Giulia.

But it was his relationship with his brilliant, beautiful, sexually promiscuous daughter Lucrezia that has captured the attention of scholars over the centuries. She had a remarkably modern look, with long blond hair, a small mouth, and fine features. For years it was believed that a portrait of St. Catherine disputing philosophers, painted by the renowned artist Pinturicchio in the Sala dei Santi of the Borgia Apartments, was of Lucrezia, but now scholars are doubtful.

It is said that on the night of his daughter Lucrezia's wedding to Giovanni Sforza, Alexander personally escorted the couple into an ornate bedroom with a gigantic bed and proceeded to stay, and watch, to make sure the marriage was consummated. A few years later, in order to use Lucrezia to form another political alliance, Alexander arranged for her marriage to Giovanni to be annulled on the grounds it was never consummated (despite having witnessed such consummation with his own eyes). Giovanni was indignant. He insisted he had consummated his marriage to Lucrezia "an infinite number of times" and even offered to make love to her in public as proof that he was satisfying his obligations as a husband (a not-uncommon test, by the way). In the end, fear for his life—and a papal payment of 31,000 ducats—convinced Giovanni to sign an affidavit of impotence. To guarantee the outcome, Alexander had Lucrezia swear before a marriage tribunal that she was a virgin, testimony that caused shrieks of laughter throughout Italy.

Rumors of other, more shocking events—including late-night orgies in the Vatican in which Lucrezia participated—were current in Rome. When Giovanni fled the Vatican and returned to his estate, fearing for his life, he alleged that Lucrezia had been carrying on an incestuous relationship with her father, the pope. Alexander "wanted his daughter for himself," he charged, adding that he had "known her carnally on countless occasions." This is not as preposterous a charge as it may seem at first. Four years after her marriage was annulled, Lucrezia bore an illegitimate son—the mysterious Infans Romanus—and many historians believe that Alexander was indeed the father. Certainly, his trust in Lucrezia was total; he frequently left her in de facto charge of the papacy in his absence on business.

All of this did not escape the notice of ordinary Catholics, of course. Even to the jaded people of Italy, accustomed to dissolute clerics and rapacious popes, the behavior of Alexander VI was shocking. Eventually, the pope had to endure the fiery polemics of the courageous Florentine reformer Girolamo Savonarola, who, like Martin Luther, combined righteous indignation with political extremism. For five years the fiery Dominican friar raged against the corruption of the clergy in general and the pope in particular:

> *They sell benefices, they sell the sacraments, they sell nuptial Masses, they sell everything. And then they are frightened of excommunication. When evening comes, one will betake himself to the gambling table, another to his concubine. This poison has reached such a height in Rome*

that France, Germany, the whole world, are sickened by it. Things have come to such a pass that we must counsel all men to keep clear of Rome, and say, "Do you want to ruin your son? Then make him a priest."

As for Pope Alexander VI, Savonarola did not mince words.

I assure you that this Alexander is no pope, nor can be considered as such. Leaving aside the fact that he purchased his pontifical throne through simony, and that he assigns the ecclesiastical benefices to those who pay highest for them; and leaving aside his other vices, well known to all men, I assert that he is no Christian, and does not believe in God's existence.

Protected by the powerful Republic of Florence, Savonarola was able to keep this up for five years. Eventually the people of Florence tired of his stern morality, however—his "bonfires of the vanities"—and he was examined under torture by the Florentine government and burned at the stake. Alexander himself may have been accidentally poisoned with a vial intended for an enemy cardinal at a papal banquet, and died in 1503.

The Borgia pope's excesses were the beginning of the end of papal promiscuity.

After the brief reign (twenty-six days) of Pope Pius III, the formidable warrior pope Julius II (1503–1513) was elected, again with the help of numerous bribes. He was ruthless, tough, and ambitious. He fathered three daughters, but he was more interested in military than sexual conquest. And while Alexander attempted to plunder the Papal States for his family's personal gain, Julius was motivated solely to strengthen the papacy, not weaken it. Despite his military ambitions, he became one of the great patrons of the arts, commissioning such artists as Michelangelo and Bramante to begin the construction of the new St. Peter's Basilica.

The building of St. Peter's cost the popes a lot of money and it was financed largely by simony—the sale of "sacred things," primarily the cardinal's hat and indulgences. Pope Leo X (1513–1521), a "lover of boys and liquor," fathered several illegitimate children despite his homosexual preferences. Under Leo, the sale of indulgences became so crass that eventually, in 1517, a young Augustinian theologian named Martin Luther posted his ninety-five theses, opposing the practice, on the door of the church in Wittenberg. Disgust with the corruption of the papal court was so strong throughout Europe that Luther's public defiance was the spark that caused the flames of the Reformation to spread across the continent like a forest fire. When it was all over, much of the Catholic Church lay smoldering, in ruins.

As a result, there were only a few more corrupt popes. Pope Clement VII (1523–1534) had a beautiful black woman as a mistress whom all of Rome called simply "the Moor." It was Clement who so enraged the holy Roman emperor that he sent a vast army of German mercenaries to sack Rome. Clement escaped to the safety of Castel Sant'Angelo, along the Passetto, only because the first Swiss Guards sacrificed their own lives in his defense. The German soldiers, many partisans of the Reformation, stripped St. Peter's clean, stealing the famed Golden Cross of Constantine (which was never recovered). Thousands were slaughtered; nuns were raped; churches desecrated.

The one-two punch of the Protestant Reformation and the Catholic Counter-Reformation, launched by the Council of Trent, pretty much put an end to papal partying. Despite desperate digging on the part of muckraking journalists and Protestant polemicists, no one has been able to dig up evidence of pontifical fornication for at least three hundred years.

The last pope we know for certain had sex was Pope Gregory XIII

(1572–1585), the reformer of the calendar, because we know the names of his illegitimate children. One of them, Giovanni, he made a cardinal.

Gregory's successor, the pious and stern Franciscan Sixtus V, who greatly expanded the Inquisition, more or less put an end to sexual shenanigans in the Vatican. He reorganized the Curia, fixed the number of cardinals at seventy, and in general tried to get the papacy's ship in order.

The legacy that Sixtus left to his successors was an expectation that popes live upright, moral lives. Future popes may have been somewhat dissolute as cardinals—including fathering illegitimate children—but once elected to the papacy, they had to straighten up.

XVI

Overdue Books at the Vatican Library

Sauntering around the Vatican, I wilted from exhaustion, and when I got home, my legs felt as if they were made out of cotton.

ANTON CHEKHOV

I had heard the rumors, over the years, as you may have: The Vatican Library allegedly has the largest collection of erotica in the world. That naturally captured my attention, as I like a good racy novel as much as the next fellow.

Maybe they'd let me check a few out?

Years ago, I discovered a simple trick to help me when I was studying a foreign language: I would find myself the raciest story I could lay my hands on and then plunge right in. When studying French, I found a collection of Anaïs Nin's in French (she actually wrote in English, so it was a translation), and so, instead of giving up after twenty or thirty pages, as I invariably did with Victor Hugo or Flaubert or even Jean-Paul Sartre, I would keep flipping the pages, eagerly looking up words so I could figure out what exactly was going on.

A few years ago, when I took up the study of ancient Greek, I tried the strategy out with a little Sappho, but unfortunately all that is left are a few sentence fragments ("Her skin was smooth as . . . Never . . . Oh, yes! . . .") and, besides, the gentle poet of Mytilene was entirely too ethereal for my needs.

As I was having considerable trouble with my Italian, I decided to call up the prefect of the library and ask him if he might have any really wild novels, ribald poems, or lascivious limericks that he could recommend to help me along.

"Certainly, my good fellow," the prefect replied. "But I'm afraid you have to read them here. We don't allow anyone to take books home with them, not since that Napoleon chap borrowed a few thousand volumes and neglected to bring them back. You wouldn't believe the fines he's managed to rack up!"

The prefect, a charming, friendly, erudite Irishman who enjoys ribbing his interlocutors to test their mettle, said he could see me the following week, and so we set a time.

The next Monday, I set out. To go to the working part of the library—not the tourist exhibits that you see as part of the regular Vatican Museums tour—you have to enter through the ground-floor entrance in the Cortile del Belvedere. But first, you have to go through the Porta Sant'Anna, past three frosty Swiss Guards in their blue "night uniforms," and obtain a special visitors' pass from the Vigilanza office fifty feet up on the Via del Pellegrino (the street of the pilgrim).

This is actually not that big of a deal. Ordinary Roman citizens enter here all the time to take advantage of the Vatican pharmacy, which stocks drugs and other items (such as the largest collection of perfume and cosmetics this side of a duty free shop!) not found in Italy. You simply go into the little office, fill out a form, making sure you have your passport or other ID with you, and they give you a pass. Show the slightest disorientation or hesitation outside on the streets, however, and immediately a blue-uniformed Vigilanza guard will strut over to you, say, "Prego," and snap his fingers to see your pass. If you can't show one, you'll be escorted out through the Porta Sant'Anna faster than you can say "sneaky tourist."

I collected my pass (feeling like I was back in high school) and set out for the library. I walked straight up the Via del Pellegrino, past the massive round tower at the base of the Apostolic Palace on my left and the Vatican Post Office on my right, and ahead about a hundred yards to a large arched entryway in the long six-story building that is the Vatican Library and Museums complex. It's a gigantic building, believe me.

Of course, most of the buildings in this area were long ago connected to one another, so it gets a bit confusing trying to figure out where one ends and another begins. Inside the arch, in the Belvedere Courtyard, there is a fountain, but mostly it is now one vast parking lot. I turned to the right and headed for the entrance on the far right-hand side of the courtyard.

There was a guard inside and visiting scholars had to sign in. It was nine-thirty in the morning. The scholars straggled in, dressed in everything from three-piece suits to blue jeans. I noticed that after they signed in the registration book, they handed the guard an ID card and he in turn gave them a key. There was a little locker room off the main entry hall (hence the key) where the scholars had to leave their purses and briefcases. Security was tight to prevent theft. In the early 1990s, a retired American art history professor, Anthony Melnikas, admitted smuggling three pages of a six-hundred-year-old illuminated Bible out of the Vatican Library and attempting to sell them in the United States.

A guard took me in an elevator up to the prefect's office on the top floor, right next to the manuscript reading room. The prefect, an older priest with black hair and ruddy cheeks, greeted me affably, asking me to sit in his office while he gave touring advice to some visiting Canadian scholars. I glanced through facsimile editions of various eleventh- and twelfth-century books, none of which, by the way, looked the slightest bit pornographic.

When the prefect returned, he gave me the grand tour. The library is divided into two basic parts, he said: The manuscript division—made up of irreplaceable, hand-copied documents dating all the way back to the second and third centuries—and the printed book division. There are separate reading rooms for each, although they are next door to each other.

Contrary to popular belief, the library itself does not date all the way back to the dawn of the papacy. Many of the earliest books and records of the Church were lost in various plunderings of Rome by invading armies—or simply lost when the popes moved around, from Rome to Avignon and other places.

The current library was founded by Pope Nicholas V only in 1451, earlier than the Secret Archives next door. The pope wanted to establish a permanent repository and avoid the dispersal of valuable manuscripts that had occurred in earlier centuries. For the next five hundred years, some of the most valuable private collections in Europe would be bequeathed or sold to the Vatican Library.

Unfortunately, just three centuries after it was founded, in 1797, a little French general named Napoleon Bonaparte thought the Vatican's fancy books would make a nice addition to his personal collection and so he ordered that the rarest volumes and manuscripts be boxed up and shipped to Paris. Of course, Napoleon then decided that the pope, Pius VII, would also make a nice addition to his personal collection, and he ordered that he be boxed up and shipped to Paris as well.

Much of the Vatican's library was returned to Rome eventually, along with the pope, but the dangers continued. During World War II, the library became a safe haven for many of the world's rarest books when the mightiest armies in world history blew much of Europe to bits.

On October 14, 1943, German officers gave advance warning to the abbot of the ancient Benedictine Abbey of Monte Cassino that the upcoming battle for the strategic hilltop site would put the abbey's vast collection at risk. As a result, forty thousand parchments—including works by Seneca, Cicero, and Augustine—were hurriedly loaded onto trucks and moved to the Vatican. But throughout the German occupation of Rome, there were worries that the Nazis were planning to follow Napoleon's lead and ship the Vatican's vast treasures, and the pope, back home to the Fatherland.

Scholars come to the Vatican Library from all over the world to do research, and the library admits only about two thousand people a year. "We get a lot of wanna-bes," the prefect said. "People who would love to put on their résumés that they researched this or that topic at the Vatican Library. Many important scholars come here and put on this attitude that the Italians call *prepotente*—you know, that they're renowned in their field and by God they have a right to see this or that book." The prefect flashed a wry Irish smile. "That, of course, is *fatal*."

He showed me the reading rooms. In the manuscript reading room, about two dozen scholars, many surprisingly young, sat hunched over desks, large volumes in alien scripts perched on book stands. Some had laptop computers on their desks. To get the manuscripts, the scholars must first deliver special request slips along with their locker key to staffers at a desk in the front of the reading room. The appropriate manuscript is then fetched.

Next door, at the printed book reading room, a similar procedure was followed. Although scholars can use reference materials on shelves there freely, no one is allowed into the stacks, which the prefect showed me (just rows and rows of old books on steel-gray shelves). A large white marble statue of St. Thomas Aquinas, his pudgy Dominican face looking somewhat stern, watches over the printed-book scholars as they do their work.

After all that, the prefect escorted me to what he called "the most important room" in the library—the bar!

Located upstairs in an old alcove that was once some kind of fountain, the bar serves mostly coffee and fruit juice to the scholars and library staff—although a large shelf of more powerful stimulants is clearly on display. Having spent a considerable amount of time trying to untangle the mysteries of the Greek aorist participle, I can imagine some medieval scholar, faced with a particularly knotty paragraph of ecclesiastical Latin, repairing to this little watering hole for a quick shot of Scotch before returning, with new courage, to do battle again.

Over a cappuccino in the bar, I brought up my problem of finding suitable reading material to advance my study of Italian. I asked the prefect if the rumor about Vatican erotica is true. He looked me straight in the eye, for a moment incredulous . . . and then laughed out loud. "Why, certainly it's true!" he said, still chuckling. "Mind, how good is your Latin? And of course, a solid knowledge of medieval Persian would be helpful."

The prefect explained that the library has many excellent first editions of ribald classics by such authors as Boccaccio, Rabelais, Chaucer, and Apuleius; but if it's the illustrated *Kama Sutra* I'm looking for, I was out of luck, he said.

What the library does have, however, is probably the most valuable private collection ever assembled—1.5 million books and 150,000 rare manuscripts. The manuscripts include the oldest known copy of the entire Bible (Codex Vaticanus B), the Galesian Sacramentary, a copy of St. Thomas Aquinas's *Commentary on the Sentences* written in his own hand, early editions of Dante's *Divine Comedy,* original letters from King Henry VIII and Martin Luther, and so on.

Because of its past experience with emperors and others borrowing books and neglecting to return them, the Vatican Library views its primary mission as one of preservation, not facilitating research. As a result, many of the rarest of the rare manuscripts have been diligently copied in facsimile form and are now stored in the steel and polished aluminum underground vault in the Vatican Secret Archives I visited earlier.

Before I left the library, I decided I wanted to actually hold one of these really old books in my hands. I knew that many of them are already available now for reading via computer—in digital form—but that's just not the same.

I saw my chance after the Prefect introduced me to a scholar from the University of California, Santa Barbara, named Larry, an art historian researching large illuminated Bibles from the eleventh century.

Larry has visited some of the world's greatest libraries—including the British Museum, the Bibliotèque Nationale in Paris, the Staatsbibliothek in Berlin, and the Nationalbibliothek in Vienna—but, he told me, he likes the Vatican Library the best. For one thing, there's the bar. And secondly, you can leave your rare manuscript on your desk, go get coffee or check a reference book, and come back. Other places make you check your manuscript back in whenever you leave your desk.

Larry said he would let me look at his rare manuscript, the Bible of Santa Cecilia in Trastevere, an eleventh-century illuminated "large Bible" made out of parchment.

We walked back from the bar to his desk near the front of the manuscript reading room. The young blonde next to him was glaring at a large Hebrew text, her annoyance palpable. To his left, a gray-haired professor in a red sweater was standing up at an easel and studying a large volume of medieval music.

Larry opened his own illuminated Bible and very carefully turned the pages. He showed me how the scribes used a sharp edge to make creases, still visible on the page, so they could keep their sentences on a straight line without using pencil marks. The parchment felt thick but very durable (obviously). The Latin text was very easy to read (assuming, of course, you read Latin), and there were copious cross-references and notes in the margins, just like in contemporary Bibles.

Larry couldn't put a number on how much this Bible was worth, but I quickly gave it a shot. When Anthony Melnikas was arrested for trying to hock two pages of an illuminated Bible similar to this one, but dating from two centuries *later,* curators estimated their worth at about $500,000 for the pair—or $250,000 each. This was a complete Bible I was holding in my hands, at least two hundred pages, perhaps more. That would make it worth—maybe not in one piece but page by page—at least $50 million.

I don't think I've ever held anything worth that much money in my entire life. I left the library a bit disappointed by the paucity of erotica available in the Vatican collections, contrary to what I had been led to believe. But the altar boy in me sort of likes to think that the most valuable item I've ever held in my two hands was not gold or diamonds, but a Bible.

XVII

The Only Man in Rome
Who Speaks Latin

Omnia praemium rara.
(All the best things are rare.)

CICERO

The Reverend Reginald "Reggie" Foster, OCD, was a legend among the thousands of seminarians, theology students, and postgraduate nuns who flock to Rome for advanced study.

He was, to put it bluntly, the only man in Rome, perhaps in the entire Catholic Church, who really knew Latin.

Most ecclesiastics, including most bishops and cardinals, know only enough Latin to decode Church documents with the help of a good dictionary—or to sprinkle a few select phrases through their canon law theses to make them look suitably Roman.

Foster actually *knew* Latin—better than the ancient Romans did. According to experts I've spoken with, he wrote better Latin than Augustine. Maybe better than Cicero.

Foster was the official Latinist for the Roman Catholic Church, the man responsible for translating official Church texts into Latin for all posterity. He was also a certifiable lunatic, categorically and demonstrably insane.

In an institution as paranoid and tight-lipped as the Vatican—where clerical advancement depends above all else on discretion—Foster spoke his mind loudly and bluntly. He said the institutional church is coming to an end. He said the pope doesn't take care of business. He said the Curia is full of pious frauds. He grunted and guffawed, chortled and laughed out loud, whenever some pious student repeated what you might call the party line.

Unlike similarly obstreperous clerics in the United States—who take their predictable cheap shots against the pope to cheering crowds of students, all the while bragging about what courageous free thinkers they are—Foster did and said all these things two doors down from the pope's office.

I was told that Foster was fiercely hated by top curial officials, who would have loved to exile him to a little mission in the Sudan but who realized, if they did, they would have to translate their own damn documents into Latin. Also, the pope, surrounded as he is by yes-saying toadies, was alleged to rather like Foster's honest spirit, as bizarre as it was.

Clearly, this was a man to meet. It turned out Foster, a Carmelite priest, lived just three blocks from our apartment, at San Pancrazio Monastery up the hill on Via Vitellia, on the grounds of the Villa Doria Pamphili.

Foster worked every morning in his office in the Apostolic Palace, and then traveled over to "the Greg" to teach Latin six days a week. It was abject slavery. His classes ranged from first-year students up to fifth-year students.

I called Foster one day at his office, introduced myself, and asked if I could come meet him. He told me to come by anytime I wanted at one of his classes at the Greg. Most started at two o'clock, he said.

The issue of Latin as a liturgical and literary language was of keen interest to me because of my interest in Hebrew. In my wild, misspent youth, I spent some time in Israel, studying modern Hebrew in two successive six-month *ulpanim,* and I got to see firsthand how Jews have kept alive what was, if ever there were one, an officially "dead" language.

The secret is really simple: Jews love Hebrew!

Even when they don't speak it, and most don't, many wish they did. I knew Jewish yuppies who sent their kids to Hebrew schools, to Hebrew summer camps, to *ulpanim* in Israel. They'd buy Hebrew-language videocassettes *(Shalom Sesame)* and CDs by such Israeli rock stars as Yehudit Ravitz and Benzene. They read Hebrew newspapers and listened to "easy Hebrew" broadcasts on Kol Israel. In synagogues, Jews continue to use Hebrew as the official liturgical language, even when, as in Reform congregations, the majority of the people can't really read it. It's a badge of honor for young Jewish boys and girls to master enough of the ancient tongue to be able to read their "portion" of the Torah scroll at their bar and bat mitzvahs. I've heard Jewish teenagers, at Orthodox synagogues, flirt shamelessly with members of the opposite sex using the same words and phrases the Jerusalem prophet Isaiah used 2,400 years ago.

In contrast, Latin in the Catholic Church is a sad joke. Although still officially the language of the Church, and many important Church documents are still produced in the official *editio typica* in Latin, it is as dead and ossified as Pope Pius X is in St. Peter's Basilica. Catholic seminarians in recent years have been forced to take a year of Latin to finish their studies, but that's like saying NASA scientists are required to take a year of algebra before they are allowed to work on the space shuttle. A year of Latin is a waste of time.

Foster, however, still kept the Old Knowledge alive—somehow. He was also the last-ditch hope for many students who flunked whatever perfunctory examination they had been given and quickly had to learn enough Latin to pass. Hundreds of Latin students and teachers came to Rome every summer to study with Foster, who delighted in taking his students on his famous walking tours of the city.

Two weeks after we spoke on the phone, I showed up at the Greg. Having attended a Jesuit high school and college, I had heard about the Gregorian University all my life. It loomed in my imagination somewhere between Oxford and the Sorbonne, an ancient center of traditional but rigorous scholarship, a place where all the undergraduates knew Latin and Greek and could spot the fallacy of the undistributed middle faster than you could say *ad hominem*.

Like most venerable institutions in Rome, the Greg turned out to be somewhat of a disappointment, a bit tacky and down at the heels. Located just a few short blocks from the Trevi Fountain on Via della Pilotta, it actually looked far less impressive than my own Jesuit liberal arts college back in the States and not a bit like Oxford University—small, run-down, with far too many pony-tailed baby Jesuits dressed in berets. Not knowing precisely where Father Foster's class met, I went up the stairs to the right of the main entrance and just started wandering around the halls.

The Roman colleges, by the way, are something of a racket. I visited the venerable Angelicum too—the Pontifical University of St. Thomas Aquinas—around the bend a few blocks from the Greg. I heard a similar story there. Ambitious clerical students all come to Rome to enroll in the Greg or the "Ange"—without knowing a single word of Italian. By United States standards, pontifical universities are ridiculously cheap—something like $900 per year for tuition and $800 per month for room, board, and laundry. Because students can take their examinations, read their books, and write their papers in their native languages, Italian is necessary only if you want to attend the optional lectures. And since enterprising students long ago drafted lecture notes for each class, in each of the major languages, there was no real need to know Italian. You could try to follow along as best you could, but since no one asks questions in the Italian university system, and the professors merely read from their yellowing lecture notes, you didn't have to worry about having to think fast on your feet or seriously engage the material. As a result, while pontifical schools hold themselves out as being elitist—at least in churchy circles—in fact they are considerably less demanding than, say, a typical Catholic university in the United States or Europe. "You get none of the give-and-take between students and professors as you do in the United States," one acquaintance of mine, an American priest studying at the Ange, told me. "There's no vision, no intellectual excitement, no debate. The professors here merely read their notes in Italian . . . and then leave."

At the Greg there were three stories around a central indoor courtyard. On the second floor I saw the weirdest thing I had seen since leaving college: Two rows of about five bearded professors faced each other, quietly discussing some topic, and while one row walked forward, the other row walked backward. After about twenty feet, the row that had been walking backward started to advance while the other row walked backward. I was always in awe of progressive Jesuit educational techniques.

Finally, off in the distance, I recognized Father Foster's deep, gravelly, staccato voice and headed in that direction. I was expecting someone who looked like Anthony Quinn in *Guns for San Sebastian,* big flowing robes and pockmarked face; instead, Foster turned out to be a small, bald-headed, rather reptilian-looking man with glasses and a bright red, peeling face from too much sun. He was dressed in a weird blue two-piece leisure suit that made him look, quite literally, like a Maytag repairman. He was said to be a secret (albeit chaste) nudist and avid motorcyclist. Ironically enough, though, many of his students consider him to be one of the holiest men they have ever met—a judgment that would only have made Foster snort in bemused disbelief.

"Ah, yes, hello, how are you?" he bellowed when I approached, the voice echoing all around the building. Foster handed me some sheets of paper with Latin all over them. This turned out to be a fifth-year class and on that particular day they were going to work on some Cicero.

I spent the next two hours listening to about a dozen students— six clerics and six women graduate students—wrestle with deponent verbs and the optative subjunctive. For fifth-year students and teachers of Latin, they all seemed relatively lost. "Vocabulary, people!" Foster would snarl at them. "It's an ugly, painful fact, but you're not going to be able to handle this stuff unless you learn the vocabulary!"

At the break, Foster met me in the back of the classroom. He pulled a brown paper bag out of his briefcase and withdrew from it a liter bottle of Italian beer, Birra Moretti.

And then he proceeded to guzzle it. *Glug, glug, glug, glug.*

"Come on," he barked. "Walk with me while I get my mail."

Foster walked out of the classroom and down the hallway, continuing to sip the beer along the way. Whenever we'd pass another faculty member, Foster would raise the beer bottle in a little salute and growl, "Hello, how are ya?" The faculty members just stared back without saying a word.

Obviously, this was a guy beyond caring about what other people thought.

We talked about a mutual friend for a time, and then about my book. Foster said there was absolutely nothing interesting to write about in the Vatican.

"What are you going to do?" he snarled in a taunting voice. "Write about the Vatican Museums?"

I said, well, no, not exactly. I said I thought there must be a lot of interesting stories in the Vatican. What about the Scavi? I said. That's interesting.

"The Scavi?" he asked incredulously. "Jesus, that's ancient history! That came out in the sixties. Everybody knows about the Scavi."

I replied that that wasn't true. Maybe the chief Latinist of the Roman Catholic Church, who works every day in the Apostolic Palace knows all about the Scavi, but most people had never heard of them.

"Okay," he said. "What else?"

I told him some of my other ideas.

The Swiss Guards (he winced). The Vatican Bank (he snorted). The lesbian Queen Christina of Sweden (he chuckled).

"It's all over," he told me finally, shaking his head in a definitive manner. "The institutional church is dead. *They*"—he motioned with his head upward, referring either to the Vatican or to God and his angels, I wasn't quite sure which—"*they* just don't know it yet."

For Foster, Christianity in general, and the Catholic Church in particular, are slowly devolving into an eccentric sect as quaint and irrelevant as the Amish.

One reason for that, in Foster's view, is the loss of Latin. In his mind, a knowledge of Latin is as essential to understanding what Catholic doctrine is all about as calculus is to physics.

Strangely enough, a rabbi once told me the same thing.

I was taking a class on the philosophy of Thomas Aquinas at the time, and the rabbi, who taught Catholic theology students about the Talmud, asked me whether my Latin was up to the task. When I told him that the only Latin I knew were a few prayers remembered from grade school, he replied that I was wasting my time with Aquinas.

Just as you can't study the Talmud in translation, he said, so, too, you can't understand Aquinas without a mastery of Latin. He recommended that I drop the Aquinas class and quickly enroll instead in a remedial program in Latin. "It would be the best thing you could do for your education," the rabbi said.

Of course, I ignored the advice—since I needed the Aquinas credit to graduate, not Latin. Besides, in my day the Jesuits wanted you to study Spanish, not Latin, so you could better read the writings of Che Guevara in the original. I thought back on all this while listening to Foster.

Without Latin, Foster told me, you miss the resonances between Catholic doctrine and the Bible. You fail to hear how the same thoughts echo throughout time, over and over again, in a kind of grand symphony of the soul.

The contemporary Church has lost the ability to hear its own music, he said. Without Latin, everyone is now tone deaf. We're still doing the same ritual dance steps by rote, he explained, but no one can hear the music anymore. No wonder people are bored.

He collected his mail and we walked back to the classroom.

It was a fairly pessimistic worldview for someone in the Vatican to hold, I averred gently. Foster shrugged. He seemed resigned. Like Sisyphus pushing the rock up the mountain, only to see it tumble down again, Foster seemed to think the effort itself was worth it, despite its inherent futility. He would continue to teach his students, day in and day out, tending the tiny, sacred flame, passing on a lifetime of learning to the handful of mediocre students nerdy enough to pay attention.

The Catholic Church may be coming to an end, but perhaps a little would survive here and there. A remnant.

It reminded me very much of Hebrew, how the dispersed Jewish community, following the bloody annihilation of Jerusalem in A.D. 70, had kept alive the ancient tongue. Jews spoke the language of whatever country they lived in—whether German or Spanish, Arabic or French or Russian—but they never gave up Hebrew. They continued to use it in their synagogues, in their yeshivas and Hebrew schools. They continued to say their prayers in Hebrew. Marriage contracts, the *ketuvot*, were written in Hebrew. And the Bible continued to be studied in the original language.

When Eliezer ben Yehuda began his campaign to revive Hebrew as a spoken language in the early twentieth century, he had 2,000 years of Hebrew literature and culture to draw upon.

It is said that just as the Jews kept the sabbath, the sabbath kept the Jews. But I wondered if, at least as much as the sabbath, *Hebrew* kept the Jews. And that, in turn, made me wonder if Foster was right—if, as the traditionalists so noisily insist, the loss of Latin will result in a gradual dissolution of the Catholic faith.

Foster and I shook hands. He chugged the last of his beer with a grand flourish, wiped his mouth on the back of his hand, and opened the door to his classroom. Another group of students was gathered for another class. "Be good," he snarled, and walked inside.

XVIII

Haute Couture in the Vatican

I was strolling lately through the vast temple, equally impressed
with reverence and delight, when a cardinal entered by a side door.
He was a young man, with a marked air of gentility; and I presume his
early rise in the church was owing to his high birth. He was in his official
dress, and carried the red hat pressed against his bosom.

JAMES FENIMORE COOPER, *Gleanings in Europe*

M ale denizens of the Vatican—from the pope on down—do not
dress like ordinary people or even like ordinary priests. They wear
funny short capes and sport extra-large yarmulkes on their heads. In
fact, they look a lot like Sherlock Holmes, if Sherlock happened to have
been an Orthodox Jew.

I was curious about the Vatican's dress code. Early on in my stay
in Rome I decided to find out more about it. I began to frequent the

various ecclesiastical clothing stores that are found around St. Peter's and in various other places in Rome. It wasn't an easy story to look into. Like everything else having to do with the Vatican, simple, seemingly inocuous facts are hidden behind centuries of tradition.

It turns out that the Savile Row of ecclesiastical high fashion is a series of tiny shops just off of the Piazza della Minerva, about a block from the Pantheon. The shops have names like Gherri, Baraggio, and De Ritis. They have mannequins in their windows, but unlike the half-naked mannequins that can be seen on Rome's famous Via Condotti, these displayed priestly chasubles, the ornate kite-shaped gowns worn at Mass, and contemporary nuns' habits. The most exclusive of these tiny boutiques is a small shop by the name of Gammarelli, the pope's personal tailor.

It thought I'd take the bull by the horns and try Gammarelli first. I met Luca, my faithful Italian translator, on the portico of the Pantheon, and we walked the block or so to Gammarelli. I explained to Luca that what I wanted was a crash course in Vatican high fashion. I wanted to know what all the clothing was called and what it signified.

He looked nervous. "What if they won't talk to us?" he asked.

"They'll talk to us," I replied, with a confidence I didn't actually feel. "These aren't clerics. The Vatican has no direct power over them. People *want* to talk about their jobs. Usually the problem is getting them to shut up."

"Okay," Luca said.

Gammarelli is located at 34 Via di San Chiara, across the piazza from the beautiful Dominican-run Basilica of Santa Maria sopra Minerva (where St. Catherine of Siena is entombed under the high altar).

The shop is small and elegant, its two windows framed in dark wood. Luca and I walked in, with Luca carrying a motorcycle helmet under his arm and looking like some kind of thug. Inside, there were no displays whatsoever, merely a large table covered with green felt, and racks with bolts of cloth on them.

It occurred to me that the pope probably wouldn't paw his way through racks of white papal outfits as if he were at some department store on Fifth Avenue. On the wall to our right were framed certificates announcing that this establishment, for as long as anyone can remember, has been the official tailor of the papacy.

The place was as hushed and quiet as a tomb. There were two Trappist monks, their distinctive strip of black cloth over their white robes, standing on one side of the table. They were obviously customers and appeared to be whispering. On the other side of the table stood a saleswoman and a man of about forty, who turned out to be the scion of the Gammarelli family and looked exactly like an aging version of the former tennis pro Bjorn Borg, with long, greasy blond hair, big bushy blond eyebrows, and a hideous orange tie.

As soon as Luca and I walked in, everyone ceased talking and stared. Luca froze. I quickly elbowed him in the ribs and he jumped forward.

He explained that I was an American writer working on a book about the Vatican. We wanted to speak to someone about the clothing worn by cardinals and bishops.

Instantly, Bjorn started wagging his head back and forth like a goat.

"No way," he told Luca in Italian. "*Non è possibile.* We've had lots of bad experiences in the past with journalists, and, because we don't want to discriminate, we simply have a blanket policy not to do interviews. Sorry."

Luca, who was learning the journalistic discipline of not taking no for an answer, did his best. He explained that we weren't looking for any secrets, just basic information about what everything is called, what the different colors mean, and so on.

Bjorn kept shaking his head. "Try around at the other stores," he said. "Someone will be glad to help you."

Strike one.

I had to admit Bjorn was probably right: If you can't trust your tailor to keep his mouth shut, who can you trust?

"Well, that sure went well," Luca said as we walked out the front door. "Now what?"

"Simple," I replied. "We try someplace else. Someone will talk. Just wait."

It was getting dark, and the post-siesta sales cycle was beginning. We walked down Via di Santa Caterina da Siena, next to Santa Maria sopra Minerva, until we came to a large shop with the name Barbiconi on it. We walked in the swinging glass doors, told a salesclerk what we wanted, and waited. And waited.

Finally, a lively, middle-aged woman with blondish-silver hair came rushing out of the back of the shop, harried but with a big smile on her face. Her name, she said, was Manina, and her family had owned this establishment since the 1820s. Until the 1950s they made only hats for the clergy, especially the richly embroidered *cappello romano*. The "Roman hat," with wide, slightly rounded brims, went out of fashion in the 1960s—although you sometimes see a baby-faced "more traditional-ist than thou" priest, probably a Legionary of Christ, strutting around St. Peter's Square dressed in his cassock and *cappello romano.*

Luca explained to Manina, who spoke only Italian, what we wanted: A crash course in dressing like a cardinal.

Manina sighed. It was obviously a big job, but she took a deep breath and said okay. She took us into the room where the tailor worked. He and she began taking garments off the racks and showing them to us.

"The first thing you have to understand," Manina said, "are the basic garments, and then we'll talk about the colors. Out on the street, prelates dress just like ordinary priests, in a black suit or black cassock; but 'around the office,' so to speak, they wear special clothes reserved just for the hierarchy.

"The basic outfit consists of three parts—a garment called a *simar,* which looks like a regular black cassock with a short shoulder cape attached to it; the *fascia,* a six- to eight-inch sash that is worn high up on the sternum, and which has two pieces that extend almost to the floor; and the skullcap, or *zucchetto.*"

Manina told me that only bishops and cardinals may wear the *zucchetto,* but I found out subsequently, during visits to other shops, that this is not strictly true. In theory, any priest may wear a *zucchetto,* which was originally used to cover the bald spot, or tonsure, given to monks; but in practice, at least around the Vatican, it's considered somewhat presumptuous for the lower-level monsignori to do so, and they don't. However, only bishops, archbishops, or cardinals may wear the *simar.* Monsignori in Rome wear a black Roman cassock with red or purple piping and buttons, but no little cape.

These three garments—capelike *simar,* sash, and skullcap—are the basic uniform, so to speak.

The next element involves color. You can tell a prelate's rank by the colors he is wearing, but it is all a bit complicated. Just as there are three basic garments, there are also three basic colors—purple (actually a kind of fuchsia or magenta color); amaranth red (or crimson), which is a reddish-purple; and scarlet (which looks like an orange-red), used only by cardinals.

The reason things get a bit confusing is that the piping and buttons on a *simar* and/or cassock can be one color and the *zucchetto* and *fascia* another color.

The cardinals are the easiest to spot: They go with scarlet all the way, for *zucchetto,* sash, and buttons. The pope just wears white, so he's easy enough to spot as well. Patriarchs, archbishops, and bishops will wear a *simar* with amaranth-red piping and buttons but will wear a purple sash and *zucchetto.* Lowly monsignori, who are not bishops, will wear purple piping and buttons on their black cassock (not a *simar*) and a purple sash.

"Wait a minute," I said. Now my head was beginning to spin a little. "Let me get this straight. If I see a guy *without* a little cape over his shoulders but *with* a purple sash around his waist, that probably means he's a monsignor, not a bishop, right?"

"*Esattamente,*" replied Manina.

"But both monsignori and bishops wear purple sashes, right?"

"Correct."

"But only cardinals wear red or red-orange or whatever it is."

"*Sì.*"

There was a final complication.

Some of the sashes and *zucchetti* had a kind of moiré pattern that is part of the actual cloth. This moiré pattern—which gives the material a kind of 3-D effect—is made by using what is called watered silk. The *zucchetti* and sashes of all cardinals and the pope automatically have this moiré pattern, but not those of all bishops and archbishops. The use of watered silk is considered a special honor. Manina said that it is usually reserved for Vatican diplomats or nuncios, not the ordinary "working bishops" you see around St. Peter's.

"So, all I will need are a *simar,* a skullcap, and a sash once I'm made a cardinal?" I asked.

Manina smiled. Not quite, she said. What she described so far was merely what my day-to-day working uniform would be. I would need special garments for church, which is where, after all, a cardinal spends a good deal of time.

Cardinals, archbishops, and bishops must buy a special cassock to be worn during solemn ceremonies. This is called a choir cassock. Cardinals wear choir cassocks that are scarlet and have special watered-silk cuffs. Archbishops and bishops wear purple choir cassocks.

On top of this colored cassock is worn a lacy white silk garment called a rochet (in English-speaking countries pronounced, incredibly enough, "rocket"), which looks like the surplice once commonly worn by altar boys; and on top of the rochet is worn a short wool cape called a *mozzetta,* which is the same color as the cassock (scarlet for cardinals, purple for bishops). Unlike the cape on the *simar,* which is worn open and does not cover the front of the wearer's chest, the elbow-length *mozzetta* completely covers the person wearing it and is buttoned up the front. On top of the *mozzetta* the cardinal or bishop will wear his pectoral cross, hanging from a special colored cord (a *cordoniera per croce*) around his neck, and a simple stole. The stole is a long, narrow strip of cloth worn by all priests at Mass.

On his head, over his *zucchetto,* a carninal will wear the funny square hat with three or four ridges on top known as a biretta, once commonly worn by all Catholic clergy but now worn only by cardinals (in moiré-ized scarlet, of course) and a few traditional-minded bishops (in purple). The biretta is *not* the traditional "red hat" that was once given to newly created cardinals. This was called a *galero* and looked like a kind of flattened sombrero. It is seen still in the coat of arms of bishops and cardinals. Today, however, newly created cardinals are presented with the red silk biretta during the special gathering, called a consistory, that confers membership in the College of Cardinals.

Manina stopped for breath.

"How much is all this stuff going to cost?" I asked.

"Not too much," she replied. "Seminarians spend a lot more on their clothes than do cardinals. A cardinal starting out will normally buy just three cassocks—a plain black one, a black one with scarlet buttons and piping, and an all-scarlet one. These vary in cost according to the materials, but a black cassock with scarlet buttons usually costs around 700,000 lire (about $450). The *fascia,* or sash, costs around 70,000 lire ($45), unless it's moiré-ized, in which case it costs 200,000 lire (or $130). The *zucchetto* is just 28,000 lire ($19)."

"I was going to ask you about accessories," I told Manina. "What do aspiring cardinals have to buy in the way of crosses, rings, and such?"

Manina laughed. She took me over to a glass case and showed me her line of pectoral crosses.

"Contrary to popular belief, the jewelry is actually quite modest," she said. "These crosses run from one million to four million lire," which at the time was between $700 and $3,000. "It depends upon the type of semiprecious stones used, whether they're made of silver with gold plating or just silver. Often they are bought for the cardinals or bishops by their family members, wealthy friends, or former parishioners. A cardinal's day-to-day ring costs just 150,000 lire ($100). If the cardinal wants a solid gold ring, it can cost more like 500,000 lire ($350)."

Manina repeated that cardinals really don't spend much on clothing. Because of their age (most are elderly), they don't wear their clothes out like the wild young bishops; and there are so few of them (only 150), and they are so scattered around the world, that they don't constitute much of the day-to-day business for the Vatican tailors. Bishops, priests, and fashion-conscious young seminarians are their bread and butter.

"How long does it take to make everything?" I asked.

"A month and a half."

"Do you have, you know, a catalogue or something? Something I could take with me?"

"No. No catalogue. In the old days there were more choices and people spent a lot more money. Not today. Now we just have a few simple line drawings to show people when we take measurements. That's it."

I thanked Manina for all her help. I told her that if I ever needed a *zucchetto, fascia* or matching *mozzetta,* I would come to her and not to those stuffed shirts at Gammarelli's.

She just smiled weakly as Luca and I walked out into the night— glad, no doubt, to be rid of us.

Luca was upbeat. He was discovering that in journalism, if not in life, persistence usually pays off. Slowly, very slowly, we were getting answers to our questions.

Manina had also shared with us a little curial gossip—revealing which cardinals were known as the Vatican's dandies—but we promised not to repeat it. We had to keep some secrets, after all.

XIX

Weird Relics

The priests showed us two of St. Paul's fingers and one of St. Peter's;
a bone of Judas Iscariot (it was black) and also bones of all
the other disciples; a handkerchief in which the Saviour had left
the impression of his face.

MARK TWAIN, *The Innocents Abroad*

I was roaming around the Gesù like a good tourist one sunny afternoon
in late October. It's the Jesuit mother church, located a block from the
Piazza Venezia on the Via del Plebescito. I had had lunch at the little
trattoria across the square from the church, including a beer or two, and
was in a very good mood. Rome is beautiful in the fall.

Eight years in a Jesuit high school and college had made me somewhat familiar with this famous, albeit rather ordinary Counter-Reformation church, and I was enjoying all of that lush Baroque painting side by

side with the pro-Castro posters on the bulletin boards, when I happened to glance up and see on display . . . *an entire human arm!*

Yikes! I couldn't believe my eyes.

It was ghastly. Up on a high side altar there was an elaborate oval gold-and-crystal reliquary with a full-sized golden angel floating languidly on his (or her?) side above it. Inside the reliquary was what looked like an entire human arm from the elbow socket on down.

Black, moldly, utterly withered flesh still clung to the bones!

If you wanted to see it better, or take pictures, you had to drop a 200-lira coin in a little metal box on the side, and large floodlights, hooked up to a timer, popped on. I took pictures.

It turned out the arm once belonged to St. Francis Xavier, the great Jesuit missionary to India and Japan. My mind reeled as I struggled to remember what happened to old St. Francis, one of those genuinely heroic saints I had heard so much about in my youth. Did he lose his arm to some Japanese samurai, who lopped it off in rage during a sermon? I couldn't remember. I should have paid more attention during seventh-grade religion class.

Later I found out that, in fact, St. Francis went to his grave with all his limbs quite intact. He died of a sudden fever in early December 1552 on Sancian, a desolate island off the coast of China, and was buried there. The Jesuit general back in Rome, Claudio Acquaviva, ordered that Francis's body be dug up, his right arm cut off at the elbow and brought back to be enshrined in the Gesù, and the rest of his body reburied on Goa.

My encounter with St. Francis Xavier's right arm left me somewhat rattled. But I had had similar gruesome encounters all over Rome. The cult of relics is an aspect of Catholicism rarely seen in the United States—if only because America is too young, or has had too few saints, for such a cult to develop.

But in Rome, relics are everywhere.

Catholicism has always had a macabre fascination with *reliquiae*—

pieces of saints' bodies or clothing that are collected and preserved after they die. This has gone way beyond clipping a lock of someone's hair to keep as a memento; there isn't a body part that we Catholics haven't snipped off and enshrined in an elaborate reliquary.

Bones, entire skulls, drops of maternal milk, blood, internal organs, fingernails, skin, spit, you name it—if it was part of a dead person, we Catholics have saved it.

Among the relics venerated in Rome and elsewhere are the skull of John the Baptist, bones of the magi, Mary Magdalene's foot, the incorrupt heart of St. Vincent de Paul, the wristbone of Christ's grandmother (St. Anne), the heads of both St. Peter and St. Paul (in the Lateran), the liquefying blood of St. Januarius, the vocal chords of St. Anthony of Padua, the hands of St. Catherine Labouré, the gallstones of St. Clare of Montefalco, the tongue of St. John Nepomucene, and so on. The head of St. Thomas, the first Christian skeptic and apostle to India, is said to reside in the Basilica of Ortona. There is even a shrine in Calcate, north of Rome, that claims to have the *foreskin* of Jesus Christ, allegedly collected and preserved following his *bris* or ritual circumcision, encased in a ruby-and-emerald-studded box.

Sometimes it doesn't even have to be a *part* of a body. Like the ancient Egyptians, Catholics have even gone in for what amounts to full-body mummification. The body of St. Bernadette Soubirous, for example, the seer of Lourdes, now lies encased in wax and on public display in a glass reliquary at the Convent of St. Gildard, in Nevers, France. A similar fate has befallen St. Charles Borromeo, on display in the Cathedral of Milan.

You can see the same thing right in St. Peter's. Pope St. Pius X is mummified in an altar display case on the left side of the basilica. St. Pius X (1903–1914) was the energetic and saintly pope best known for his war against modernism (the "heresy of all heresies"), which is basically a broad name for virtually everything people in the world today believe. For this reason, Pius X is much beloved by Catholic traditionalists, particularly followers of the late schismatic French archbishop Marcel Lefevbre, who named his breakaway society after this pope.

In any event, there is this creepy bronze statue of St. Pius X, wrapped in red pontifical robes, lying in a crystal case under an altar on the left side of St. Peter's, near the baptistry.

Every time I walked past, I had to stop to look at it. And I had always wondered if . . . well, if . . .

"Yes, it's his actual body," a guide finally told me one day when I worked up the nerve to ask. "The face and hands are covered with a type of silver."

My God, I thought, they bronzed him! Just like a pair of baby shoes.

The face looks like a statue, but the *hands* . . . the hands look too realistic, twisted and bony, shriveled up, veins popping. Rather than discreetly bury the poor fellow down in the grottoes with the other popes, the Vatican put him in a glass box so that gum-snapping teenage tourists, dressed in T-shirts and jeans, could forever stare at his veiny hands.

I found out later that the pope died in 1914, but his body was exhumed in 1951, when he was beatified, and found to be "incorrupt." (Catholic officials have a very generous understanding of what the term "incorrupt" means, applying it to any human remains that are not merely dusty bones.) The papal physician in 1951, Dr. Galeazzi Lisi—an incompetent quack and secret press spy who later mucked up the embalming of Pope Pius XII—injected the body of Pius X with chemical preservatives that gave him what looks like a permanent suntan.

The tour guide saw the shock and horror on my face and laughed. Just like a tourist, he probably thought.

Of course, we Catholics are not alone in this bizarre obsession. Most of the world's religions have, at one time or another, indulged in the passion for anatomical collectibles. Tibetan Buddhists build large shrines for relics called stupas; and the mortal remains of Confucius have been revered since the year 195 B.C. Moslems keep two hairs from the prophet Mohammed locked in a special reliquary in Jerusalem's Dome of the Rock. You don't even have to be religious to have a cult of relics—as the embalmed, carefully preserved bodies of Lenin and Mao attest.

But we Catholics, as usual, take things to extremes.

And just how far we take this relic business can be seen by visiting the weirdest tourist site in all of Rome—the infamous "bone house" of the Capuchin monks.

One of Irish Bob's Italian writers, the dapper Antonio, hold told me several times about one of the "secrets" of Rome he would show me, the Capuchin ossuary. Of course, I quickly discovered that this "secret" has been written about by every writer who ever came to Rome, although many contemporary guidebooks now discreetly pass over it.

Luca and Anne had seen the bone house, too, and said that, yes, it's creepy beyond belief. I decided to wait until Halloween, just a few days away, to visit the bone house. Until a few years ago the American holiday of Halloween was mostly unknown in Europe, but in recent years the French and, now, the Italians, recognizing another opportunity to dress up for a wild party, have begun to observe the holiday as well.

Luca told me the Capuchin ossuary was located right by the Piazza Barberini, where Bernini's famous Fontana del Tritone has been spouting for 350 years. Also, I knew there was a metro stop nearby, which would make getting there easier.

As a result, on Halloween morning I took my usual buses down the hill to the Vatican, puttered around the Sala Stampa for a half hour, and then walked the six blocks or so to the Ottaviano metro stop, at the corner of Viale Giulio Cesare. The Barberini metro stop, on the A line, is just one stop after the Spanish Steps and takes all of five minutes.

I stepped out of the metro right onto the beginning of the Via Veneto, the famous (now somewhat shabby) street featured in Fellini's 1960 film *La Dolce Vita*. I walked what seemed like just five steps up the street and there, on my right, was the tiny church I was looking for, Santa Maria della Concezione. It was a very tall, narrow building made of thin orange bricks with a double staircase leading up to a landing in front of the main door. Off to the right there was an entryway into a basement vault next to the church.

I walked through a door into a small gift shop. There was an old, white-haired, somewhat surly monk dressed in ragged brown robes, sitting on a chair in the near darkness. He pointed to a sign in Italian that indicated I had to make a donation. After I dug a 5,000-lira note out of my pocket, the monk turned on some lights and showed me down a hallway into the cemetery proper.

Even though I had had some idea what to expect, I still couldn't believe my eyes.

In a series of six chapel vaults all in a line, the monks had created elaborate decorative montages entirely out of human bones—thousands and thousands of them. Entire walls were lined with skulls two or three deep. The ceilings were covered by intricate patterns made out of pelvic girdles, rosettes of vertebrae, archways of ribs and collarbones. One entire crypt, the Crypt of the Pelvises, was covered by nothing but pelvic bones. Another was dedicated to skulls, yet another to leg and thigh bones. Above one of the chapels was a quotation from Romans 14:8: "Alive or dead, we belong to the Lord."

It was like something you'd see in a campy Hollywood horror flick. Some of the skulls still had tufts of hair and leathery skin attached to them. Even more chilling, the Capuchins had taken full skeletons, dressed them up in the brown habits and white rope belts of their order, and positioned them in various poses facing out to the visitors. In one of the chapels, a full skeleton, without a habit, was holding a scythe in one hand and a balance scale in the other—both made, of course, out of human bones.

Creepy doesn't begin to describe the feeling I had walking through this place. Ghoulish is closer.

These were not anonymous bones. The friars actually knew who almost everybody was. "Oh, that's Brother Alexander," they'd say. "He died in 1867. And over there is Bartolomeo; he died in 1784." For literally three centuries they've buried their brothers in the dirt floors of each of the chapels, as well as in other burial vaults, waited a few years for the flesh to decompose, and then dug up the bones to use in further decorating. It wasn't until the late 1700s, though, that work began on creating chapels made entirely out of bones.

The Capuchins are a reform branch of the Franciscan Order begun in 1525 in Italy, known for their strict poverty, pointed hoods, and beards. As a result, they explained this ghoulish monument by referring to the teaching of St. Francis of Assisi about "our sister, bodily death."

On a wall plaque was written: "This dramatic presentation of the final end of human existence rises out of the soil, specifically brought from Jerusalem for the burial of these bodies. Using the exhumed bones themselves to build a series of niches, arches, and symbolic designs, they remind us of the biblical truths about death, which are also a message of hope. As the apostle Paul says, the world as we know it is passing away—shown in the symbol of the clock and the hourglass. Death is swallowed up in victory, redemption, and resurrection. Let us perform works of justice and mercy while there is still time."

The reaction of visitors, of course, has alternated between macabre fascination to outright horror. Charles Dickens, that Victorian scourge of all things papish, was revolted. Mark Twain got in a few digs. "From the sanguinary sports of the Holy Inquisition, the slaughter of the Colosseum, and the dismal tombs of the catacombs, I naturally pass to the picturesque horrors of the Capuchin convent," he wrote.

Noting how the monks divided up the skeletal parts into separate rooms—the skulls in one vault, the pelvises in another—Twain couldn't resist asking a monk, when he visited in 1869, if that wouldn't lead to a chaotic scramble "if the last trump should blow."

The most chilling part of the entire spectacle, however, comes at the end, near the last of the six bone-covered rooms. Near a skeleton of one of the monks—dressed up in brown habit—was a sign. And on the sign were these words in Italian:

QUELLO CHE VOI SIETE NOI ERAVAMO,
QUELLO CHE NOI SIAMO VOI SARETE.

What you are now, we used to be;
What we are now, you will be.

In Search of the True Cross

Pieces of the True Cross had already been scattered throughout the land.

ST. CYRIL OF JERUSALEM, *Catechetics* (A.D. 350)

Perhaps the most famous relics in Rome are those of the Passion, kept in what has to be the ugliest church in Christendom, the Basilica of Santa Croce in Gerusalemme.

After seeing St. Francis Xavier's withered arm and the Capuchin bone house, I decided the time had come to go to see the Passion relics. Every time I had visited the great Basilica of St. John Lateran, the pope's "home church"—which is just a block or two from Santa Croce—I had meant to go see them, but for one reason or another I never got around to it. Every smart-aleck writer who ever visited Rome, from Dante to Henry James, goes to see the True Cross at Santa Croce and then makes some snide, ironic remark about it.

Who was I to break such a long tradition?

190

And so, about a week after my visit to the Gesù, I set aside a day to go exploring. I walked up from our apartment to the Piazza San Giovanni di Dio and took the number thirteen tram out around the Colosseum, past St. John Lateran and down Viale Carlo Felice toward the ancient, famous but horribly ugly Basilica of Sante Croce.

I'm not kidding when I say it's the most repulsive church I've ever seen. The basilica consists of a central eighteenth-century Baroque facade topped with statues (similar to those on top of St. Peter's), with two large four-story wings branching off to both sides. The outside walls of these wings are made of gun-metal-gray plaster, with many of the windows covered over with old boards and black plastic or, in some places, patched over with gray plaster.

The church looks more like a tenement apartment in the Bronx than the repository of the holiest relics in Christendom.

It didn't help, of course, that I got off the tram a few blocks past the church and in the middle of a torrential early morning rainstorm. I arrived in the portico of the basilica soaking wet. Because of the storm, the cleaning ladies and I were the only ones in the church.

From the inside, the basilica wasn't so bad. Like many of the crumbling churches of Rome, Santa Croce still contains works of art that would be considered priceless anywhere else in the world—such as magnificent fifteenth-century frescoes, a bas-relief Pietà, a marvelous statue of St. Helena, and so on.

The core structure of the building actually dates all the way back to A.D. 325, when it was adapted as a church. You can still see those ultra-thin early Roman bricks—the kind visible down in the Scavi— around the back of the basilica. This makes it, along with St. Peter's and Santa Maria in Trastevere, one of the oldest churches in the world.

According to tradition, St. Helena, the mother of the emperor Constantine, brought back from a pilgrimage to Jerusalem pieces of the Cross, as well as numerous other relics now on display, and placed them in this church. She also allegedly carried back a couple tons of dirt from

Jerusalem, used as ballast in her ships, and placed them on the floor of the basilica, in an old chapel that is still used today. The story of the finding ("invention" is the Latin word) of the True Cross was observed as a Catholic feast day (May 3), until it was suppressed by Pope John XXIII in 1960.

St. Helena's relics of the passion are now on display in a side chapel built in 1930 out of dank-smelling concrete. It took me quite some time to find this little chapel, but finally, after I had wandered all over the basilica, I saw a doorway in the left wall, near the front. There was a sign that said SS. RELIQVIARVM SACELLVM. I went through the doorway and walked up some stairs into an inner chamber that, in turn, led to a long series of marble steps up into a small chapel with an altar. On the way up these steps, set into a wall, was a grid of iron bars and bulletproof glass that contained—not a sliver as I expected—but a five-foot-long beam of what looked like fairly fresh (pale brown) wood. Above the iron bars were chiseled the words PARS CRVCIS BONI LATRONIS, the cross of the good thief.

At the top of the marble stairs was the main chapel, which contained a small tablelike altar, surrounded by a baldachin made of green marble pillars, topped by a cross. Behind this structure, in an illuminated glass case set into the back wall, was a series of six reliquaries, each containing one or more relics—including three fragments of the True Cross, one of the holy nails, two thorns, the "title" placed on the Cross, the finger of St. Thomas the Apostle, and fragments of the column of the flagellation, the holy sepulcher, and the crib. The reliquaries were about a foot high each and looked like fancy candlesticks topped by a little oval glass orb or holder.

I couldn't decide one way or the other whether the various relics looked real or fake. The thorns were huge, about two inches long, from an as-yet-unidentified plant. The nails looked like thick railway spikes. St. Thomas's finger looked like a thin piece of gray concrete about an inch long.

The only thing that was truly unusual was the title, the board that the Romans, according to the Gospels, placed above Christ on the Cross with the mocking words "Jesus of Nazareth, King of the Jews." Encased in a silver reliquary, the board was riddled with tiny termite holes, but I could just barely make out a few letters. Nearby, there was a plaque with a reconstruction of what scholars have found on the board—letters in Hebrew, Greek, and Latin spelling out the words described in the Gospels. I could read the Hebrew easily enough, as it was written correctly (right to left); but the weird thing about the relic is that the words in Greek and Latin were also written from right to left—that is, backward.

Defenders of the authenticity of this relic like to say that had a Jew in Roman-occupied Palestine, accustomed to writing right to left, been ordered to write this down, he may have done just this—written the Hebrew correctly (right to left) but screwed up with the other languages, writing them right to left as well. The only problem with this theory is that the letters are not merely written backward in the sense of CAT being written TAC; the letters are reversed as well, so that the C is facing left instead of right, as though the writer had used a mirror. In fact, when I got back to the apartment, I took a postcard that I bought of the "title," held it up to a mirror, and could read the Greek and Latin just fine: IESVS NAZARENVS REX IVDEORVM.

But that raises an interesting question: Why would some medieval forger go to such trouble?

The title was not discovered until 1492, the year Columbus set forth for America, when it was found in a wall in the basilica, behind a mosaic that was then being repaired. Until that time there had been no record of any such relic in existence; but in the late nineteenth century the writings of a fourth-century Spanish nun, Aetheria (Egeria), who went on pilgrimage to Jerusalem, were discovered, and she described a relic similar to this being venerated in Palestine.

None of this proves anything, of course, which is probably why writers have so much fun poking fun at the "True Cross."

I was fully prepared to be openminded about the True Cross, however—if only because no one else seems really to believe the relics are genuine. As we've seen, people have been laughing at the Vatican for centuries for its insistence that St. Peter was buried beneath his eponymous basilica, and then, lo and behold, they dug down and found a first-century Roman grave marked with a Greek inscription that said "Peter is here."

Then, too, I knew from reading I'd done before visiting Santa Croce that the literary evidence is strong that a search for the True Cross was undertaken early in the fourth century. The emperor Constantine did build elaborate churches in Roman-controlled Jerusalem (then called Capitolina) on a site where Christ was believed crucified; and St. Cyril of Jerusalem, writing in A.D. 350, assures his readers that the True Cross had been in the Church's possession in Jerusalem for some time and that pieces of it had been scattered throughout Christendom. This is supported by an inscription found at Tixter, in Algeria, that mentions a relic of the Cross in the year 359. And the fourth-century Spanish pilgrim Aetheria, in her *Itinerarium,* describes the care with which deacons guarded the True Cross during Good Friday liturgies—to make sure that pilgrims, when kissing it, did not attempt to bite off a sliver as a relic.

Contemporary Bible scholars claim that the Cross was more likely merely a single crossbeam (the Roman *patibulum*) that condemned prisoners carried on their shoulders and which was hoisted up, with the prisoners tied or nailed to it, and placed on a more or less permanent stake, used for regular executions. It's not impossible, therefore, and perhaps even likely, that the friends and family of Jesus, when taking his body down from the cross, might have removed this crossbeam as well. They could very well have hidden it away for safekeeping. If the Cross somehow survived the annihilation of Jerusalem by the Romans in A.D. 70—when an estimated 100,000 inhabitants were killed and the city burned to the ground—it's possible that it might have been preserved for two more centuries, until it was rediscovered by visiting Roman dignitaries, such as Helena.

On the other hand, it's just as likely that even if some piece of wood were found, it was simply a fake. A Jewish legend, preserved in a medieval book called the *Toledot Yeshu,* states that Jewish leaders, under pressure by the Roman empress Helena to help her find the True Cross, secretly buried three large pieces of wood. When the empress demanded that a rabbi take her to the secret burial place of the True Cross, he simply took her to the place where these three pieces of wood were buried. Perplexed by which of the three could be the real Cross of Christ, the empress asked the rabbi what he would suggest. He recommended that the three pieces each be put in contact with a dead man, and the one that brought the dead man to life would be the real thing. Fortunately, the rabbi knew that by the power of the name of God, the secret of which he knew, the dead man could be brought back to life. This was duly accomplished, the empress had her "True Cross," and the rabbi spared his people further suffering at the hands of the Christian leaders.

I hate to admit it, but my skepticism toward St. Helena's relics has little to do with the scholarly evidence and stems primarily from the decrepit condition of the basilica. I would have been more inclined to fall on my knees had the relics not been consigned to this concrete block chapel, in a dank and seemingly abandoned church.

If the Vatican *really* thought these were relics of the Passion, wouldn't it give them at least the same billing as those of St. Peter—which, as we've seen, lie at the center of the most expensive monument in history? It's pretty pathetic, but architecture, not archaeology, guided my attitude toward the Passion relics.

I looked around a little more.

Off to the side of the chapel was a room, almost like a storage room, filled with old reliquaries and a life-sized model of the body of Christ on the Cross. It was made of resin perhaps and was supposed to be a prodigy of anatomical reconstruction. It's a very horrifying portrait of the crucifixion. The body is covered with thousands of small, bloody punctures, supposedly from the scourging with a cat-o-nine-tails, and the face is awash in blood.

The rector of the basilica, a Monsignor Giulio Ricci, apparently fancied himself an authority on the Shroud of Turin, and his life-sized model is his attempt at reconstructing the crucifixion based on the evidence found on the shroud. He was the founder of something called the Centro Romano di Sindonologia. The Italian word for the shroud is *sindone,* and so this was something like the Roman Center for Shroudology—I think.

I actually found the life-sized statue of the crucifixion in the Gesù, the Jesuit mother church, to be even more horrific, because the figure, carved out of wood, looks down at you with such agonized, pleading eyes. While visiting the Gesù, I saw two or three middle-aged Italian men fall on their knees in front of this statue, kiss the feet, and pray.

I headed for the ubiquitous gift shop in the vestibule of the basilica. There I found a few postcards and a book about Monsignor Ricci's model, *Chemin de Croix Selon le Saint-Suaire.* I had to wait outside while the shop owner, a dour Italian woman, ran down the block to get change for the 50,000-lira note I tried to give her.

By this time the rain had stopped. The woman returned, gave me my change, and I left. I had had quite enough of relics.

XXI

On Pilgrimage with Martin Luther

"[The church] was too crowded, and I could not get in;
so I ate a smoked herring instead."

MARTIN LUTHER, *Collected Works*, 14, 6

Time and again in Rome, I was struck by the contrast between the smug churchy professionals—the burned-out bureaucrats, the cynical monsignori, the world-weary prelates, the grim church ladies—and the good-natured, even buoyant faith of the hapless pilgrims.

We laity may not be too bright . . . and we're certainly no angels . . . but at least we know how to have a good time.

The Vatican's working elite naturally evinces a certain condescension for the fun-loving pilgrims—although, like tourists everywhere, they provide the money that greases the wheels and keeps the operation running smoothly. They flock to St. Peter's quite literally by the bus-load—day after day after day, in good weather and in bad, seven days a week, twelve months a year, nonstop. They pour into Rome, enduring the surly Italian shopkeepers, the overpriced cardboard sold as pizza, and the docents in the Vatican Information Office.

Many of these innocent, trusting, half-tipsy pilgrims appear to be sincerely interested in whatever religious experiences Rome has to offer, unlike the scurrying bureaucrats who work in the Vatican. Indeed, like many a Catholic who comes to Rome, if I had merely spent all my time in the Vatican—speaking to the priests, bishops, and assorted hangers-on who work there—I would have chucked the entire religion, lock, stock, and holy water font.

I kept thinking of one particular pilgrim, old Martin Luther, as I went around Rome. Most Catholics have never read Luther, but they should. He's an enormously entertaining writer, with a hilarious talent for polemic. Early in 1511, while still a pious Augustinian monk, Luther spent an entire month in the Eternal City on official business for his religious order. I couldn't help making a special trip out to the former Augustinian convent where he stayed—the Convent of Santa Maria del Popolo, right next to the Porto del Popolo—just to see what he saw there. Despite his later condemnation of such pious practices, Luther was a zealous pilgrim. "When I made my pilgrimage to Rome, I was such a fanatical saint that I dashed through all the churches and crypts, believing all the stinking forgeries of those places," he wrote.

What he was not impressed by, however, were his fellow priests. "I was not in Rome very long, but I celebrated many Masses there and also saw many Masses; it horrifies me to think of it. I overheard the officials at mealtime laughing and boasting about how some Masses were done, saying over bread and wine, 'Bread you are, and bread you will remain,' and then holding up the bread and wine [at the elevation]. Now, I was a young and truly pious monk, and I was shocked by such words. Indeed,

I was disgusted that they could celebrate the Mass so flippantly, as if they were performing some kind of trick. Before I had even gotten to the Gospel [reading], the priest beside me had already concluded a Mass and shouted at me: *Passa, passa*—enough now, finish it off." Luther added that "we were simply laughed at because we were such pious monks. A Christian was taken to be nothing but a fool."

But you quickly see, if you spend any time at all in the hundreds of churches, shrines, and sanctuaries of Rome, that such clerical impiety, even if it still exists, is largely beside the point. The Holy See is merely an outward symbol—a unifying symbol, to be sure, but a symbol nonetheless—for a faith that is somewhat larger than what is found in the 108 acres of the Vatican. Whenever I was put off by some particularly ill-mannered Vatican bureaucrat, I would go visit one of the major pilgrim centers, with tour buses parked outside, and be instantly cheered up.

You run into so many good-natured, happy pilgrims—rather like the lusty Wife of Bath in Chaucer's *Canterbury Tales*. Most of them are not the doddering old ladies clutching their proverbial rosary beads either—as the weary cliché would have you believe. They look like prosperous, well-educated, chic Europeans—Dutch and Swiss, Germans and French and Austrians, some Brits, a few Americans. You see tweedy German professors peering at a relic, bifocals balanced precariously on their noses, side by side with characters who look and sound like Danish bikers—who in fact *are* Danish bikers.

And most amazing of all, a lot of them are young . . . and surprisingly devout. Wherever I went in Rome—from the catacombs to Santa Maria in Trastevere, from St. Peter in Chains to the Lenten station churches—I would run into groups of smiling European teenagers and young adults, studying their guidebooks, buying religious souvenirs, praying at the holy sites. The Youth Day celebrations that bring hundreds of thousands of cheering young Catholics to Santiago, Denver, Manila, and Paris mystify the sour, middle-aged clerics trotted out on CNN, their triple chins wobbling in indignation at such old-fashioned piety, but are utterly understandable when you see all the youthful pilgrims in Rome. They bless themselves with holy water, wear smooth the feet of St. Peter's statue, toss coins into the fountains, and pray.

One late afternoon, when I was getting the usual runaround by a particularly smug Vatican priest, I decided to go visit the Scala Santa, or Holy Staircase. The Scala Santa is, of course, one of those traditional holy sites it's so easy to ridicule but which continues to draw, year in and year out, millions of benighted pilgrims. I had avoided it up to then, mostly because the story sounds so incredible.

According to late medieval legend, the empress Helena—the mother of Constantine and Catholicism's first serious relic nut—brought back from the Holy Land, in the year 326, the twenty-eight marble steps up which Christ walked to see Pilate. Supposedly, the stairs are mentioned in the *Liber Pontificalis* dating from the time of Pope Sergius II (844–847) as well as in a bull issued by Pope Paschal II. But that is hardly evidence that would stand up in court.

Today the stairs are located in a small two-story building kitty-corner across from the Basilica of St. John Lateran. This small building is one of the few surviving parts of the old Lateran Palace, where the pope and his court lived until the Avignon Papacy of the fourteenth century. The stairs were originally located on the north side of the palace, but in 1589 Pope Sixtus V (1585–1590) commissioned the architect Domenico Fontana to move the steps from that location to where they are today. There existed then, and still does today, a papal chapel known as the Sancta Sanctorum—the "holy of holies" of all Christendom. Pope Sixtus thought that the Scala Santa should be positioned directly in front of this very old papal chapel.

For centuries, pilgrims have climbed these hard marble stairs—on their knees. In 1723, Pope Innocent XIII had the stairs covered with walnut to keep them from being worn down. The architect Fontana built four other staircases, parallel to the Scala Santa, so that pilgrims and tourists could walk up to the chapels above and not use the venerated stairs. To this day, no one walks on the Scala Santa.

I arrived late in the afternoon, around three o'clock. As usual, I had taken the number 13 tram from Piazza San Giovanni di Dio, which winds its way down the Gianicolense, up through Porta Portese, around the Colosseum to the Lateran. A helicopter was just landing on the grass outside the basilica when I got there, delivering a patient to a waiting ambulance that would whisk him to nearby San Giovanni Hospital. I scuttled across the Piazza di Porta San Giovanni, and found the sanctuary of the Scala Santa. You can easily see it from the main entrance of St. John Lateran. There is an ornate triclinium, or templelike facade on one side with an elaborate mosaic built by Leo III in the eighth century and completely restored in 1996.

I went in the main entrance and there, directly in front of me, were the five sets of steps, the middle one being covered with wood. There is a small atrium area at the bottom of the steps, where are found a number of nineteenth-century statues of Christ and, I was surprised to see, a large sculpture of Pope Pius IX, whose body rampaging Roman nationalists attempted to toss into the Tiber after his death. Apparently, Pius had come here in 1870, on the eve of Italian troops conquering Rome, and crawled up the staircase.

But what amazed me most of all were the pilgrims.

Every few minutes, one or two pilgrims would approach, most of them under age forty, dip their hands in a holy water font at the base of the stairs, kneel down, and begin to climb the stairs on their knees. They would climb one step at a time, pause for a minute or two in silent prayer, and then climb another.

I was astonished. I was seized with a sudden, crazy thought to make the ascent, but, I'm ashamed to say, felt too embarrassed to perform such a crass act of pious devotion.

I'm not exactly the devotional type. My idea of devotion is reading Kierkegaard in front of a fire, a large snifter of warm cognac in hand. But what finally convinced me to have a go were all the kids. First a group of what looked like French eleven-year-olds arrived, and they went up. Then I saw four or five college kids and a young Asian woman in her mid-twenties. They went up. Then a young couple, holding hands, came. They went up.

Finally, I said to myself, what the hell? I knelt down on the first step. Following directly after me was a large group of German teenagers, obviously part of some pilgrimage group.

The first thing I noticed, once on the stairs, was that . . . *it hurt like a son of a bitch!*

I mean, it *really* hurt. I've never felt anything quite like it. I've knelt down on the marble floors of churches before, during the Consecration, but the walnut wood covering these steps, with ridges and valleys centuries old, was far harder and more unforgiving than mere marble. Each movement of my legs was agony. Everywhere my knees touched burned. And as I took my weight off one leg to move it up to the next step, putting all my weight on my other kneecap, the pain became excruciating. I quickly felt my calves begin to cramp up, and I started to sweat. I honestly felt, after just three or four steps, that I might not be able to make it. I was afraid I might pass out. Which astonished me no end! I had had no trouble whatsoever climbing St. Peter's dome, after all. I glanced over at the pretty German girl next to me, dressed in blue jeans and a sweater, her ponytail tossed over her shoulder. Her name was Sabine, from Munich. She smiled in encouragement, plainly in pain herself, but for some reason bearing up better than I (perhaps because I was putting an extra seventy pounds or more of pressure on my knees). Behind us, her fellow teenage pilgrims, especially the boys, were also making muffled sounds of mock agony—in between giggles—so I didn't feel quite so embarrassed. Everyone seemed to be having a hard time, so I pressed on.

As you looked up to the top of the staircase, you could see a large painting of Christ crucified on the Cross with Mary on his left and St. John on his right. There were also paintings on the sides of the staircase, but no one was bothering to look at those. Everyone kept bending over, pulling themselves up to the next step, putting as much weight as possible on their hands to relive the pressure on their knees. But the effect of this pious devotion was undeniable. As you looked up at the large painting of Christ on the Cross, your knees in agony, you definitely spared a thought or two for what he must have gone through—if not on this staircase then on one like it.

Somehow, I made it halfway and stopped to rest. I found myself rocking back so most of my weight was on my shins, not my knees, but I felt guilty, looking at the teenagers, and did my best to straighten up and pray. Sabine was a step ahead of me now.

I pressed on. *Thirteen, twelve, eleven* to go. My mind drifted back to the time I had spent in Jerusalem, to the dirty, urine-besotted Via Dolorosa, the Church of the Holy Sepulcher, the Kidron Valley with its dusty ancient tombs, the Garden of Gethsemane on the opposite side, the smell of diesel from the Egged buses. In the interest of journalistic accuracy, I tried to remember what the Roman Antonia fortress looked like in the scale model of first-century Jerusalem at the Holyland Hotel, and whether a staircase like this would have fit in it at all.

Six, five, four more left. Thank God! Whereas I used my hands to drag myself up to the next step, Sabine simply lifted her knees and climbed up, her hands remaining folded in front of her. Two more left. One more.

Done. I dragged myself to my feet, bending over to massage my aching knees.

I thought once again about Luther. One of the last places he visited during his month in Rome was the Santa Scala. "In order to release my grandfather from purgatory, I climbed the stairs of Pilate, praying a Paternoster on each step, for it was the prevailing belief that whoever prayed in this way could free a soul," he wrote. Supposedly, halfway up the stairs Luther suddenly realized the futility and impiety of such a practice, stood up, and walked out. The reformers liked to say that from that moment forward Luther understood he would have to seek God's grace elsewhere.

Perhaps. But having climbed those stairs on my knees myself, I now have a simpler explanation for Luther's sudden decision to quit halfway.

It hurt like hell!

XXII

Speak Softly and Carry a Big Halberd

The papal Swiss guards stood in their bright festal array. The officers wore light armor, and in their helmets a waving plume: this was particularly becoming to Bernardo, who was greeted by the handsome young ladies with whom he was acquainted.

HANS CHRISTIAN ANDERSEN, *The Improvisatore*

Next to Michelangelo's shining dome, the most recognizable symbol of the Vatican is probably the Swiss Guards, resplendent in their baggy red, blue, and yellow felt uniforms and tin helmets. Since 1509, this tiny band of Swiss soldiers has been the pope's personal bodyguard, sworn to protect his life even at the cost of their own. A pair of them is always standing at attention, halberds at the ready, beneath the Arch of the Bells to the left of the steps leading up to St. Peter's Basilica.

Although they look a bit ridiculous with their pointy metal helmets and Wizard of Oz uniforms, the members of the Guardia Svizzera Pontificia are, like the beaver-headed sentries posted in front of Buckingham Palace, deadly serious soldiers. They suffered an embarrassing setback in recent years—when a bug-eyed Turkish terrorist named Mehmet Ali Agca plugged John Paul II as easily as saying howdy-do—but the Swiss Guards have a reputation for typical Swiss military efficiency. All carry Mace and some carry nine-millimeter pistols under their blue cloaks. Most are towering Helvetian lummoxes with thick necks and, judging from Rome police reports, quick tempers. Around the time we were living in Rome, some Swiss Guards, after closing down a few bars, got into a nasty altercation with the local Roman police that nearly caused a minor international incident.

About a dozen off-duty Swiss Guards were returning from a bar in the Prati district, where they had been watching on TV their favorite soccer team, Grasshoppers Zurich, battle it out with another team from the Valais. According to the account by legendary Rome journalist Paul Hofmann, the Swiss were drunk out of their minds on that six-percent Kronenbourg beer and were smashing out the headlights of parked cars. Near the Piazza del Risorgimento, close to the Vatican's walls, a half-dozen Rome police cars came careening up and a small army of Italian cops leaped out. By this time, the Swiss were standing right outside Porta Sant'Anna, waiting for it to open to let them in. The Italians and the Guards got into a nasty fistfight, and the Italians managed to handcuff two of the Swiss before the remaining ones slipped through the electronic gate. At that point the Swiss allegedly attempted to drag one of the Italian policemen onto Vatican territory. "The idea was apparently to use the policeman as a hostage to be traded for the handcuffed guardsmen," Hofmann explained dryly.

The hapless Italian somehow managed to escape, however, and his colleagues took the Swiss to police headquarters and booked them for assault.

You can imagine what happened next. By this time it was two or three o'clock in the morning. The Swiss Guards' commandant had to be awakened and he had to go wake up a top-ranking curial cardinal, who probably preferred sleeping in his nice soft bed to getting involved in a minor international scandal in the middle of the night. The cardinal, in turn, had to call some Italian officials at their home, waking up their wives and all that, and ask for a little favor. The net result of all this predawn telephone diplomacy was that the Swiss Guards vice commandant drove down to Rome police headquarters, issued a formal apology, and retrieved the now-sober and chastened Swiss, who were promptly shipped home.

The tourists, though, can't get enough of them—and my kids were no exception. My five-year-old son, Robert John, became a Swiss Guards fanatic while in Rome.

Every time we visited the Vatican, Robert and his brother James wanted to go see the Swiss Guards. They would run up to the barricade in front of the Arch of the Bells and jump up and down in excitement. Eventually, Robert took to marching around the apartment with a plastic halberd at his side and his mother's blue beret cocked jauntily on the side of his head, "standing his post in a military manner," as his grandfather commanded.

Getting in to see the Swiss Guards, however, took more than the usual amount of Vatican string-pulling. For one thing, they rarely grant interviews to the press and almost never to non-Swiss journalists. My friend Greg Burke, the Rome bureau chief for *Time* magazine, had tried and been politely rebuffed. The commandant at this time, the Guards' thirtieth, was a no-nonsense career soldier named Colonel Roland Buchs-Binz, who looked like a professional boxer: severe crew cut, red nose squashed flat like a lump of clay, and round head. He looked like he could crush a block of party ice with his face.

But like most things in the Vatican, getting in to see the Swiss Guards merely required patience, persistence, and a few personal favors.

And like most things in the Vatican, once you finally got inside, you wondered what all the fuss was about.

I started out calling a Guard named Stefan Meier, a corporal, and one of the ten or so Guards who had received permission to marry. One Vatican contact assured me that Meier would certainly talk to me, at least off the record. But the Code of Silence being what it was, and since Meier didn't know me from Adam, he refused to talk. "I'm afraid I can't speak to you without the colonel's permission," Meier told me nervously. There was a quiver of fear in his voice, as though he might get fired just for telling me no. A friend of mine told me that Meier was more voluble in years past; now that he was a corporal, and perhaps making a career out of the Guards, he was being more careful.

I could see this was going to require what the Israelis call *protectia* . . . contacts. I started with Martine Zaug, a beautiful Swiss journalist based in Rome, who had once written an article about the Guards for a Swiss magazine. Her father was a high-ranking officer in the Swiss Army and, technically speaking, the superior of the Swiss Guards' commandant. Martine gave me all her notes, a thick stack of research material (in French, German, and Italian) and offered to contact the commandant, Colonel Buchs-Binz, on my behalf.

"The Swiss are a very secretive, very closed people," Martine confided to me over lunch one day. "They're not very smart. Conformity is everything. That's why I had to leave." Martine explained that while she was Swiss by birth, she felt more at home in the bon vivant *départments* of France than in the practical cantons of Switzerland. Like many Swiss, her native language was French, but she felt a far stronger connection to France than did most French-speaking Swiss. Her husband, for one thing, was French. They had just bought a house in Provence, where they planned to live in five years, when they left Rome.

A month passed, then two. Finally Martine called me one day and explained that she had tried her best with the colonel but it was no use. He said the Guards granted interviews only to Swiss journalists. I would have to get special permission from the Cardinal Secretary of State himself.

As a result, I had Luca help me write a letter to the cardinal, in Italian, and waited. I had some friends in the Curia put in a good word for me. Another month passed and still no word. I called the colonel's office and, in my broken French, tried to find out what the situation was. Finally, I received a letter from the colonel himself. I was welcome to come visit them!

The hundred or so Swiss Guards are headquartered in a long ocher-colored building situated between St. Peter's Square and Porta Sant'-Anna, off the Via di Porta Angelica near the number 64 bus stop. Only Swiss citizens who are Catholic, single, of "good character," and under thirty years of age may apply. When I visited them, three quarters of the recruits came from just four of Switzerland's twenty-six cantons—Luzern, Aargau, Wallis, and Sankt Gallen. The Guards take a special oath to protect the pope—the *Giuramento*—and, in the period between the death of one pope and the election of a new one (*sede vacante* or "empty see"), the entire College of Cardinals.

Although the Vatican has a regular police force, the 120-man Vigilanza, it is the Swiss Guards who still hold the primary responsibility for protecting the pope. They guard the Apostolic Palace and the main gates of Vatican City.

This unusual arrangement came about as a result of one of those quirks of history that determines so much of everyday life in the Vatican. On May 6, 1527, an army of 20,000 German foot soldiers and Spanish mercenaries, sent by the Holy Roman Emperor, laid siege to the Holy See. All the other troops protecting the Apostolic Palace quickly fled, but the tiny band of Swiss Guards, known even then as fierce mercenaries, held their ground. Out of 189 guards, 42 survived because they helped Clement VII, an unsavory Medici schemer, escape along the secret corridor, the Passetto, that an earlier pope had built on top of the wall connecting the Apostolic Palace to Castel Sant'Angelo. The rest of the Swiss, 147 of them, were massacred to a man on the steps of the High Altar in St. Peter's Basilica along with two hundred fugitives. The Swiss captain, Kaspar Roist, was taken to his quarters, tortured and executed in front of his wife, Elizabeth Klingler. The unpaid German mercenaries, most of whom were sympathetic to Martin Luther, proceeded to sack Rome, stripping it of art treasures and rare books that have never been recovered. They marched up and down in front of the impregnable Castel Sant'Angelo, inside of which the pope was kept safe, shouting *Vivat Lutherus pontifex!* ("Long live Luther, Pontiff").

The Swiss Guards still observe the anniversary of May 6 every year with a special ceremony. And it is their reputation for loyalty to the papacy that probably accounts for why the Swiss Guards survived, unscathed and unchanged, the reorganization of papal security units after Vatican II. In 1970, Pope Paul VI disbanded all the other Vatican military units, such as the Palatine Guard and the Pontifical Noble Guard (who sported really ridiculous horsehair helmets and even stranger uniforms, now on display at the Lateran Palace Museum), but he kept the Swiss Guards intact.

On a cool fall morning shortly after his sixth birthday, Robert John and I set out to visit the Swiss Guards barracks. Robert was dressed in his sharpest blue suit, with shirt and tie, and nearly beside himself with excitement. We took the 144 bus down the hill to the Vatican and arrived at ten A.M. outside Porta Sant'Anna. Most of the Guards speak only Swiss German and a little Italian, but to our good fortune the guard who met us at the front gate was from a French-speaking canton. As a result, he and I were able to trade a few pleasantries while Robert and I waited for our guide, Vizekorporal Frowin Bachmann, Colonel Buchs-Binz's aide-de-camp, to arrive.

The French-speaking guard was near the end of his two-year hitch and therefore willing to speak freely. He took us into a small wardroom just inside Porta Sant'Anna, with security video screens and a ring of small flags, each representing one of the Swiss cantons. The guard said, yeah, it was fun getting out of Switzerland and seeing the sights, but being a papal guard got old fast. He was definitely eager to get home. For one thing, they had practically no time off. Even though the Guards were supposed to have regular days off, in fact they almost always had to pull extra duty for the never-ending ceremonies of the Vatican (such as the Wednesday papal audiences, canonization ceremonies, and so on). The pay was nominal, the food only so-so, and the opportunities to chase women extremely limited. Guards are strictly forbidden to bring anyone, even a male friend or a relative, to their rooms.

I asked him if it was true that female tourists threw their hotel keys at the Swiss Guards . . . or flashed bared breasts at them like some crazed tourists do at Buckingham Palace. He laughed and said no. "We don't really have many opportunities to speak with the tourists," he explained, and even then most Guards spoke only Swiss German. "They let us out to have a few beers, but we have to be back in our barracks very early."

Just then Vizekorporal Bachmann showed up, dressed in regular street clothes. Thirty-one years old, married with one child, Bachmann was smaller than most of the Guards, with short brown hair and a quiet demeanor. He had spent eleven years in the Guards and planned to make a career of it.

After a few pleasantries—he spoke careful, heavily accented English—Bachmann gave Robert and me a complete tour of the barracks. There was an armory filled, ironically enough, with armor: walls and walls of bright, shiny breastplates and pauldrons (a kind of metal shoulder pad). On a top shelf was a line of the silver tricornered helmets emblazoned with the papal seal and topped by a red plume. Besides the armory, there were also a dormitory (with one to three guards to a room), showers, a large cafeteria (with a colorful mural painted by a former Guard, Robert Schiess), a study hall, gym, kitchen, and outside courtyard. The guards also have their own chapel, dedicated to saints Martino and Sebastiano—of whom, like most of the saints in Italy, I've never heard. After chatting for a few minutes with the guards who spoke English, it seems that they would have preferred to spend more of their free time out drinking in the nightclubs in nearby Trastevere than praying in the chapel.

The armory was an experience, I must admit. It was down a flight of stairs, in a kind of basement, and consisted of two rooms. One held all the Guards' uniforms, the other all their weapons, many of them centuries old. There were hundreds of weapons of all types, including various designs of halberds (the long, spearlike things the Guards always carry), swords and sabers, pikes and lances, maces, axes, blunderbusses, muskets, carbines, crossbows, mortars, a cannon or two, and a special long, undulating broadsword (called a flame sword) once used during papal processions.

Many guidebooks say that it's a big secret whether the Swiss Guards carry guns or not, but Bachmann didn't hesitate a moment when I asked him about it. "We are armed, yes," he said matter-of-factly. Corporals carry nine-millimeter pistols hidden discreetly under their uniforms. "And," Bachmann added, "wherever we are on duty, we have the ability to arm ourselves very quickly," implying that they keep rifles or other guns at the ready. During World War II, when the Vatican was surrounded by Nazi troops, the Swiss Guards manned their posts carrying carbine rifles, but today the only weapon tourists see them carrying is the halberd.

In the uniform room, Bachmann explained the complicated Swiss Guard uniform, said to consist of 109 separate pieces. Contrary to what most guidebooks say, neither Michelangelo or Raphael designed the Swiss Guard uniform. Old paintings show sixteenth-century Swiss mercenaries wearing a uniform, bearing the colors of the Medici family, similar to the one worn today. In 1914, the Swiss Guards' twenty-fourth commandant, Jules Repond, researched the history of the uniform and came up with a simplified design based on uniforms of the past. This is what the Guards wear today.

The basic uniform, the one most tourists see, consists of loose two-inch-wide strips of orange, red, yellow, and blue felt attached to underlying fabric along with a black metal helmet topped by a red feather plume. Normally, the Guards wear a simple black beret and reserve the helmets (either the black ones or the special full-dress silver ones) for special occasions. The plain black metal helmets are worn inside St. Peter's during regular ceremonies, such as a papal Mass, and the more elaborate stainless steel helmets, embossed with the papal coat of arms, are reserved for special feast days such as Christmas and Easter. The Guards wear the cuirass, or breastplate—which the Swiss call a *panzer,* German for "tank"—only once a year, during the May 6 ceremony commemorating the fall of their predecessors. At that time they also wear a round pleated *gorget,* or collar, and white gloves with red sleeves.

I asked Bachmann if the uniform is a pain to wear, if the helmet is heavy. "Oh, it weighs about two kilos," he replied. "If you don't have a good fit, it can begin to bother you." He thought about the question for a moment, and then added, "If you're not careful, the uniform catches on doorknobs and things a lot."

There is another uniform, the night uniform, that is worn at night as well as by the Guards at Porta Sant'Anna. It is a very simple all-blue uniform with silly-looking blue knee socks, a black beret, and a white schoolboy collar. The Guards also sometimes wear a calf-length cape or cloak, dark blue, over either the regular or night uniform.

Bachmann took Robert and me up to the *Gardeschneiderei,* or tailor shop, where the uniforms are made. An ancient couple are the Guards' personal tailors. The man, Elio, a bald-headed little guy with tufts of curly white hair on the side of his head, had been working as a Swiss Guard tailor for fifty-six years; his wife, Juliana, for forty years. They make an average of 170 uniforms a year—or roughly three and a half uniforms a week.

When I expressed surprise that they would need so many, Juliana explained there are actually both a summer and a winter uniform, the latter made with felt and the former with a lightweight material called *castilano.* Plus, Guards who serve for a certain amount of time are allowed to keep their uniforms when they leave. And there is a lot of wear and tear associated with the job.

The Guards are divided up into three *Geschwader,* or squads, two of which work while one, at least in theory, has time off. The squad that is off duty, though, frequently has to perform *Sonderdienste,* special services, such as standing guard inside St. Peter's during a Mass or attending the regular papal audiences or concerts in the Audience Hall. On the day a Swiss Guard is on duty, he'll work between eight and eleven hours, depending upon the complicated rotating shifts. A typical shift will be from eight A.M. to two P.M. and then continue from three to seven P.M.

"The real difficulty with being a Swiss Guard is the personal knowledge you have to have of the people who work in the Vatican," Bachmann said. "You have to check the people as they go in and out. Who can go inside? Where are they allowed to go? And so on. Many people come into the Vatican to work; others come inside to buy things." In other words, a Swiss Guard has to learn who's who, otherwise he may challenge a top curial official and get in big trouble.

The Guards sign up for two-year hitches. Most leave after their first tour. "They come here for the experience, to get away," Bachmann explained. "Also, many like the idea of serving the pope. Most go back, though, to start a career."

The starting pay, while peanuts by Swiss standards—1.8 million lire per month—is actually comparable to a typical Italian salary. In addition, the Guards also receive free room and board, free medical care, and so on. If a Guard elects to stay on beyond his two-year term, and wishes to marry, he has to wait until one of the handful of apartments reserved for the Swiss Guards opens up.

Our tour completed, I asked Bachmann about the alleged tension between the Swiss Guards and the Italian police. Italian carabinieri handle security in St. Peter's Square, and it is said there is no love lost between them and the Swiss.

Bachmann winced, plainly uncomfortable discussing the topic.

"Let's just say we each have our own sphere of duties," he said carefully. "We stay out of each other's way."

I decided not to press him. He was a most courteous and amiable host, after all. And I'd hate to make him mad.

XXIII

Queen Christina Comes Out

With her downright, manly disposition she lacks any sense of obligation
to act with feminine reserve and comply with the Italians' own deliberate
circumspection. She gives full vent to her natural high spirits and that
excitability which makes it impossible for her to stay still for long or
maintain gravity of voice and expression. . . .

CARDINAL SFORZA PALLAVICINO, 1658

On the right side of St. Peter's Basilica, just a few feet before Michelangelo's *Pietà*, there is an unusual monument to an unusual Catholic
heroine. The monument itself—a large bronze medallion of a woman's
head above a marble sarcophagus—is a testimony to the ambivalence the
Vatican no doubt felt in having it commissioned. Most tourists never
notice it. In fact, it's omitted entirely from many guidebooks.

That's because this monument is a tribute, in the very heart of
the Catholic Church, to a freethinking lesbian who, despite a lifetime of
deliberately scandalizing Church authorities, is buried with the popes

in the grottoes beneath St. Peter's Basilica, a few steps from Pope John XXIII.

Her name was Christina. She was a rather plain-looking blond woman with a long face and a big nose, but she was also brilliant, free-spirited, generous, fiercely independent, autocratic, passionate, and, at times, dangerous. She was the absolute ruler and queen of Sweden for ten years, beginning in 1644 when she was eighteen. In 1654 she shocked her subjects and the world by announcing she was renouncing her throne, converting to Catholicism, and moving to Rome.

Christina's story had fascinated me from the first time I heard it. It wasn't so much that she was a seventeenth-century intellectual and libertine committed to exploring new ideas wherever they took her—whether into a married woman's bed or into the very religion she had been brought up to revile. What intrigued me was that the Vatican was more or less forced, because of the politics of the time, to welcome Christina with open arms.

I was determined, while in Rome, to visit at least a couple of the scenes from her life there—especially since I had my own personal Swedish assistant, Anne, to fill in the cultural gaps. I knew that Christina's home in Rome, the sumptuous Palazzo Riario, had been taken over and expanded in the eighteenth century into the Palazzo Corsini, located in the beautiful gardens of the Lungara at the foot of the Janiculum Hill. One morning I decided I'd walk there.

Normally, to get down the hill I'd take the number 41 bus up Via Vitellia to Via Giancinto Carini, where I'd walk across the street to the number 144 bus. This bus normally passed through a "porto" in the Aurelian Wall and then through a large metal gate into what is called the Passeggiata del Gianicolo. On this bright morning, however, I skipped the 144 bus and simply walked down to the large iron gate and continued downhill on the Via Giuseppe Garibaldi—past another magnificent papal fountain, the Fontana Paola, built from an aqueduct constructed by the emperor Trajan in A.D. 109.

It was, as usual, a beautiful winter morning in Rome. The air was crisp, and full of the scent of junipers. The Via Garibaldi was a series of switchbacks, but there were these delightful little staircases that allowed me to take shortcuts down the hill. At the bottom, I walked through the Porta Settimana into a very old, very quaint district in Rome—narrow streets, small shops, little trattoria—and went in search of the Palazzo Corsini. I found it, right at the base of the famous Botanical Gardens of the Lungara.

Although the palazzo now houses the Galleria Nazionale d'Arte Antica, the building was almost completely deserted. It took me quite some time to locate the rooms, on the second story, where Queen Christina's original suite was located. The old Palazzo Riario was completely renovated, but her bedroom has been kept just as she left it—covered by the paintings and bronze nudes she had collected throughout her life. Gustave Flaubert visited the gallery in 1851, aroused by Murillo's *Madonna*. I walked through the silent Galleria, each room of which was guarded by a bored college student, thinking about Christina.

Christina was born on December 8, 1626, the only child of the "lion of the north," King Gustavus II Adolphus of Sweden, and his wife, Maria Eleonora of Brandenburg. When her father was killed during the Battle of Lützen, Christina, then only six years old, became queen-elect. The nation was ruled by a council of regents headed by a chancellor, Axel Oxenstierna, until Christina was eighteen. Meanwhile, her father had left strict instructions that she was to be given the finest education available—the same that would have been given a prince. As a result, the famous Lutheran theologian Johannes Matthiae became her tutor, although all her life she was a fervent student of Stoic philosophy and might be better considered a cheerful pagan than a Christian, whether Protestant or Catholic.

In 1644, at the age of eighteen, Christina assumed the throne—and immediately opposed the powerful chancellor Oxenstierna. Sweden at that time was involved in the bloody Thirty Years' War that pitted Catholic nations against Protestant. Christina is credited by historians with being a powerful force for peace and the success of the Treaty of Westphalia, which ended the war.

She remained throughout her life a woman of contradictions. Personally imperious, Christina nonetheless ruled with tolerance. Although committed to peace and social civility (in later years she was considered the personal protectoress of the Jews of Rome), she once had her equerry summarily executed for betraying her plans to the pope and gave up her pension to help prolong the Christian war against the Turks. At the same time that she was embracing the Catholic Faith, she was also an enthusiastic champion of French freethinkers and the joie de vivre of libertinism. She saw no contradiction between her religious beliefs and her openness to new ideas—even radical and potentially blasphemous ideas.

Despite a fierce discipline and prodigious intellectual energy, Christina was a woman of passion—and her greatest passion was for knowledge. Throughout her life she rose every morning at five to study, and as queen invited the most brilliant minds of Europe to her castle. These included such luminaries as René Descartes, who personally instructed her in philosophy and wrote a book about her life. Too lavish in her spending, generous to a fault, Christina was a patroness of education, launched the first Swedish newspaper, and, in general, ruled in a tolerant and benign manner.

That is why Christina's decision to abdicate her throne, after only ten years of rule, shocked all of Europe. She claimed she was ill, that the burdens of office were too much for a woman, but that wasn't, of course, the real reason. Christina had secretly converted to Catholicism—which was illegal in Lutheran Sweden—and she wanted to avoid, at all costs, getting married. The idea of being dependent, especially sexually dependent, was abhorrent to the proud queen: She did not want to be, she said, "a field for a man to plough." On another occasion, Christina remarked: "I am unable to marry. That is how it is. I need not give my reasons. I have no inclination to marry. I have earnestly prayed to God to let me change my attitude, but I have not been able to do so." Had she remained queen, the pressure for her to find a suitable consort and produce an heir, would have been considerable. As a result, on June 6, 1654, at the age of twenty-eight, she signed the elaborate accord of abdication with 307 seals attached, now kept in a special box in the Vatican Secret Archives.

After a brief stay in Innsbruck, where she was publicly received into the Church on November 3, 1655, Christina moved to Rome permanently. She was received with elaborate ceremony by Pope Alexander VII, who had a special suite of eight rooms prepared for her in the Tower of the Winds—as far from the Apostolic Palace as possible. While touring the Secret Archives, I saw these rooms, which have not been changed at all since she lived in them. Small and spare, with elaborate murals painted on them, they clearly were not adequate for the needs of a former queen. Christina did not stay there long.

She moved in succession to the Polazzo Torlonia, which still exists a block from the Vatican on the Via della Conciliazione, then to the Palazzo Farnese, and finally to the more elaborate Palazzo Riario (now Palazzo Corsini). Christina turned this palace into a cultural center for all Rome. She founded the Accademia dell'Arcadia for philosophy and literature, which still exists. She pushed for the creation of the first public opera house in the city, the Tordinona. She counted among her friends some of the greatest artists and musicians in Italy—such as Bernini, who built the famous colonnade of St. Peter's, and the composer Alessandro Scarlatti, who became her choirmaster. Her palazzo was filled with the largest private collection of Venetian painting then in existence.

Almost unknown today, in seventeenth-century Europe Christina was notorious for her alleged sexual appetites. Europe at that time, while wracked by innumerable religious wars and theological controversies, was also characterized by the upper-class society depicted in Molière's *Précieuses Ridicules,* and later in *Les Liaisons Dangereuses.* It was a society in which women frequently could be almost as sexually aggressive as men, in which a Catholic matron might visit her confessor in the morning before entertaining her lover in the afternoon. It was therefore quite plausible, for upper-class Europeans, that an absolute monarch such as Christina may have used her position to indulge her appetites as she saw fit.

It didn't help matters that Christina, throughout her life, was largely indifferent to social convention. Her commitment to personal freedom was total. While in Rome, she shocked the papal court by her brazen defiance of convention, and by her frequent custom of dressing in male clothing. On more than one occasion, papal envoys complained that the queen seemed to enjoy a deliberate display of décolletage in the presence of cardinals and other ecclesiastics.

The truth is that Christina was a sexual adventuress who enjoyed liaisons with woman and perhaps with men as well, so long as they did not impinge upon her freedom. She had a passionate fondness for feminine beauty and filled her palazzo with nude paintings and sculptures of both men and women. She scandalized the pious in Rome by ordering that fig leaves be *removed* from the famous marble statues she bought. Ironically, while Christina cherished female beauty, she preferred the company of men—often men of a decidedly unintellectual and rowdy cast. She cursed like a sailor, loved ribald jokes and stories, and openly mocked the pious.

Christina never saw any conflict between her interest in the Catholic faith and her enthusiasm for the French free thinkers. It may be difficult to understand today, but in Christina's time Roman Catholicism was considered, in contrast to the austere Lutheran and Calvinist movements, to be a haven of freedom and philosophical speculation. The Lutheran pastors of Sweden struck Christina as a rather grim, joyless lot, while the representatives of Catholicism she encountered—the French, Spanish, and Italian diplomats and philosophers—were by and large worldly, fun-loving men who did not allow their religious beliefs to impinge upon their having a good time. Also, philosophically Christina found Catholic belief more in harmony with her own stubborn views on the importance of a strong will. Whereas orthodox Lutheranism taught the total depravity of man and "the bondage of the will," Catholicism was decidedly more optimistic: Original sin weakened but did not destroy freedom of the will, and human beings possessed many good qualities that God's grace "perfected."

It was not as difficult for freethinking Christina to convert to Catholicism as one might imagine, therefore; but it is quite true that the Rome that Christina discovered—full of worldly cardinals and scheming Jesuits—was not exactly the arcadia of free inquiry that she expected. The pope soon discovered, moreover, that Christina was far from being a docile convert, and it was not long before numerous papal entreaties were forwarded to Christina that she be more discreet in her personal habits. Christina, of course, cheerfully ignored all such requests. "Her behavior is only gradually improving," complained her future biographer, Cardinal Sforza Pallavicino, "for this is such a delicate matter that no one dare speak to her about it."

There is some controversy concerning whether Christina was bisexual. There is little doubt concerning her lesbianism; the question is whether she also felt sexual desire for men. She seems to have had a genuine if mild disinclination toward heterosexual intercourse, perhaps stemming from her revulsion of childbirth and determination never to marry. Yet in her letters and unfinished autobiography, she was frank that she was by temperament "hot-blooded" and would have abandoned herself to "excesses with women" (la débauche des femmes) had she been born a man. All her life Christina enjoyed erotic paintings and books.

Yet while Christina had numerous passions for women—perhaps most famously for the beautiful and married Ebba Sparre, with whom she shared her bed for years—she also seems to have genuinely fallen in love with men. The greatest love of her life, in fact, was probably a cardinal—the worldly, cultivated, emotionally icy Decio Azzolino.

During her early years in Rome, Christina already had quite a reputation. She was known as an outspoken libertine with a sharp tongue, a sexual amazon whom one Spanish diplomat called "the biggest harlot in the world." This was a great exaggeration because it is by no means clear that Christina ever had sexual relations with a man. Nevertheless, all Rome believed that she was carrying on an affair with a cardinal—what the Italians called *il concubinato scandaloso*—a judgment historians tended to doubt. Then, late in the nineteenth century, Christina's most intimate love letters to Azzolino were discovered. Written in code and deciphered, the letters revealed a passion on Christina's part that may or may not have been reciprocated.

Azzolino, a young, powerful, cautious politician, seems to have had a weakness for beautiful women, although to what extent he physically indulged the weakness is uncertain. Christina made bitter remarks concerning his fondness—no doubt for purely "pastoral reasons," she said—for pretty actresses. Despite this, Azzolino appears to have been an at least outwardly devoted friend to Christina and helped her in every way he could, particularly with regard to money. She in turn never got over her love for him and named him as her sole heir in her will.

While the evidence is strong that Azzolino merely used Christina for his own purposes, it is clear that she was deeply in love. Her decoded letters are full of tears and passionate yearning. She speaks openly of her desire to be his "lover" and insists she will love him "until death." Apparently, however, Azzolino did not share her feelings, because her letters became increasingly shrill and bitter. "All your coolness cannot stop me from worshipping you until death," she wrote. On another occasion she wrote angrily, "My lot it is never to experience other than imperfect joys . . . I shall never love anyone but you, and you are determined to make me for ever unhappy." My favorite letter is full of sarcasm and open jealousy:

> *You edify me with the theological and moral meditations you draw from whatever happens, and I do not doubt for a moment that your mind*

*was, as usual, turned to God when you listened to a comedy being read
at the French ambassador's, and the two young ladies who recited, used
as they were to giving some degree of pleasure to the whole of Rome,
did not inflict mortification on you by attracting your glances to
themselves. But no doubt you were following our Lord's example, in
order to convert them. . . .*

Christina gradually settled down to her life in Rome. Her misfor-
tunes in love and eventual financial difficulties slowly softened the fierce
pride of her youth, when she had the Stoic's belief in her ability to
master her emotions and subject everything to her own indomitable
will. She quoted La Rouchefoucauld approvingly: "If we conquer our
passions, it is because of their weakness rather than our strength." It
appears that her religious beliefs, while purely intellectual in the past,
became more heartfelt as she aged, although never exactly orthodox.
Christina had a lifelong dislike of "external piety," and she was quick to
mock anyone who came before her in any pose of holiness. Her love of
ribald jokes and erotic comedies were part of that protest against false
piety. Yet following a meeting with the blind Marseilles mystic François
Malaval in the 1650s, she spent the last twenty years of her life deeply
involved in the Quietist movement—which, like her, eschewed external
religious practices and taught that a person could be inwardly in contact
with God even in the midst of dissolute activities. Her interests were, as
usual, varied, including even alchemy; but she apparently became quite
interested in mysticism.

Despite this later religiosity, however, Christina remained fiery and
independent until the end. While recuperating from what would be her
final illness, she discovered that a randy Italian abbé had attempted to
seduce (or rape) one of her ladies-in-waiting. She promptly hired a thug
to kill the man. Two days before her death, when Christina discovered
that the thug had thought better of murder and had merely encouraged

the would-be rapist to flee, Christina, then sixty-three years old, threw herself in fury upon him, collapsing unconscious from the effort.

Attended by her beloved cardinal Azzolino, Christina died at six o'clock in the morning on April 19, 1689. In her will she was quite explicit about what she wanted: To be buried in the Pantheon with little ceremony. "The body should not be displayed and we forbid all funeral pomp and suchlike vanities," she said. Her wishes were almost completely ignored. After her body was displayed for four days, her face fitted with a silver death mask, she was buried along with the popes, with considerable pomp, in the grottoes of St. Peter's. Christina was no doubt the most publicly skeptical, impious and ribald Catholic queen in history, and she alone is buried in the papal crypt.

The bedroom where Christina died is rather small by the standards of a monarch. It has an very ornate vaulted ceiling rising above marble columns. There is a large painting of her as Diana the Huntress by J. van Edgemont, as well as other paintings. Her beloved nudes are everywhere.

On the wall there is an inscription in Swedish, a quotation from her that sums up her life. It says simply:

Jag Fóddes fri,
Levde fri,
och skall dö frigjord.
    —Christina

I had our Swedish baby-sitter, Anne, translate it. It means:

I was born free,
I lived free,
and I died free.
    —Christina

XXIV

Opening a Savings Account at the Vatican Bank

The state of affairs in Rome beggars description. You can find there a buying and selling, a bartering and a bargaining, a lying and trickery, robbery and stealing, pomp, procuration, knavery, and all sorts of stratagems bringing God into contempt, till it would be impossible for the Antichrist to govern more wickedly.

MARTIN LUTHER, *An Appeal to the Ruling Class of the German Nationality*

I f it's scandal you're looking for, there's no better place to find it than the Vatican Bank. In recent years the bank has been involved in international intrigues right out of a James Bond thriller, complete with charges of money laundering, Mafia contacts, corrupt Italian politicians, sinister Masonic conspiracies, scheming bishops, and even a suspect "suicide."

Naturally, then, I wanted to see the bank myself, even though I knew it would look just like any other bank. And naturally, the Vatican didn't want to let me see it. It was the one place the Sala Stampa told me flat-out was off limits.

This seemed ridiculous to me. Of course, the then-most-recent Vatican Bank scandal—having to do with money laundering to Italian politicians—happened to involve a journalist who had an account at the bank. So maybe the Vatican was a little touchy about writers.

But I wasn't going to let a little multimillion-dollar money laundering stop me from my appointed tourist duties.

I asked around and found out that a journalist named Jesús (yes, Jesús!), who worked for the Spanish daily *ABC*, happened to have an account at the bank. I knew someone who knew Jesús, and so I called him up. He didn't speak much English, but his wife was French, so we managed to communicate in French. Jesús said he'd be glad to show me around the bank. We agreed to meet at ten o'clock in the morning the following week outside Porta Sant'Anna.

In the meantime, I spent most of my time reading up about the bank. Its real name is the Istituto per le Opere di Religione (IOR), the Institute for the Works of Religion. It was founded (with a slightly different name) in 1887 to provide the Vatican with an independent financial center after the fall of the Papal States. At that time Pope Leo XIII kept most of the Vatican's liquid assets, in the form of gold coins, locked in a chest under his bed. (I'm not making this up.) When the Vatican found itself surrounded by hostile forces—such as Fascist Italy and then, later, German panzer tanks—the IOR allowed the Church to transfer large amounts of cash in and out of Italy without hindrance. Nations have the nasty habit of confiscating or restricting the use of people's money, and the Vatican Bank allows international religious communities, with branches in many different nations, to keep their money safe from politicians.

The IOR continues to be the Vatican's last big secret. Despite all the new openness and accountability in almost every other area of Vatican finance, the IOR remains stubbornly tight-lipped. No one knows precisely how much money the bank has, although in recent years reports have claimed the bank has about seven thousand depositors and total deposits of between $3 and $5 billion—chicken feed for a bank. But that's not counting how much of its own money the bank has in working capital, which has been estimated to be as high as $1 billion.

Vatican officials like to claim that the Vatican Bank really has nothing to do with the Vatican. It's completely independent. In fact, however, the IOR reports directly to the pope and is, in a sense, his personal piggy bank, to do with as he pleases. In the past the bank was, and today still is, nominally supervised by a council of five cardinals, appointed by the pope, but recently these cardinals have in turn appointed another council of five lay banking experts to oversee operations. One reason for this is that the council of five cardinals was largely considered window-dressing in the past. Supposedly, the cardinals met rarely, were not allowed to take any written reports with them, and were always given a $5,000 check "for Your Eminence's personal charities." Considering that in those years a cardinal's salary was less than $20,000, there was plenty of incentive not to ask too many questions.

No one would have asked any questions either. The Vatican Bank was and is like a little Switzerland in the middle of tax-happy Italy. In fact, it's better than Switzerland. It publishes no financial statements. It answers to no government regulators. It reports no financial transactions to tax authorities. It is, in a sense, a money launderer's dream.

For years, critics have claimed that wealthy Italians with the right connections were smuggling millions of dollars out of Italy through secret Vatican Bank accounts. Considering the way business is done in Italy—at a prestigious Rome hospital, where my wife briefly stayed, we had to pay each of the doctors in *cash* and in little envelopes—it's safe to say that this must have gone on, at least in the oh-so-distant past. In fact, though, the truly wealthy, and the Mafia, do not need the Vatican Bank to do their money laundering for them; there are far more reliable and time-tested channels for that.

What brought the nasty glare of publicity, and the dreaded Italian *fiscali* (fiscal police), to bear on the Vatican's private banking arrangements was the wholesale collapse of a major Italian bank, the Banco Ambrosiano of Milan, and evidence that the Vatican had at least something to do with it. In the 1980s the Vatican Bank was run by a burly, tough, but inexperienced Chicagoan, Bishop Paul C. Marcinkus, nicknamed the Gorilla, who also moonlighted as the pope's personal bodyguard. Because of his arrogance and inexperience, Marcinkus got the Vatican Bank involved with some shady financial operators—including a Sicilian financier with Mafia ties and a Milanese banker named Roberto Calvi. Calvi, it turned out, was a member of the infamous Italian Masonic organization P2 that Luca was always raving about.

To make a long story short, Calvi was involved in bilking Italian banks out of more than a billion dollars through a series of dummy offshore corporations. Marcinkus had lent the Vatican Bank's name and prestige—with rather vague "letters of patronage"—to Calvi's operations. When Calvi's scheme collapsed in 1981 along with $1.3 billion of depositors' money, the Vatican Bank was partially implicated. Calvi himself, already convicted in an Italian court and out on appeal, was found hanging underneath Blackfriars' Bridge in London in 1982, an apparent suicide. Although the Vatican's lawyers insisted the Vatican Bank was not *legally* responsible for Calvi's actions, the Vatican Bank agreed in 1984 to pay $244 million in cash as part of a settlement without admitting wrongdoing. Nevertheless, the Italian government issued an arrest warrant for Marcinkus, who was forced to hide out in the Vatican and forego his customary weekly eighteen holes at the prestigious Acqua Santa country club near the Appian Way.

The whole scandal brought unwelcome attention to the IOR—and led to giddy speculation concerning its holdings. By some estimates, Marcinkus's high-stakes wheeling and dealing made the IOR more than

$1 billion. At the very least, it became apparent that the Vatican Bank could afford to pay the $244-million settlement in cash without noticeably disturbing its operations or touching its depositors' money.

In recent years the Vatican Bank has initiated various efforts at reform. After yet another scandal in 1993, for example, in which a journalist claimed he had laundered more than $50 million through the bank as part of a scheme to bribe Italian officials, the Vatican allowed an outside company, the American accounting firm Price Waterhouse, to audit its operations. The results of that audit, however, were never made public.

All this makes the Vatican Bank slightly more exciting than your typical savings and loan. I was full of anticipation as I stood outside Porta Sant'Anna, waiting for Jesùs.

He was late, but finally a tall, thin man in his thirties, with a slight stubble of a beard, showed up. He introduced himself and we chatted briefly about mutual friends. Jesùs was typical of many journalists I had met in Rome—friendly, multilingual, married to someone of a different nationality, loyal to the papacy. Like many journalists, he had come to Rome representing a Catholic magazine and ended up working for a much larger secular newspaper. He had met his French wife, a translator, in Rome, and they were then expecting their first child.

Jesùs told me he likes American writers and American journalism. "It's an old cliché, but it's true," he said. "The Americans are interested just in the facts. The French are interested just in philosophy. The Italians are primarily interested in gossip, in human relations."

I asked Jesùs why the Italians were primarily interested in gossip, and he said it had to do with the twisted, nepotistic way Italians did business.

"Italians don't have business deals or political programs as such," Jesùs explained. "They have friends, and they have enemies. Everything you do in Italy, in business or politics, depends upon who your friends and enemies are. As a result, the most important thing to know about in Italy is gossip and human relations, who is getting along with whom."

"And the Spanish?" I asked. "What are the Spanish interested in?"

Jesùs laughed. "It's a mixture between Italian and French. We have some journalists trained in the United States, and so they emphasize the facts. But in Spain people like to know about people, and that shapes Spanish journalism as well."

Finally, Jesùs nodded toward Porta Sant'Anna. He pulled out some sort of Vatican Bank identity card, showed it to the Swiss Guard on duty, and we were quickly waved through.

I'm not sure what I was expecting exactly. Probably some old, non-descript, typically Vatican office, with ancient wood paneling, old ledger books (like I once saw used in a London bank I visited), and so on. I was astonished when Jesùs and I walked about ten feet to the bottom of the Tower of Nicholas V, a very old part of the Vatican, at the base of the Apostolic Palace and directly behind the Swiss Guards' barracks. I had walked by it at least two dozen times. The "public" part of the bank used to be in another part of the Apostolic Palace complex, Jesùs explained, but recently was moved to this tower, where the Vatican Bank offices have been for some time.

At the base of the tower was the entrance, and this is what really made me stop in my tracks. It looked like something out of *Star Trek*. The doors were two glass tubes, next to which were a green and red light and the word *ingresso* next to them. You pushed one of the lights and a portion of the glass tube spun around with a whooshing sound, allowing you to step into the tube. Once you did so, a guard on the other side pushed a button and that opened the tube to the inside of the bank. Very high-tech. I stepped inside the tubes, half expecting to be beamed up to the *Enterprise*.

Once inside, a pair of curving staircases led to an upper level, where the bank's main business area was located. It was an extremely modern facility, with large circular windows, a vaulted dome on the ceiling, and gray tile. The upper level was divided into two tiers with seven tellers, each of which had his or her own computer and worked behind a shield of bulletproof glass. The only noticeable difference between this and an ordinary bank was the large crucifix found on the main wall.

I asked Jesùs how he, a mere layman, was able to have an account at the Vatican Bank. He replied that it wasn't really his account but belonged to a Catholic magazine he once worked for. That he was allowed to continue using this account, when he no longer worked for the magazine, says a lot about how the past scandals could have developed.

With one last look around, Jesùs and I walked back down the stairs and out through the space tubes.

That was it: the Vatican Bank. It was as unexceptional as I had expected—just like an ordinary bank, except for the security entrance—which made the Sala Stampa's declaration of it as off limits seem strange.

Jesùs and I chatted for a few more minutes, standing in the middle of St. Peter's Square. Then I offered to buy him lunch for his trouble, but he said he had to get back home to his pregnant wife. We waved good-bye. I made my way to a little restaurant I had just discovered, on Borgo Pio, that made the best carbonara I had found in Rome—not too slimy, with a generous amount of prosciutto. All that investigative journalism had given me a tremendous appetite.

XXV

Auditing the Pope

Italy for fifteen hundred years has turned all her energies, all her finances, and all her industry to the building up of a vast array of wonderful church edifices, and starving half her citizens to accomplish it. She is today one vast museum of magnificence and misery. All the churches in an ordinary American city put together could hardly buy the jeweled frippery in one of her hundred cathedrals.

MARK TWAIN, *The Innocents Abroad*

The alleged wealth of the Vatican has exercised less prejudiced minds than that of Mark Twain over the centuries. But his was and still is a common reaction.

You can see his point simply by visiting the Vatican Treasury Museum. The entrance is located inside St. Peter's on the left side of the basilica, near the Altar of the Transfiguration. You go down the corridor toward the sacristy (where, by the way, you can arrange for a Mass to be said for a 15,000-lira stipend), past the wall on which are chiseled the names of all the popes from St. Peter to the present. The treasury entrance is at the end of the corridor. The fee is just 5,000 lire, and it's money well spent.

The first few rooms are taken up by historical artifacts of interest. These include the famous Dalmatic of Charlemagne, which looks like a big square burlap bag in which someone cut out holes for arms and neck and upon which a grandmother did some elaborate needlepoint. Supposedly, old Charles wore this outfit when he was crowned Holy Roman Emperor in the old basilica on Christmas Day A.D. 800—a miraculous feat if ever there were one because the garment, said to be a masterpiece of Byzantine embroidery, actually dates from the eleventh century. There are also a couple of cruciform reliquaries each containing slivers of the True Cross not locked away at the Basilica of Santa Croce. There is a copy of the oak-wood throne donated by the Emperor Charles the Bald to Pope John VIII on Christmas in 875. The actual chair, widely believed at one time to have been St. Peter's, is now inside the bronze throne created by Bernini immediately below the apse of the basilica.

But all of this stuff is merely a warm-up to the really big exhibition. After the Room of the Candelabra and the Room of the Angel—in which are featured dozens of crosses, reliquaries, and tabernacles all made out of solid gold, silver, and crystal—you reach the Gallery. This is where some of the most awesome treasures this side of the Tower of London are kept. The York Chalice, for example—a large cup of chiseled gold studded with 130 diamonds, was a gift of Henry Cardinal Stuart, the Duke of York. Then there is the Triple Crown, the papal tiara with three crowns symbolizing the Three Powers of the pope (Father of Kings, Ruler of the World, Vicar of Christ), made of priceless jewels.

My personal favorite was a display case in which were found a dozen large five-pointed stars, each made of dozens of large diamonds, all set in gold. The day I visited, a few of us were gazing at these stars in wonder, trying to figure out what they were exactly, when I heard an old white-haired tourist turn to his wife and say, "These must be the stars that God took from the sky with which to crown Mary." He said it with such a humble awe, and erudition, I was impressed. And he was right: It turns out they were a gift from the Catholics of France to Pope Pius IX on the fiftieth anniversary of the proclamation of the dogma of the Immaculate Conception (December 8, 1854). The reference is to the Book of Revelation: "A great sign appeared in the sky, a woman clothed with the sun, with the moon under her feet, and on her head a crown of twelve stars" (12:1).

All this magnificence has both astonished and appalled visitors over the centuries. On the one hand, the Vatican is obviously one of the greatest collectors and patrons of art in the history of the world. If the popes had not collected all this stuff or had it commissioned, Catholic churches throughout history would all look like they now do in the United States—big cinder-block barns decorated with felt banners covered with butterflies and Susan Polis Schultz slogans. On the other hand, some people find it unseemly, even vaguely blasphemous, for a Church that claims to represent Jesus Christ on earth—a man who, whatever else you may say about him, certainly made some rather astringent remarks about the rich—to display such ostentatious wealth.

Figuring out how much money the Vatican really does have, though, is no easy task. Because it is a sovereign nation, accountable to no one on earth—not the United States Congress, not the United Nations, not even *The New York Times*—the Vatican doesn't have to tell the world anything it doesn't damn well feel like.

But then again, the world doesn't have to give it any money either, and in recent decades the Vatican has gone begging.

The bishops at the Second Vatican Council created all these new agencies and mandates without figuring out—just like typical politicians—how they were going to pay for them. As a result, the Holy See had been running a large deficit until the mid-1990s and was forced to beg for money from Catholic dioceses around the world. This wasn't the first time the Vatican was desperate: In the early decades of the twentieth century, the financial situation got so bad it required an emergency loan from the U.S. Knights of Columbus to keep the Vatican solvent.

I decided the only way to find out the truth about the Vatican's wealth was to ask the man charged with supervising all the various financial organizations in the Vatican.

He was the cardinal in charge of the Prefecture of the Economic Affairs of the Holy See, sort of the General Accounting Office of the Vatican. Although the prefecture does not actually handle the Vatican's investments—another organization does that—it audits almost all of the various Vatican agencies and provides financial services to most.

I had interviewed this cardinal on one other occasion in the U.S., when he was first appointed. As a result, when I had a staff member of Irish Bob's office contact him about a follow-up interview, he agreed.

The unassuming, totally unmarked office of the prefecture is located on the corner of the Palazzi dei Propilei, directly across from the right-hand colonnade of St. Peter's. I used to walk right by it on my way to the Leonine Bookstore on Via Corridori.

The morning I arrived, a young Italian man in an elegantly tailored suit met me as I walked through the ground-floor entrance. He knew who I was, and escorted me to one of those bouncing ancient Italian elevators (cables stretching and groaning all the way) that make Americans so nervous. The offices of the prefecture were located on the top floor of the building. When I stepped out of the elevator, I went through a glass door into a waiting area, where another young man was seated at a small wooden table. He, too, seemed to be expecting me and showed me into a waiting room where I, well, waited. After about ten minutes, the cardinal's personal secretary, a monsignor named Blair, ushered me into the cardinal's modest private office.

The cardinal was a tall, white-haired, very old American. His skin was powdery and pink, and he wore bifocals. He was gracious, suspicious, down-to-earth, and quick-tempered. We shook hands. I liked him immediately.

For one thing, the cardinal, like most of his brethren in scarlet, had no pretense of sanctity. The higher up the hierarchy you go in the Vatican, I found, the more down-to-earth and no-nonsense the people tend to be. This guy seemed more like a crotchety bank president than a possible future pope.

As soon as we had settled ourselves in chairs for a lengthy interview, the cardinal discovered that I didn't have a copy of a fact sheet he had recently distributed at the Sala Stampa. He quickly rushed to his telephone to track down his secretary, the monsignor, who, it soon turned out, had taken this opportunity to sneak out for a quick cup of coffee.

The cardinal tried in vain to locate this fellow, struggling with increasing impatience with his own limited Italian and the obtuseness of the Italian telephone operators. Finally, his patience exhausted along with his Italian, he ended up screaming plaintively into the receiver, "Blair! *Dov'è* Blair? Where is Blair?!"

Despite this seemingly disorganized beginning to our interview, the cardinal was actually responsible for bringing the Vatican's finances into the twentieth century, at least from an accounting point of view. When he took over, there were no computers at all and the prefecture had only three full-time accountants. He oversaw the installation of a fully computerized accounting system, the hiring of more accountants and assistants, and the publishing, for the first time ever, of a consolidated financial statement for all the Vatican's departments.

The financial statement was what we were supposed to discuss. Published each year, in Italian and English, it was a detailed analysis of the Vatican's overall financial situation—with a few very significant omissions. The Vatican City-State and Vatican Bank operations were not part of the consolidated financial statement.

At this hour-long meeting—and a subsequent two-hour session the following week—the cardinal attempted to give me a thorough overview of the Vatican's money.

"How much do you know about reading a balance sheet?" the cardinal started off once he had given up on Blair.

"Well, I can balance my checkbook," I replied.

He sighed. He didn't particularly like writers or journalists, especially those with no financial background, waltzing into his office and expecting to understand a billion-dollar organization in one hour. "See, this is the problem with you people," the cardinal scowled good-naturedly. "I have to end up giving you a crash course in basic accounting."

But he did it. And he let me read the Consolidated Financial Statement sent to all the bishops of the world—although he wouldn't let me take it with me at first. I finally managed to talk him out of a copy when he insisted, at our later meeting, that the Vatican has no financial secrets and that he would *gladly* give the Consolidated Financial Statement to any journalist who asked him—but, alas, none ever did.

I smiled. He winced, quickly realizing what he had done. He now had to give me the document or seem like a liar. He handed it over with all the enthusiasm of a condemned man giving the firing squad the bullets they would use to shoot him.

"Why are you always talking about secrecy, the Vatican's secrets?" he finally demanded to know. "We don't have any secrets. Nobody keeps any secrets." ▸

"Maybe not from you, Eminence," I quickly shot back, determined not to take any crap from this guy. "But trying to get the simplest questions answered from the Vatican is a pain in the neck. You should try it sometime."

At that, he smiled. The cardinal had fought his own battles, plainly, with the Curia's old-boy network, which resented an upstart American coming in to tell them how to run their shop. After all, who needs computers when quill pens have worked so well all these centuries?

"Well, those people don't know anything anyway," the cardinal growled back with a softer note.

We spoke for an hour about the Vatican's overall money situation, which had, at this time, finally stabilized after decades of deficits.

Throughout most of its history the Vatican had relied on rents and taxes on its vast lands, the so-called *Patrimonium Petri*, given to the church over the centuries. But in the mid-1860s, Italian nationalists, in the drive to unify Italy under its first king, Vittorio Emanuele I, conquered the Papal States in central Italy. The loss of the Papal States created a real financial squeeze, especially since the Vatican refused to cash the (admittedly small) checks Italy offered in payment for expropriated lands.

The precarious financial situation was finally resolved by the so-called Lateran Treaty signed by the Vatican and Mussolini's Fascist government on February 11, 1929. In compensation for the annexation of the Papal States and other properties (including the Quirinal Palace), Italy gave the Holy See 750 million lire in cash (about $39 million in 1929) and one billion lire in five percent Italian state bonds (worth about $52.3 million in 1929). The pope created a new organization which eventually became today's Administration of the Patrimony of the Apostolic See (APSA), which cautiously invested the money (mostly in gold, Italian banks, and utilities).

For accounting purposes, the Vatican is actually divided into two basic parts—the Vatican City-State, which takes care of the physical operations in Rome; and the Holy See, which is the seat of government for the universal Catholic Church. It's actually more complex than that—there are dozens of other semiautonomous organizations, such as the Archdiocese of Rome—but for our purposes this is true enough. In a nutshell, the Vatican City-State, with such money-making activities as the museums, stamps, and gift shops, has historically made a small annual profit, while the Holy See, which has a lot of costs and relatively little income, posted increasingly large deficits for twenty-three consecutive years (until 1992).

The cardinal's Consolidated Financial Statement concerned only the finances of the Holy See—not the Vatican City-State or the Vatican Bank. Still, it was interesting.

The cardinal thumbed his fingers through the document, bound in an inexpensive green cover. It showed income of $194 million and expenses of $192.4 million, for a net operating surplus of $1.6 million. In the past, the Vatican had been losing up to $25 million a year. (The Vatican City-State, which at this writing has kept its finances a secret, reportedly has an annual budget of around $130 million with a profit of $5 million.)

Half of the Holy See's money comes from investment and real estate income; the rest comes from donations from Catholic dioceses and religious orders. The Holy See's Big Four media organizations—Radio Vaticana, *L'Osservatore Romano*, Libreria Editrice Vaticano, and the Polyglot Press—either lose millions of dollars or post very small profits each year.

As for the Holy See's financial assets, the Consolidated Financial Statement lists $317 million in cash, $347 million in stocks and bonds, $19 million in gold, and $308 million in land and buildings. (The Vatican used to hold 235,765 ounces of gold, bought in the 1930s for $35 an ounce and held at the New York Reserve Bank, but in the early 1990s it sold off most of its gold and now holds only 47,772 ounces.)

That doesn't really tell the whole story, however. For one thing, the Vatican values its stocks at their purchase price, not current value (unless the current value is less than the purchase price). Even so, it doesn't appear that the Vatican's money managers, for all their alleged shrewdness at currency speculation, have done that well. Warren Buffet they're not. If the Vatican started out with $91 million in 1929 and today, after seventy years or more, has non–real estate assets of only $650 million, it has been earning less than three percent on its money on an annualized basis. In contrast, had it invested in the equivalent of a United States stock market index fund, which averaged ten percent (dividends and capital appreciation) over the same time period, the Vatican would now have between $1.6 and $3.5 *billion.*

As for the real estate valuations, they, too, raise more questions than they answer. For one thing, the Vatican lists only "income-producing buildings and agricultural properties" among its official assets. Secondly, it allows the various Vatican departments to estimate the value of each property under their control—not an independent appraiser. Most experts consider a valuation of the Vatican's real estate holdings at $308 million to be a laughably low figure. Even the Consolidated Financial Statement at one point admits that the market value of land and buildings located inside the Vatican's sovereign territory—which it lists on its books officially as worth one Italian lire—is an estimated $1.2 *trillion* (1,850 trillion lire).

The Vatican's defenders quickly point out, however, that most of this real estate wealth is not liquid, and indeed can even be seen, from some points of view, as a financial liability.

"What are we going to do, sell St. Peter's?" the cardinal asked me sarcastically at one point. "Besides, who would buy it?"

This is the standard Vatican line—although it begs the question of whether more mundane real estate, such as office and apartment buildings, might be sold.

The truth is that while the Vatican owns at least thirty buildings in Rome, many in prime locations, most of them are used for office buildings and subsidized apartments for Vatican workers. It's far cheaper for the Vatican to keep the buildings in use than it would be for it to sell the buildings and then have to pay market rates for apartment rents, offices, and so on.

After an hour and a half, the cardinal stopped talking. My head was spinning from all the numbers being thrown at me, most of which the cardinal was sure I'd get wrong. His secretary, Blair, reappeared, sheepish at being caught sneaking out.

Like so many things in the Vatican, the Holy See's finances were far less interesting than outsiders imagine them to be. It turns out the Vatican has less liquid assets than many large U.S. Catholic dioceses, such as New York or Chicago, and certainly less than large American universities.

Running your own country doesn't appear to be a money-making enterprise.

The cardinal looked tired. He was battling the flu. I felt sorry for him. The media image of a cardinal—an energetic schemer—didn't seem accurate. Most of these guys look like very old professors, their joints aching, their skin pale and dusty, who have not been allowed to retire in peace to write their memoirs. Instead, they're stuck in drafty offices, at the age of seventy or more, and forced to work late on things like consolidated financial statements.

The cardinal walked me to his door. "Do you have any kids?" he asked suddenly, tired but still solicitous.

"Yes," I replied. "Three."

"Are you Catholic?"

"Yes, of course." It hadn't occurred to me that a non-Catholic would even be interested.

He smiled warmly and rushed over to a large wooden bureau, from which he pulled out five cheap rosaries. They were in little black cases with the papal seal on them.

"Here, give these to your wife and kids," he said. "Tell them they're from me."

It was a nice gesture, something I hadn't expected. It was as if, after all this talk about filthy lucre, the cardinal wanted me to know that he was, after all, still a cardinal, not a banker.

"Thank you," I said warmly. "They'll appreciate these."

The errant monsignor fetched me and walked me to the elevator. In my hand I held the green Consolidated Financial Statement and five black rosaries—not a bad metaphor, I thought, of what the Vatican is like.

242

XXVI

The Last of the Crusaders

When you attend some sort of major papal event such as a canonization of a saint or Christmas midnight Mass, you see people dressed up in the usual formal attire. Diplomats wear white tie and tails. Cardinals are all decked out in their finest scarlet and lace. Americans wear their cleanest jeans.

But you'll also see a whole bunch of strange-looking men that, unless you hang around a lot with French viscounts and British earls, you've probably never seen the likes of before.

They have gray hair, most of them, but they sport all sorts of colored satin sashes, thick gold chains, mammoth silver and gold stars like some kind of super-sheriff's badge, medals, buttons, collars, hanging pendants, and so on. The amount of decorative froufrou and aristocratic puffery looks like it weighs as much as ten pounds and must take literally an hour to put on, if not longer.

Some of these preening peacocks are officially members of the papal household, laymen who are given the honor of hanging around the pope's residence for formal events, greeting visiting dignitaries, and basically keeping up the image of the papacy as a kind of European monarchy. These men have a variety of titles, such as Lay Assistant to the Throne, Prince Assistant to the Throne, Gentleman of His Holiness, and Lay Familiar of the Holy Father. They are remnants of a time when the papacy, as a royal court, had a regular detachment of lay courtiers dressed in satin hose and ermine.

Most people would be surprised to discover how much the papacy remains enmeshed in the traditions, habits, ceremonies, and weird get-ups of mostly vanished European nobility. While long ago tossed out of their castles and forced to work for a living, these aristocratic families still cling tenaciously to their elaborate pageantry, the pretense of chivalry, and, most of all, to their satin sashes and gold chest chains.

Pope Paul VI formally did away with much of the pageantry and privileges associated with these lay courtiers, in his *motu proprio Pontificalis Domus,* which reorganized the Curia; but the traditions, and the sashes, persist.

In addition to the official members of the papal household, there is an entire class of aristocrats, large and small, who still hang around the Vatican. Some of these folks are the last surviving remnants of the old "black" or pontifical nobility—formally abolished in the 1960s—but others are merely European traditionalists who enjoy dressing up in the elaborate robes of this or that chivalric "order," even if not formally recognized by the Holy See.

The origins of the papal aristocracy lie, naturally, in the traditional tit-for-tat practices of Roman politics. For hundreds of years, corrupt Italian popes thought nothing of using the power of the papacy to enrich their own families by arranging for huge transfers of lands, castles, dukedoms, and palaces to their illegitimate sons, mistresses, brothers, fathers, nephews, cousins, and so on. A handful of powerful Italian families—the Barberinis, the Borgheses, the Pamphilis, the Boncompagnis—thus became the foundation of what was known as the "black" nobility. (Remember the strategic placement of the Borghese family name front and center on the facade of St. Peter's?) The corruption got so bad that a reform-minded pope, Innocent XII (1691–1700), issued a bull in which all future popes had to swear, upon their election, that they would not use their new office to enrich their relatives. But the families nevertheless continued to play a crucial role in Vatican politics and ceremony. In 1870, following the defeat of papal forces and the occupation of Rome by Vittorio Emanuele, a number of powerful Roman families remained loyal to the pope and refused to recognize the new Italian government. These aristocratic families became what is known as the "black" nobility. Until the 1960s, a department of the Vatican, the Heraldic Commission of the Pontifical Court, actually kept a formal registry of four hundred or so of them.

Two families in particular were singled out for special privileges— the Colonnas and the Orsinis. These families—who had battled each other since the time of Dante in the manner of Shakespeare's Montagues and Capulets—had one member appointed to the position known as Prince Assistant to the Pontifical Throne. Like modern-day gangs, the Colonnas and Orsinis and their feuding private armies had been a threat to public safety. As a result, in the sixteenth century Pope Julius II (1503–1513), himself a warrior, decided to keep the peace by quite literally keeping one member of each of the warring families in his household. The position of Prince Assistant was purely ceremonial, of course, but it had a tremendous amount of prestige.

This state of affairs continued from the sixteenth century until the late 1950s. That's when the Orsini family appointed a notorious playboy, Don Filippo Napoleone Orsini, to be "its" Prince Assistant. In 1958, the married Don Filippo attempted to kill himself after a tumultuous affair with the sexy British actress Brenda Lee. When, after he had recovered, the papal prince began appearing as an extra in Brenda's movies, the pope, Pius XII, finally had had enough and ended the Orsini family's role in papal pomp and circumstance. Don Filippo even had to return his Vatican license plates (with the telltale SVC initials). For some time, the only Prince Assistant was a Colonna; but finally the Torlonia family (part of the Borghese clan) was allowed to take the place of the Orsinis and have one of its members be a Prince Assistant.

There is more than one way to skin a cat, and so tradition-minded European Catholics continue to keep alive various orders of knighthood. In addition to a handful of official pontifical orders—primarily honorary associations of heads of states—there are also dozens of weird Catholic chivalric "orders," not recognized by the Holy See, that dress their members up in wild costumes and continue to insist that they are the direct descendants of medieval knights. Some of my favorites are the Order of the Elephant, a Danish organization that pins its blue sash and elephant only on royalty and victorious Allied generals (not a lot of those these days!); the Order of the Garter, of course; and the Order of St. Sylvester. Only a few of these chivalric orders are recognized by the Holy See; the rest are purely self-appointed and function like college fraternities, only without the panty raids and keggers.

Two large and ancient chivalric orders, long rivals for papal attention, are recognized by the Vatican—the Knights of Malta and the Knights of the Holy Sepulcher.

The Knights of Malta—actually the Sovereign Military Hospitaller Order of St. John of Jerusalem, of Rhodes and of Malta—is one of the world's oldest and strangest institutions. Although the order no longer has any territory, it likes to pretend that its 10,000 members constitute a sovereign nation under international law—and a few Catholic countries, and the Holy See, humor them in this belief. The order dates back to the eleventh century and the foundation of a hospital in Jerusalem to care for pilgrims. For centuries, the Knights of Malta fought the Muslims—on land and particularly on the sea—but eventually they were evicted from their strongholds on Rhodes and Malta. In recent years, the Knights of Malta have stressed their medical mission origins, running a series of hospitals and medical missions around the world. In the Vatican, the Knights have a small first aid station off St. Peter's Square, near the post office, usually open on Sundays and during large Catholic festivals.

The worldwide "capital" of the Knights of Malta is not on Malta but three doors down from the Foot Locker retail store, on Rome's ultra-chic shopping street, the Via Condotti, at the base of the Spanish Steps. The distinctive flag, with the eight-pointed Maltese Cross, flies proudly above an arched doorway that leads into a large paved inner courtyard. Although technically limited to members of the European aristocracy, the Knights in recent years have prudently created a special class of membership, a Knight of Magisterial Grace, to permit rich plebeians, such as Lee Iacocca, Alexander Haig, and William F. Buckley, Jr., to join.

The other main chivalric order is the more ancient Knights of the Holy Sepulcher—formally the Equestrian Order of the Holy Sepulcher of Jerusalem. Dating back literally to 1070 and the First Crusade, the Knights of the Holy Sepulcher were organized to protect the Church of the Holy Sepulcher in Jerusalem and took as their symbol the bloodred Jerusalem Cross. The order appears to have more or less died out by the Renaissance, but in the nineteenth century, with a revived interest in Palestine, it was resurrected. Less pretentious than the Knights of Malta, and nearly twice as large, the Knights of the Holy Sepulcher today have as their primary mission providing aid to the Christian Church in the Holy Land. You see the "chevaliers," as they call themselves, at large papal events, clad in their distinctive white capes with red Jerusalem crosses.

Given my background, I was more curious about this order than about the Knights of Malta. I've visited the dusty Church of the Holy Sepulcher in Jerusalem many times, when I was studying Hebrew in Israel. During my first Hebrew *ulpan,* conducted at a kibbutz in the Jez-reel Valley, I used to go to Mass every Sunday (said in Arabic) in Naza-reth, at the beautiful and modern Church of the Annunciation. The Knights of the Holy Sepulcher have contributed millions of dollars over the years to the upkeep and maintenance of these Christian churches in Israel.

I made an appointment to see an official of the Knights of the Holy

Sepulcher at their venerable headquarters, the old Palazzo dei Penitenzieri, about a block from the Vatican on the Via della Conciliazione. Most of the palazzo, built by Cardinal Domenico della Rovere around 1490, now houses the Columbus Hotel, which at one time was run by the order as a revenue source but which has recently been sold to a private company. The Knights' headquarters are in a wing of the palazzo, where the hotel guests are not allowed. The entrance to the hotel is actually hard to find, merely one small door in a long line of tourist gift shops and tobacco stores. If you enter the palazzo from the back, along Largo Ildebrando Gregori, across from the Church of San Spirito in Sassia, you see a large vaulted entrance that leads into an inner courtyard with a koi pound and a few outdoor tables and chairs. Above the entrance is a sign that reads ORDO EQVESTRIS S. SEPVLCRI HIEROSOLYMITANI.

The Knights were expecting me. I had an appointment with Graziano Motta, an Italian representative of the order who lived in Jerusalem and spent most of his time working with the Latin Patriarch of Jerusalem, Michel Sabbah. Motta spoke no English, but his French was fluent, so we struggled though our interview in the latter.

The palazzo was amazing. It looked like something out of a Gothic novel—towering ceilings, a throne room (for the Grand Master, a cardinal), various dark meeting rooms, ancient wooden furniture, dusty tapestries. I kept expecting to see a group of hooded knights, swords drawn, kneeling in some ancient hazing ritual.

But after spending a couple hours with Motta, I was a little disappointed. There are currently about 18,000 Knights—11,000 men, 5,400 "dames," and 1,800 priests. Half of the Knights, surprisingly, are in the United States, with another large contingent (about 3,500) in Italy. They get together sporadically and have an investiture ceremony once a year.

I was hoping the Knights would turn out to be some sort of Catholic secret society, a powerful, vaguely sinister group—sort of like the Masons or what the Jesuits insist Opus Dei is. I thought of the Knights as an ancient order of warrior-priests who passed on long-forgotten rites in underground caverns in the basements of old Crusader castles, and practiced ascetic disciplines not seen for centuries.

Instead, what the Knights do mostly is write checks. They're primarily a large fund-raising organization for the Catholic Church in Israel and Jordan. It turns out they have even less ritual than the Knights of Columbus, who at least practice the Sacred Ceremony of the Ale Keg.

Motta was apologetic. "Well, we do have get-togethers at least once a year," he said, sensing my disappointment. "People wear their vesture then."

But no secret meetings in ancient crusader castles? No quasi-pagan rituals? No blood oaths?

He was afraid not. Their primary mission is no longer battling the Turks. It's raising money.

I couldn't understand it. What's the sense of putting on all that chivalric ornamentation if you can't at least *pretend* to be a knight, part of some ancient secret society?

Motta walked me out. He understood my disappointment. He invited me to attend that weekend the beatification of one of the Knights, Bartolomeo Longo, who built a Marian shrine, Our Lady of Pompeii.

I said thank you, but I couldn't make it. I was thinking perhaps I should give the Knights of Malta a second chance. They had a more sinister reputation, after all.

XXVII

Living in Rome

At last—for the first time—I live! It beats everything: it leaves
the Rome of your fancy—your education—nowhere. It makes
Venice—Florence—Oxford—London—seem like little cities
of pasteboard.

HENRY JAMES, Letter (1869)

At this point, I should say a few words about Rome as a city, as it was
obviously so much a part of our lives during our stay there.

You hear so many different things about Rome, it's difficult, from a
distance, to sort out the reality from the myths. For example, we had
heard, before and during our stay, that "nothing works" in Rome . . . that
it is a dirty city in which foreigners have a hard time adjusting . . . that
Romans are rude and arrogant.

I found none of that really to be true—or, more precisely, it *is* true
but not in a way that really matters.

The reality is that Rome is a very modern city that exists on top of, around, and in a place where people have been continuously living for three thousand years. When you sit out in the piazza in front of the Pantheon, gobbling a late lunch of *costoletta alla milanese,* you have to keep reminding yourself that the building in front of you, standing perfectly intact and still in use, was built in A.D. 118. Much of what is difficult about Rome grows out quite naturally from its very antiquity. Many of the roads, for example, were quite literally built by people who put the word "Caesar" in front of their names, and were designed for horse-drawn chariots rather than for double-decker German tour buses. The Aurelian Wall, which snakes its way through the city and through which are found the various "portas"—as in Porta San Pancrazio, by our apartment—was built in A.D. 270 by the Emperor Aurelian. Most of the wall has survived. Its soaring brick battlements have shaped the geography and life of the city for more than one thousand seven hundred years.

Despite continual complaints from Italians, things *do* work in Rome, more or less—the buses, trams, and metro run quite efficiently, the telephone connections are fine, the electricity goes off only when you turn the lights on while also using the washing machine, the garbage is (sort of) collected, the automatic teller machines at banks spit out money when you insert your credit card.

Rome *is* dirtier and shabbier than most suburban North Americans are used to, but it is probably not dirtier than downtown Los Angeles or New York or Mexico City. Garbage is not collected at your house but at large green plastic Dumpsters left on street corners, usually overflowing and with bags stacked around them.

Graffiti is absolutely everywhere, literally covering virtually all the buildings and even some monuments. In this, Rome looks more like a New York City subway car than a city, which is a shame. Paris, in contrast, has somehow figured out a way to keep the graffiti to a minimum, either by making it punishable by guillotining or by having such fierce civic pride that ordinary Parisians routinely chase down and garrote anyone they see approaching the Arc de Triomphe with a can of spray paint.

The buildings in Rome are a strangely mixed lot. You see brand-new brick apartment buildings existing side by side with what can only be called seventeenth-century tenement slums. I was struck, near the Trevi Fountain, by the contrast between the glistening white marble monument behind the fountain—and the fountain itself—and the shabby, nearly collapsing tenement next to it, its sagging walls covered with crumbling red plaster. When Romans speak about nothing working in Rome, however, what they are usually referring to are public services that usually don't impact the average foreigner, at least until they think about settling in permanently. The phones work, but trying to get one installed in an apartment can take months.

I forgive Rome all its petty sins, though, because it has one redeeming quality that it shares with a few other large European cities and which strikes Americans with particular force: It's tremendously safe.

It's not until you spend an extended period of time in Europe that you realize what a horrible aura of *menace* surrounds many large American cities. As I write these words, some American scholars are beginning to write about how America is, in many respects, degenerating into a Third World nation, at least regarding the safety of its streets. In truth, that's an insult to the Third World, because most Third World nations are safer, from the perspective of the average person strolling down a city street, than America. So many European tourists have been gunned down while minding their own business in Florida, for example, that the European Union actually put out a security alert advising its citizens to avoid that state.

One reason European cities are safer—from Paris and Rome to Vienna and Prague—is that they have radically different philosophies of urban planning than their American counterparts. When crime and poverty came to American cities, the American middle classes simply picked up and fled to the suburbs, allowing the cities to degenerate into urban jungles of violence, abandoned buildings, and crime.

In Europe, though, the opposite was the case. Europeans are proud of their cities, with all those beautiful buildings and ancient monuments, and so, rather than fleeing to the suburbs, they *stayed* in the inner cities and pushed the poor and criminals to the suburbs. The suburbs of Paris, the *banlieux*, are dangerous places, but the city center of Paris is as safe as a walk through St. Peter's.

The same is true of Rome, perhaps more so. There was no place in Rome I didn't feel safe taking my wife and kids. There were no teenage gangbangers strolling around, looking to pick a fight. No drive-by shootings. No ghetto blasters booming on the buses. Very few panhandlers, and those were mostly old Gypsy women, backs bent by osteoporosis. The Italian kids, while rambunctious as all teenagers, were friendly, polite kids, strangely lacking the surly thuggery of their British counterparts. The buses were completely safe. The only time I saw any vaguely threatening behavior on the public transit system was when some British soccer players got on the metro at the Ottaviano station. They were pink-faced louts right out of *A Clockwork Orange*, loudly commenting on the deficiencies of Italian rail transport.

I have another pet theory for why Rome has been able to maintain a certain civility while large American cities, such as Washington, D.C., have degenerated into urban barbarism.

That theory involves . . . nuns.

There are nuns in Rome. Lots of nuns. Of all shapes, sizes, and colors. You see them everywhere. In the piazzas. On the buses. In the bookstores. (You also see lots of priests, but they still exist in the United

States and Europe, while nuns do not. Priests also don't travel as much in packs, while nuns do.)

I'd talk to them whenever I got the chance. I'd just ask them, in English or broken Italian, what order they were a member of, and, if they were at all friendly and didn't immediately call the carabinieri, a little bit about their lives, their habits, what they were doing in Rome. Some of their habits were really colorful. Outside the Sala Stampa one day, my first week in Rome, I spied a beautiful young religious sister with long hair sporting what looked like a sky-blue cassock with a Roman collar. At first I thought the nun must have been a female Anglican priest or something, what with the Roman collar; but after striking up a conversation with her, she told me she was a member of an Italian order, the Oblates of Our Lady of Fatima, and that this colorful get-up was their everyday habit.

Back in the United States, nuns have all but become extinct. Following the Second Vatican Council, more than half the nuns simply . . . walked out. The few that remain, with an average age somewhere around 110, strut around proudly in drab secular clothes, looking like spinster schoolteachers. The only identifying symbol of their religious vows is a wooden cross worn around their necks.

Don't get me wrong: I fully sympathize with modern nuns' desire to be, well, modern. If I were they, I wouldn't want to walk around looking like Sister Bertrille in *The Flying Nun* either. I would make the same arguments that they do: That religious habits were merely the common clothes worn by ordinary women in the century in which a religious order was founded, appropriate to, say, the sixteenth century, but a bit ridiculous today.

But from the point of view of a selfish layperson, I found I truly liked seeing all the nuns scurrying around Rome, dressed in their colorful habits. They lent an air of civility and civilization to the streets. How degraded and violent can a place be if it has groups of nuns walking down the street?

The one area in which Rome truly lives up to its sinister reputation, however, is on the road. Italians in general, and Romans in particular, live in a different mental universe when it comes to driving.

It's not merely that it's every man for himself, regardless of the gender of the driver; it's more that there is an almost mystical disregard for physical reality, for the limits that steel and fiberglass impose on flesh and bones.

I saw this almost every day at my favorite "intersection" in Rome, the Piazzale Aurelio near Porta San Pancrazio, about two miles from our apartment. Whenever I took the number 41 bus or a taxi up the hill from the Vatican, I would marvel. At the Piazzale Aurelio four different major streets converge, resulting, since this was Italy, in six to eight different lanes of traffic, all attempting to squeeze into a one-lane, one-way street, Via di San Pancrazio, that was quite literally the size of an average alley.

This created a funnel unlike anything most Americans have ever seen. There was no traffic light, of course, but what was astonishing was that none was necessary. Each car, each big orange city bus, inched its way forward, attempting to squeeze into any possible space, and somehow, despite all the laws of physics as we know them, the cars got through in a remarkably brief amount of time.

I noticed this same phenomenon when the electricity went off one afternoon and shut down all the streetlights in the Piazza San Giovanni di Dio. The Anglo-American solution to this type of a situation would be to "queue up," calmly taking turns, letting one car go at a time, as you would at a four-way stop in the United States. On this occasion, though, all the Roman drivers merely dashed simultaneously to the center of the intersection, honking their horns continuously as they did so. Again, no one gave the least bit of ground, and each car simply waited for a tiny space in which to inch forward, eventually pushing its way through. I must say, having witnessed this on a number of occasions, I think the Italian method is at least as efficient, albeit substantially more nerve-wracking, than its American or British counterpart.

Foreigners believe that there are no rules when driving in Rome but, in fact, there are quite obviously rules—they are just the reverse of what you find in North America or Britain.

In North America you slow down when you see a pedestrian crossing a street; in Rome it's considered customary to accelerate.

In North America you are fined if you intentionally block traffic for, say, five or ten minutes; in Rome it's the only way to make a left-hand turn.

In North America sexual prowess is usually proven in bed; in Rome it's proven on the autostrada.

Both pedestrians and drivers must quickly acquire the ability to place their bodies and/or vehicles squarely in front of onrushing traffic. This is very difficult for an American (at least one not born in New York City) to do; but without this essential ability, it is virtually impossible to cross a street in Rome, whether on foot or in a car.

Finally, a word about the Romans. They *do* take some getting used to. It sounds silly, but it really does appear that no one has quite had the heart yet, lo these past 1,500 years, to break the news to them that Caesar no longer rules the world.

Romans still do seem to harbor the belief that their great city is, and always shall be, the center of the known universe, and nothing will shake them from this belief.

When we first arrived, Glenn and I naturally thought Romans were inexplicably rude. That's because they, well, act rude. But later I came to realize that we were mistaking rudeness for something else—mostly a real indifference to commerce.

As Americans, we had come to equate the cheery, snap-to efficiency of a fast-food franchise with civility; and so, if people in Rome
didn't immediately respond to a question, or appear interested in having
our business, we assumed that they were rude.

For example, I would walk into a bar to order a beer. Rather than
the chipper "What can I do for you, sir?" typical of a British pub or
American bar, the typical Roman proprietor would instead put on this
look of grave annoyance, as though I were intruding upon his dinner
rather than simply giving him some business. *"Vorrei una birra, per favore,"* I'd say. "I'd like a beer, please."

The owner would sigh, and look at me as if to say "What do *you*
want?"

Invariably, I'd look around to make sure this was really a bar. Had
I accidentally walked into someone's home by mistake? No, no, there
were tables with people sitting around them, sipping their Camparis. It
must be a bar.

Maybe he didn't understand my lousy Italian, so I'd repeat the
question: *Una birra, per favore.*

The proprietor would then turn his back in genuine disgust, ignoring me for five minutes or so. Finally, he'd slouch over to where the
kegs were, and reluctantly, very reluctantly, pour a beer, putting it down
in front of me with a scowl.

At first this annoyed me no end—because it occurred in restaurants, at newsstands, at the local Enoteca. Romans seemed pissed off
whenever I wanted to buy anything from them. The taxi drivers would
invariably wave me off whenever I got into a cab, angry that I had disturbed their reading of the soccer scores.

But then I finally realized that Romans, unlike Americans, have
not allowed business to interfere with life. They do business to make a
living, but they're not about to pretend that they *like* you just because
you're patronizing their bar or their restaurant or their *alimentari.*

They don't know you from Adam, and until they do know you,

personally, they feel absolutely no obligation to treat you with the least bit of respect.

After a while that sublime indifference to the work ethic sort of grew on me—although I never got completely used to it. Roman establishments close for siesta at one in the afternoon, which is usually just about the time most tourists arrive. The employees go home, have lunch, meet their mistresses or lovers for an afternoon rendezvous, and come back to work around four-thirty. If you arrive at, say, two minutes after one, you're out of luck. They're not about to be inconvenienced by anything so unimportant as a little extra business.

As a result, after a while Glenn and I got accustomed to the rhythms and attitudes of the people in Rome. They're definitely not the friendliest people in the world, at least not to strangers, but neither are they the rudest. Once they get to know you, they're okay. The owners of the *alimentari* on Via Ozanam got to know us pretty well—enough to invariably give our kids free candy. The husband, a handsome man in his early fifties, decided it was his duty to explain to me how to drink like an Italian, teaching me the difference between the different kinds of grappa.

And I must admit, now whenever I go into a restaurant in America, and a bubbly young waitress takes my order, full of warmth and good cheer, I'm a little nostalgic. I kind of miss the snarling old Roman bartenders.

XXVIII

Finding Bargains on Indulgences

I wouldn't have been much of a tourist if I hadn't gone shopping. Fortunately, coming from and marrying into large Catholic families, my wife and I both had a lot of presents to buy—and the Vatican is more than willing to oblige the bingeing tourist shopper, despite regular denunciations of Western "consumerism" on the part of the popes and the Pontifical Council for Justice and Peace.

In fact, after visiting the major Vatican tourist sites—the basilica, the museums, the catacombs, and the city center—that is what many pilgrims and tourists spend most of their time doing.

Every sort of cheap Catholic knickknack that scandalizes evangelicals and atheists alike—from 3-D Jesus posters to papal key chains, pens, letter openers, bottle openers, and ashtrays—is on display in the literally dozens of small gift shops that ring St. Peter's Square.

My wife found it all a bit much, but I enjoyed all the souvenir selling. The more the merrier! I kept looking for the official Vatican poker chips that a friend of mine, a Redemptorist priest studying law at the

Gregorian, insisted he had seen. I had to have some! As a result, every week I would spend some time in these little souvenir shops, picking up small gifts for innumerable nephews, siblings, cousins, and assorted relatives.

I got to know the specialties of the various shops. One shop facing the Vatican bus stop had the best prices on, and best selection of, the cheap marble-dust statues you see everywhere in Rome—reproductions of both religious statues and erotic classical statues. You see statues of the Virgin Mary side by side with statues of a nude and remarkably buxom Venus rising from the sea . . . or the Apollo Belvedere and Lao-coön . . . or two Roman gladiators wrestling, one of which has the other in a hold the World Wrestling Federation definitely would not sanction. It's not merely tasteless tourists who succumb to the allures of cheap classical statuary. In his Roman diary, Goethe confesses to purchasing "casts" of various masterpieces. For my part, I ended up buying a statue of Socrates, bald and beautiful, which my wife despises and makes me keep in my office.

The Ancora bookstore and art gallery, in the palazzo across the Via della Conciliazione from the Sala Stampa, had a good selection of "arty," all-wood religious statues and creches—as opposed to the ultra-cheap plaster statues Catholics give their kids for First Communion presents. But I quickly discovered that good taste is expensive. All-wood Christmas creches, while beautiful, can cost as much as 7.5 million lire—around $5,000. My wife and I decided that we couldn't afford good taste, and settled for a typical Fontanini creche made out of indestructible rubber, which our two-year-old could chew on.

The official Vatican gift shops, such as the one on St. Peter's roof and off to the right side of the basilica, tend to be crowded and overpriced. They're staffed by a group of Italian nuns in blue habits who, although innocent of any foreign language, still speak the universal language of hard cash. They take MasterCard and Visa faster than you can say "indulgences for sale."

We bought three small all-wood Madonna plaques for our god-daughters (at 45,000 lire a pop), three large Madonna plaques for presents (100,000 lire each), seven rosaries at 12,000 lire each, a couple of Swiss Guards and Vatican calendars, a poster of Michelangelo's *Last Judgment* (12,000 lire), an expensive statue of St. Francis of Assisi made out of molded wood pulp and resin (120,000 lire), and so on. As a backup, we bought thirty T-shirts with various touristy Roman designs (cartoon gladiators, the Colosseum, etc.) and a dozen large photographs of the pope. We figured we could slip these pictures into nice frames once we got back home, and they'd make quick last-minute gifts for anyone we had forgotten about.

In the past the Vatican received nothing from the shops in its immediate vicinity other than rent, if they happened to be located in Vatican-owned buildings. But in recent years the Vatican has began an ambitious effort to, in effect, license reproductions of its artistic treasures. This has led to the somewhat controversial creation of a new Vatican store, the Edizioni Musei Vaticani (Vatican Museums Editions).

Located in a small shop kitty-corner across from the St. Anne's Gate, at 13 Via delle Grazie, the store sells a line of more than four hundred "upscale" souvenirs—including beautiful tapestries, marble reproductions, plates, a deluxe gold-leafed Bible, pins, wristwatches, rings, necklaces, and so on.

I walked by this shop almost every week on my way to the bank machine down the block, and I'd glance through the windows. Invariably the price tags scared me off—such as $840 for an eighteen-karat gold medal of the Laocoön, the priest of Apollo who sought to warn the Trojans.

But one day I decided I had to go in and see what the Vatican was selling. Tape recorder at the ready, I walked into the shop and started browsing.

A pretty young woman with long, wavy brown hair offered to help me.

"*Prego, signore,*" she said despite the presence of my tape recorder.

"I'm looking for a special gift," I told the girl, "but not something really expensive."

The girl smiled. She pointed to some marble reproductions of Roman nudes—the torso of a male athlete and the goddess Demeter. Unlike my statue of Socrates, these statues seemed like they were hand-chiseled marble even though, of course, they weren't. Price: 335,000 lire.

"Maybe something not quite that special," I said.

The saleslady offered me some Ferragamo scarves and ties. Very nice. Price: 225,000 lire. I decided I'd stick to Nordstrom's.

For just a moment I thought of the incongruity of the Vatican marketing $150 Ferragamo scarves while it simultaneously denounces the "rampant materialism" of the evil Western democracies; but I quickly pushed such petty thoughts from my mind. Ever since the day Jesus accepted expensive aromatic oil from Mary at Bethany, the Catholic Church has been willing to do business with the very rich while simultaneously caring for the very poor. Robbing Peter to pay Paul and all that. If Ferragamo helps the Vatican make money off of wealthy tourists, fine.

The saleslady could see that I was squirming.

"Come with me, *signore,*" she said, and walked me over to a less expensive section of the store. This is where the Vatican kept its official Vatican plates and other knickknacks. There were some beautiful Vatican puzzles that caught my eye, including one of Raphael's *School of Athens.*

I asked the salesgirl what was popular with the tourists. She replied that people really loved the marble busts—such as the one of Julius Caesar (550,000 lire) and Mary's head from the *Pietà* (750,000).

I browsed around a little more and ended up buying an art book about the Sistine Chapel.

Besides the storefront on Via delle Grazie, the Edizioni Musei Vaticani also have more than a dozen small boutiques set up throughout the Vatican Museums complex. The Vatican Museums are actually a long series of interconnected galleries and hallways, stretching for what seems

262

like miles. Every hundred yards or so, now, there is a little boutique set up offering reproductions, posters, slides, books, and videotapes about the items you just saw. Following the Vatican's incredible Gallery of Maps, for example, there is a boutique offering a two-volume facsimile edition of these same cartographic masterpieces. Near the Sistine Chapel there is a little mini-mall full of souvenirs about Michelangelo's famous murals.

My favorite of all the various Edizioni Musei Vaticani shops was the fairly large store set up in the Vatican Library exhibit. That's where the Vatican sells gorgeous printed reproductions of its ancient books and manuscripts—including entire volumes costing $800 or more.

I eventually fell for a facsimile reproduction, complete with gold leaf, of two pages from an ancient illuminated Gospel of Mark in Greek. It cost me $100 for two pages, but I put the pages in gold frames when I came home and they turned out really nice. *These* my wife lets me keep in the house.

The Vatican Museums' administration defends its aggressive new marketing strategy on the grounds that it costs a lot of money to care for the Vatican's treasures. "We need revenues to support all the expenses that the museums have, like guards, conservationists, restorers, and researchers," said the Vatican Museums' director. More than three million people visit the museums every year, paying 15,000 lire each; but that doesn't begin to pay for all the costs involved, he added.

And so it appears that the Vatican has decided it's in the retail industry to stay. Plans are in the works to market everything from $5,000 tapestries to ceramic models of St. Peter's Basilica.

Upon greater consideration of the entire moral problem involved, I decided that I had only one qualm about all this buying and selling of religion.

I wish they'd hold a sale.

XXIX

Where Cardinals Go to Party

The Son of Man came eating and drinking, and they say, "Behold a glutton and a drunkard, a friend of tax-collectors and sinners."

Matthew 11:19

I made it a point to get out a little while we were in Rome. Because Glenn and I had a full-time baby-sitter, we actually were able to have more dates in Rome than we had had during all of our previous years together. And whenever I interviewed various Vatican officials, I tried to meet them at one of their favorite restaurants, far off the tourist beat.

I considered it my professional duty, of course, to learn all I could about Italian food. This required considerable discipline on my part, because, as A. J. Liebling once remarked, you really only have two opportunities each day for fieldwork. If you worry too much about cholesterol or other North American obsessions, you simply won't collect an adequate amount of data for a scientific analysis.

The thing about Italian food is this. You have to be very selective. Most of the "fast food" in Italy is horrible, particularly the pizza. So-called Roman pizza is nothing more than a piece of square pizza dough covered by marinara sauce and a few mushrooms, folded in half. It's about as appetizing as a cardboard box.

It's sounds like a typically American thing to say, but American pizza is, by and large, far better than Italian pizza because Americans pile on the toppings. Meat is expensive in Italy and so they use it sparingly or not at all. The average streetside pizzeria in Rome sells just Italian minimalist pizza or dry rolls with a thin piece of ham in them. When I was rushing to some interview, therefore, the trick was always to look for places that sold fresh calzone, those hot, doughy buns stuffed with ground prosciutto that cost about 1,500 lire each. They were a bargain and delicious. You can easily spend *twenty or thirty times that amount* for lunch in some of the tourist traps around the Vatican and not eat half as well.

Many of the restaurants in Rome are fairly ordinary—serving a few pasta dishes and pieces of dried-out chicken—but the good restaurants are really good. When we first arrived, a publisher friend from the States took Glenn and me to a moderately priced restaurant off the Via Veneto that was dedicated to serious eating. We didn't order a single dish. The maître d' simply told us when we walked in, "I'll take care of you," and he brought us one course after another, telling us what we should eat, when and with what beverage. We had fresh antipasti, *breschetta,* soft-shell crab on angel hair pasta, some sort of chop stuffed with ham and cheese, another pasta dish with marinara sauce, fava beans, *zuppa.* It was superb. We finished off two bottles of typically unpretentious Italian wine and then the waiter brought us our *digestivi,* the lemon liquor Limoncello. For dessert we had cheese and some sort of Roman cheesecake and cappuccino. Glenn and I and the publisher and his wife literally floated out of the restaurant on a cloud of culinary bliss, and strolled up the Via Veneto to a then-famous bar.

After a few months in the city, I got to know the better restaurants and watering holes in the Borgo, the warren of alleylike streets next to the Vatican, as well as in the Prati district and around the Pantheon. It helped, of course, that I had Friar Tuck to advise me, because he had spent twenty years in Rome and was, after all, a professional restaurant reviewer. And most other people had opinions about local restaurants. "Always peek in and see if you spot any Roman collars," one Vatican reporter told me cynically when I first came to Rome. "If there are a lot of priests in the restaurant, you'll know the food is good."

There was one restaurant in particular, however, that I was dying to try. It was the famous L'Eau Vive . . . no doubt one of the most unusual restaurants in the entire world. At that time L'Eau Vive still had a reputation as a regular hangout for cardinals and other prelates, who enjoyed its quiet atmosphere, discreet location and excellent, albeit expensive, food. It is one of the few restaurants in Rome that can truly say, *Il Papa ha mangiato qui!* Pope John Paul II was a frequent customer in the days before he was elected pope.

L'Eau Vive has played a part in more than one curial intrigue. The place was considered such an important meeting place that professional Vatican informers, who sell tidbits of curial gossip to the news-hungry *vaticanisti,* allegedly frequented the restaurant dressed in clerical garb just to eavesdrop on conversations among cardinals.

I decided that, in the interest of history if not of culinary curiosity, I should visit the place.

My father-in-law, John Duncan, was visiting for Christmas—fresh from a vacation in sunny Rio de Janeiro—and I went to fetch him at the airport. By then I had figured out how to take the local train from the Trastevere station out to the airport and back. From the station, it was a quick trip up the Gianicolense on the number 13 tram to our apartment.

This meant paying six bucks for transportation to and from the airport instead of fifty, or more, for a taxi.

My father-in-law, the father of eight children, is a big, barrel-chested man, a former attorney who ran a small oil company for Glenn's family. When his late wife, Anne, was alive, the two of them were inveterate world travelers and in general enjoyed life to the fullest. He had been to Italy a few times. As a young man of eighteen, John had been stationed in northern Italy, right after World War II, as an M.P. "Oh, man, it was tough duty, let me tell ya," he would say with a big grin. "I had to keep all those nasty Italian girls from corrupting our innocent G.I.'s." It had been his job, in other words, to make sure American soldiers didn't fraternize too enthusiastically with the natives. He likes to say that the first time he saw a bikini was on the beaches near the then-Yugoslavian border. The battle-weary soldiers couldn't believe their eyes.

After John was settled into our extra bedroom, I suggested that he, Friar Tuck, and I go check out L'Eau Vive on a Friday night. Glenn didn't want to go; she said we should have a boys' night out.

I was almost certain that John and I wouldn't be getting into any trouble at L'Eau Vive. I called Friar Tuck up and he said he'd be delighted to show us the restaurant; he'd make all the arrangements.

I knew L'Eau Vive was located on the Piazza Sant' Eustachio, about a block from the Pantheon and next to the Italian State Archives; but when I went there a few days before our visit, I couldn't for the life of me find the place. There were a number of restaurants opening out onto this tiny square, but none was L'Eau Vive. I finally had to ask a shop owner, who directed me to the restaurant's small, unmarked door a few yards down Via Monterone. I could see why cardinals liked the place: *Discreet* is an understatement. There were two flickering flame lamps on each side of the entrance.

On Friday night John and I got dressed up and took a taxi to the restaurant—or, rather, to the general vicinity of the restaurant. The traffic, as usual on a Friday night, was a nightmare. The driver was inching his way along the narrow alleys leading up to the Pantheon when we decided we'd just jump out and walk.

We arrived fifteen minutes late, but Friar Tuck—uncharacteristically dressed in clerical suit and collar, no doubt because of the restaurant we were visiting—was standing outside. After proper introductions, we headed inside.

L'Eau Vive was nothing like I expected. It was light and bright, with soaring vaulted ceilings and wooden beams. All the walls were painted a stark white. There was a large plaster statue of Mary near the front door. The tables were fairly close together, although I knew there was also a back room reserved for visitors who wished more private dining.

Friar Tuck, who had reviewed the establishment a few months earlier, introduced us to the proprietess in French, which all the servers spoke instead of Italian. Shamelessly angling for a better meal, he reminded her of his recent review and said that I, too, was a writer and was very interested in the quality of their fare.

I winced. I'm an enthusiastic proponent of journalistic freeloading—I'll gladly shill for a cruise line willing to give me an all-expenses-paid tour of the Mediterranean—but this was a little crude for my taste. Still, it worked marvelously. We were quickly whisked to a great table and were served one of the best meals I had in Rome up to that point.

It turned out that L'Eau Vive is actually a chain of eleven restaurants, sort of an ecclesiastical Benihana. There are similar establishments in North and South America, Africa, the South Pacific, and the Philippines. There is even a L'Eau Vive in, of all places, Ho Chi Minh City in the People's Republic of Vietnam. The one in Rome had been there for twenty-five years and had become a local landmark.

The restaurants were all run by a lay female group, the Travailleuses Missionaires de la Conception (Missionary Workers of the Immaculate Conception), which are a part of the lay Carmelite "family" known as Donum Dei (Gift of God). These lay "missionaries" are almost all young African or Asian women pledged, at least temporarily, to a life of virginity and service. They all wear colorful outfits inspired by the traditional clothing of their homelands.

Friar Tuck told us that the founder of the group, a French laywoman, actively recruited women in Africa and Asia. The members of the order come to work in the group's restaurants in Paris, New York, Rio de Janero, Manila, and so on.

The food was outstanding—French and very expensive. I had a fillet of beef with a Roquefort-Cognac cream sauce and potatoes. John had pasta. The good friar had a *poisson grillé* with a salad.

We enjoyed our dinner in the leisurely fashion of Italy, talking and drinking wine. There was no turnover at the surrounding tables. People came to the restaurant early, sat down, and spent the evening there. Most of the clientele were fashionably dressed laypeople, about half of whom spoke French. There were, however, about three tables with clerics. At one of them I spotted a flash of gold chain underneath a black suit—a telltale sign of a bishop.

We had a rousing good time. Friar Tuck was full of curial gossip. We chatted about books and the publishing business. Friar Tuck had just published a learned theological treatise, full of quotations from St. Thomas Aquinas, that happened to have on its cover a color painting of Adam and Eve in the Garden—stark naked.

John and I had a good laugh at his expense. We kidded him that now that he'd decided that sex sells, he should, well, turn up the voltage a little.

"I think theology books would do much better if they had racier covers," I observed. "Why stop with Adam and Eve? A book on Catholic sexual ethics could vividly illustrate all the things you're *not* supposed to do. You could have a nice tasteful nude on the cover—a Rubens, say— and change the title to something like *Sexual Sins: An Illustrated Guide*. The Leonine bookstore couldn't keep copies in stock! It'd be a best seller. We can pitch it to my New York agent tomorrow morning."

Friar Tuck laughed. We spent the next few minutes thinking up risqué titles for theology books.

As the meal was winding down, suddenly the proprietress walked out into the center of the restaurant, carrying a microphone. Friar Tuck whispered that this is a nightly ritual at L'Eau Vive. The woman read a prayer, in French, and then all the waitresses gathered around the statue of the Blessed Virgin Mary, hands clasped in front of them. The proprietress invited her patrons to join the waitresses in singing . . . a hymn.

Much to my surprise, and John's astonishment, the whole place started singing "Immaculate Mary" in French!

In case you've forgotten the lyrics, they go like this (in English translation):

In heaven the blessed thy glory proclaim
On earth we thy children invoke thy sweet name
Ave! Ave! Ave Ma-ree-ah!
Ave! Ave! Ma-ree-ee-ee-ah!

I've been to a lot of restaurants in my life. I've swigged "Arab whiskey" in the Casbah in Cairo. I've eaten couscous in Casablanca, souvlaki in Athens, falafel in Jerusalem, sauerbraten in Munich, and boiled beef and cabbage in London. And in all my culinary expeditions, this was the first and only time I'd seen the waitresses sing Marian hymns while the customers finished off their crème brûlée.

The desserts finished, the coffees and *digestivi* sipped, the customers all left en masse. The proprietress, standing next to the statue of Mary, thanked each of us, one at a time.

The air outside was cold. Friar Tuck walked John and me down to the Corso Vittorio Emanuele, where he caught a bus back to the Portuguese college. John and I found a taxi stand with a line. We stood around for ten minutes, cold but enjoying the boisterous Roman night life on parade. Finally, our turn came and a yellow cab careened up to the curb.

That was our big boys' night out—talking about theology books with a priest while consecrated virgins sang "Immaculate Mary."

Next time, I told John, we'd try Hooters instead.

XXX

Christmas Midnight Mass in the Vatican

High Mass at St. Peter's, as I saw it on Christmas Day, said by
Cardinal Rampolla, was an impressive ceremony, indeed, but it was
said mainly to a crowd of curious foreigners.

ARTHUR SYMONS, *Cities of Italy*

You know the Christmas season has begun in Rome when you visit
the Piazza Navona and see the outdoor carnival that is set up there
every year. In place of the handful of artists and street vendors who
normally frequent the colorful piazza, there are dozens of portable stands
set up, each selling toys and candy and overpriced Christmas crèches.

Glenn and I were determined that we would give the kids as nor-
mal a Christmas as possible. That was a bit difficult, because the Italians
don't seem to make as big a deal out of Christmas as do Americans. We

saw only a few Christmas lights, although the business district up and down Via Ozanam was decorated and the normally surly teenage girl in the Enoteca, where we bought milk and bread, actually smiled at me.

To make up for the lack of snowmen and Rudolfs in Rome, we bundled our kids up and took them to the Piazza Navona to do our Christmas shopping. We decided the best route was to take the number 42 bus that went down Via Ozanam, just a few blocks from the apartment, to the Piazza Venezia. From there it was just a short walk over to the Piazza Navona. Luckily, we had Anne to help us on these trips.

The Piazza Navona is a magical place anytime, of course, but especially at Christmas. It's a long rectangular space surrounded by four- or five-story buildings and featuring three beautiful fountains. In the center of the piazza there is the Fontana dei Fiumi, with the obligatory Egyptian obelisk rising up from the middle. At the southern end of the piazza is the even more impressive Fontana del Moro, remolded in 1653 by Bernini, who designed the great marble statues of the sea gods in the middle of it. We must have come back three or four times just to see the fountains. There was an ancient wooden carousel, made in Germany, which all the kids loved.

We'd shop, have lunch at one of the outdoor cafés, look at the paintings by the various street "artists" (many are merely promoters who sell other people's works). We ended up buying four or five paintings while in Italy.

Of course, Italy has its own Christmas and New Year's traditions. One weird tradition is that for Christmas husbands and wives give each other red underwear, which is then worn on New Year's Eve. Anne reiterated the importance of this rite for our conjugal happiness. "You *have* to buy some," she insisted with a smirk. I gave Glenn some racy red lingerie and she gave me these strange red Jockey shorts with a drawing of an exploding bomb on the front and the words *"Zona Minata, Limite Invalicabile."* I still have no idea what that means.

Another weird tradition concerns Befana, the "sister" of Santa

Claus, who looks for all the world like an old witch. She fills the stockings of Italian children with gifts and candy on the Feast of the Epiphany (the twelfth day of Christmas).

Everywhere we'd go in the Piazza Navona we'd see these Befana dolls, big and small. She'd normally wear a kerchief of some kind and glasses, and would carry a broom. We bought two or three as Christmas tree ornaments. According to tradition, Befana was too busy to see the Three Wise Men who came to adore the Christ Child, promising to see them on their return. But because the Three Wise Men returned home by a different route, Befana was doomed to search for them forever. If you happen to be a bad Italian child, Befana puts only coal in your stocking.

Earlier in the fall, Glenn and I had decided that we should try to take the kids to midnight Mass on Christmas Eve in St. Peter's. After all, we had watched it on television almost every Christmas Eve since we were married, as I hurriedly helped Santa Claus put together bicycles and other gifts. The kids were too little for us to go to midnight Mass at our local parish, so we'd stay up late drinking wassail punch, finishing wrapping presents, and watching the pope on TV. In those years the Vatican always had an American bishop act as a kind of "color commentator." This bishop was one of those self-important American prelates who inexplicably believe themselves destined for television greatness, and his smug, drowsy voice would narrate what was happening as though the Mass were some kind of sports event. The bishop specialized in inane bits of self-evident information: "The pope is now approaching the high altar," he would say in a hushed voice as the pope plainly walked up the steps. "The Holy Father is now sitting down in the papal throne . . ."

For once, we thought, we'd like to see the midnight Mass without having to listen to this putz. As a result, in October I wrote a letter to the Prefettura della Casa Pontificia and requested tickets. It's no big deal; tourists do it all the time. I asked for enough tickets for Glenn and me, our three kids, and my father-in-law. Within a month we received a letter back, remarkably in English and signed by the bishop in charge of the Pontifical Household, stating that we would be able to attend. The tickets would be hand-delivered to our address, by special courier, on the day before the event.

We spent the four or five days before Christmas seeing all the tourist sights we had missed before then. Our time in Italy was coming to a close, and we didn't want to miss anything. We spent most of our time in the city center, exploring the little shops around the Pantheon and enjoying long, leisurely lunches outside. Incredibly, even at the end of December the weather was usually sunny and warm, just like back home in California.

By the time Christmas Eve arrived, the weather had changed. It suddenly became freezing cold and rainy. The day before Christmas Eve we woke up to find a packet slid under our door, and inside were our special midnight Mass tickets, embossed with the papal seal.

One thing kept bothering us. We knew we'd take a taxi down the hill, but how, we wondered, would we get back? The Mass got out at two, two-thirty in the morning. None of the buses, of course, ran. Would there be taxis available? No one knew the answer to that. The Sala Stampa people insisted that there would be taxis, but I had learned long ago that they were not a reliable source of information.

We seriously considered hiring a driver to wait for us, but by the time we got on the phone and called around to various limousine and car rental companies, we found that they were all booked. Apparently, other people had had the same thought.

We decided there was nothing to do but take a chance. How often do you get to spend midnight Mass with the pope?

Glenn made sure we were all dressed up. Our three-year-old,

James, had a brand-new double-breasted suit and looked like he could have been an ambassador. Our eldest, Robert, then six, was more casual in a blue blazer. Glenn wore an elegant green suit. The baby, Kelly, had on a red plaid outfit that made him stand out.

Incredibly, the Vatican expected us to be at St. Peter's by nine o'clock. As a result, we had an early dinner in the delicious Chinese restaurant down the street, Vecchia Cina, and then all piled into a large taxi. We arrived on time in the piazza in front of St. Peter's, directly in front of the Sala Stampa, where the taxis always let you off.

It was a chilly evening but had stopped raining. A large crowd, all dressed up, had gathered in front of the life-sized crèche the Vatican builds every year in the center of St. Peter's Square. We'd been watching the workmen build it for the previous two weeks, and it seemed they would never get it completed on time. The figures were up on an enormous high platform covered by a large, barnlike roof. Glenn and I had visited the basilica only two days before, and it hadn't been close to finished then.

But now all was in place. We spent ten minutes or so looking at the crèche and having our pictures taken in front of it; then we got into the long line next to the left colonnade that led up to a police checkpoint.

Your seats at the midnight Mass, as in most papal events, were determined by the color of your tickets. Obviously, the worst seats were in the back of the nave, a couple of football fields away from the altar. The best seats were directly in front of the altar. The medium seats—reserved for people with some connections with the Holy See but without any real importance—were where we ended up, along the transept directly to the sides of the papal altar. If you were seated close up along the transept, you could actually see everything very well.

I must admit I enjoyed impressing my father-in-law and my wife with what seemed like Vatican connections. Most of the people, as we stood in line in front of the police barricade, were being directed to the main front doors of the basilica. "That's not where we're going," I said with a little swagger. "We'll go through there." I pointed to the Arch of the Bells.

And sure enough . . . I was right. John was a little surprised when the two Swiss Guards, glancing at our tickets, directed us through the Arch of the Bells, into the Vatican proper and up the polished marble steps into the sacristy area. I couldn't resist a cocky little grin, explaining that I simply told the pope that my father-in-law was in town and we really needed good seats.

I'd like to be able to say that our final big Vatican event—when our entire family attended Christmas midnight Mass with the pope—was a spiritual experience of profound depth and clarity.

But it was, in fact, mostly a pain in the rear end—quite literally.

Both Glenn and I ended up sitting on hard pews holding sleeping children in our arms. She held Kelly, and I held James. After about the first hour, I began to feel an excruciating burning feeling in my gluteus maximus from sitting immobile for so long. The children, asleep, were sweating through their dress clothes from the stuffy atmosphere of the basilica, filled to bursting with people. I was profoundly uncomfortable.

Luckily, we were sitting as far from the papal altar as possible. I knew from an earlier beatification Mass that Robert and I had attended approximately where we would be sitting. And I knew that the closer we sat to the papal altar, the more difficult it would be to escape for an emergency. With kids, there is always an emergency.

At the beatification Mass, Robert had waited right up to the moment when the pope arrived at the altar to announce that he had to pee . . . right then. No time to waste! By that time the middle aisle in our section of seats had been filled in with people and chairs, so there was literally no way to get out. We had to climb over people, with Robert squirming and yelling. And then we had to walk all the way outside of the basilica to the only public bathroom in about five square miles—the one next door to the Vatican Post Office on the left side of St. Peter's Square.

So we sat in the back. It seemed like forever, but finally the Vatican choir began singing and midnight Mass began. The pope processed up the central aisle. He was attended by various bishops and priests. He sat down on the papal throne in front of the altar, and there were readings.

It was just like I remembered it from watching on TV—only I didn't have to hear the bishop's smarmy commentary. There was the beautiful chanting of the Kalenda, sung by the same monk, his hair closely shaved, I saw every year. The Kalenda—the Latin word from which we get calendar—is an ancient chant recalling the times and circumstances surrounding the birth of Christ, taken from the Roman Martyrology. It has always entranced me:

> In the 5,199th year of the creation of the world, from the time when God in the beginning created the heavens and the earth; the 2,957th year after the flood; the 2,015th year from the birth of Abraham; the 1,510th year from Moses, and the going forth of the people of Israel from Egypt; the 1,032nd year from the anointing of David King; in the 65th week according to the prophecy of Daniel; in the 194th Olympiad; the 752nd year from the foundation of the City of Rome; the 42nd year of the rule of Octavian Augustus, all the earth being at peace; in the sixth age of the world, Jesus Christ, the eternal God, and the Son of the Eternal Father, desirous to sanctify the world by his most merciful coming, being conceived by the Holy Spirit, nine months after his conception, was born in Bethlehem of Judah, made Man of the Virgin Mary.

Later, I would try to track down a recording of the entire midnight Mass liturgy, in the Ancora bookstore across from the Sala Stampa, just for the chanting of the Kalenda, only to be told none exists (which I doubt).

We made it through the Scripture readings, the pope's homily, even the incensing of the altar. But, I have to admit, by the time the Offertory began, we knew we had to bail.

The kids woke up, hot and sweaty, squirming like wild hogs. Right at the one part of the Mass when everyone is completely silent and you could have heard a pin drop—the Consecration—they started screaming their lungs out.

"*Dominus vobiscum*," the pope said.

"*Et cum spiritu tuo*," the people in the basilica reverently responded.

"*Waaaahhhh!*" my son James bellowed at the top of his lungs, "I have to go PEE!"

I know one hundred million people watching on TV heard that.

We quickly sprang to our feet, and half carried, half walked our children down the side aisle of St. Peter's toward the back of the basilica. It reminded me of Mass back home.

The basilica was packed, of course. The nave was full of seats, presumably for people with tickets, but all along the side areas people were standing, two or three deep, straining to see the action on the high altar. We noticed that in some of the more spacious side areas, such as around the Chapel of St. Pius X, people had spread sleeping bags on the floor for their kids to rest. Some were asleep on the floor.

It felt good to walk. My butt felt numb from sitting for so long with a heavy child on my lap. When we walked out of the basilica into the cold night air, I was wide awake and relieved to be going. All I could think was: *What were we thinking taking these kids here?*

We could still hear the entire Mass. The pope's voice, quietly saying the words of the canon in Latin, literally boomed across St. Peter's Square through the massive Vatican public address system. It was strange to hear this, because it was two o'clock in the morning. The square was still full of people mingling around, listening to the Mass.

I noticed one surprising thing about the papal Masses, both at the Christmas Mass and at the earlier beatification: They were nothing special. By that I mean the Mass at St. Peter's in Rome, celebrated by the pope, is almost exactly like a typical Mass a Catholic sees every Sunday in his or her home parish. The words, the rubrics, the ceremonies, are almost identical. Therefore, traditionalist Catholics who imagine that the Vatican, in its heart of hearts, is on their side, are mistaken. Everything the traditionalists deplore about the new liturgy—including Communion in the hand—is practiced by the pope in Rome.

In a way I found this a little disappointing—not because I carry a brief for the traditionalists, but because I came 10,000 miles to Rome. I wanted to see a more elevated, more ceremonial liturgy in St. Peter's. In the past there were levels of solemnity—with a Low (spoken) Mass, a High (sung) Mass and, the ultimate, a Pontifical High Mass. But today, it seems, there is really just a one-size-fits-all ritual, with no real variations to accommodate big events. Leaving Christmas midnight Mass, I felt a little let down precisely because it had seemed just like the Sunday Mass back home in California, only more crowded.

On the other hand, the traditionalists make one point that does make sense, at least in a multicultural context such as St. Peter's. Surrounded there as you are by people from almost every nation on earth, you instantly see the utility of having a shared liturgical language such as Latin or Hebrew. In the past, every Catholic hearing Mass in any church in the world—or still today any observant Jew attending synagogue services anywhere in the world—would feel right at home because of the shared liturgical language. The fact that most Catholics, and today most Jews, understand only a little of this liturgical language is irrelevant. That's because the alternative, on display in St. Peter's, is far more confusing—the attempt to accommodate all languages simultaneously. During the Christmas midnight Mass, the liturgy was said alternately in about a dozen languages. Parts of the Mass were said in Italian, French, English, German, Spanish, Polish, Filipino, Portuguese, even Arabic.

"Panie Jezu, który w swej Ewangelii uczysz nas podziwiac piekno swiata stworzonego," the pope prayed in Polish, adding, four sentences later in Filipino, *"Kristom bukal ng pagbabalik-loob at aming tagapagpalaya . . ."*

I have to say, as bad as my Latin is, it's better than my Polish, Filipino, or Arabic.

During this liturgical Tower of Babel, I found my eyes actually drifting gratefully across the pages of the Mass program to the Latin translations! I could understand the ancient prayers of the Church in Latin, through sheer childhood repetition, in a way I couldn't in German, Polish, Filipino, or Arabic.

Just as we stepped outside, it started to rain. We made our way across the square to where the taxis normally wait for customers—only there were no taxis!

Our worst fears were soon realized. There was a line of Mass goers forming along one curb (obviously polite tourists) as well as a group of taxi pirates standing around, waiting to commandeer any taxi that pulled up (obviously Italians). Groups of tourists, including my now-shivering family, huddled in the doorways of the Palazzi dei Propilei, as I stood in the rain with the other tourists, hoping to hail a taxi. After twenty minutes, and only one or two taxis, I was beginning to get worried.

My father-in-law was carrying James, Glenn the baby, and Robert bravely stood up. I ran over to a pay phone, put in a phone card, and called the four-digit number of a taxi company. I asked them, in my broken Italian, to send a taxi to the Columbus Hotel, where I had met the Knights of the Holy Sepulcher. I figured a hotel is a better place to get a taxi than standing with three dozen tourists in front of St. Peter's.

We then gave up on the tourist line, crossed the Via della Conciliazione, and walked about a block down to the Columbus Hotel. There we found one or two other people waiting for taxis as well. After another twenty minutes, and only one taxi, I was getting desperate. When a freelance taxi hustler approached, asking if we needed a lift, I jumped at it—even though that is a dangerous thing to do. I figured that unless he had a gun, John and I could overpower him if he tried to rob us.

The taxi hustler asked where we were heading, and I asked how much he'd charge to take us up to the "Gianicolo." He named a price about four times the regular rate, and I reluctantly agreed. All six of us piled into his Mercedes, much to his surprise and protest, but he took us home. He let us off in the Piazza Ceresi, next to our apartment compound, and then haggled for more money. He had gone farther than the Gianicolo, he said, and so we had to pay more. At that point I wanted to slug him; but then he said, hey, listen, it's Christmas and I'm out here working instead of being with my family. I stood there, drenched, with sleepy children, a long-suffering wife, and my stoic father-in-law, and gave in. I gave the bastard an extra twenty bucks.

We staggered into our apartment at three-thirty in the morning, stripped the clothes off the kids, and fell, exhausted, into our beds.

Thus: Christmas in the Vatican.

Epilogue

Behold! I am with you always, until the end of the age.

Matthew 20:28

Three days later we were on the Air France jet for Paris.

Europe that year had the worst snowstorm in thirty years, and we barely made it out of Rome. Our plane had to be de-iced, we were late leaving and missed our connecting flight to Los Angeles. Air France put us up in a beautiful hotel near the airport and gave us 150 francs per person, per meal, to eat—which is what we did. Fresh, delicious French food soothed our tired bodies after the recent days' adventures.

The only unpleasant thing about the trip home was coming back to the United States. The immigration authorities, in Los Angeles at least, treat every arriving person as a potential drug smuggler or illegal alien, regardless of your citizenship. European customs officials wave you through with hardly a glance; snarling American customs agents give you the third degree, make you walk past drug-sniffing German shepherds, and threaten to search every bag you own.

The culture shock you feel returning to America, after living overseas, can be enormous. After I lived in Israel, coming back to a two-day weekend, instead of the single Saturday Sabbath, felt like an enormous luxury. After Rome, Glenn and I reveled in the Los Angeles freeway system . . . fully stocked supermarkets . . . and unlimited hot water.

But we soon missed Rome and the Vatican. I realized, coming home, just how much Christianity is a historically embedded religion. The story it has to tell, and the lessons it has to teach, make sense only if you understand the history. Judaism, I suppose, is the same way—inextricably tied to specific events that happened in a specific land in a specific time. The problem for both Christianity and Judaism in America is that they are so far from their historical roots.

And perhaps that's why Rome is so important to the Catholic Faith: It's one of those special places on earth, like Jerusalem, where history itself is concentrated in a kind of interdimensional whirlpool, where the crumbling buildings and distant voices of the past intrude upon the transcendent visions of the future. In Rome you soak up Christian history like a sponge. Progressive thinkers want to transform Christianity into a transcendent philosophy, like Buddhism or stoicism, without the nasty cultural baggage that comes with having a history. But that would strip Christianity of what is unique to it—the memory of a specific human being who lived in a specific time.

Memory, after all, is what makes Christians, and specifically Catholics, what they are: "Do this in memory of me." The daily Masses, the monks chanting the daily office, the feast days, the lives of the saints, the rosaries and devotions, the statues and crucifixes, the monuments and churches and roadside shrines: These are all merely ways of remembering. And that, of course, is also the primary mission of the pope—to guard the memories, the *paratheke,* the "deposit of Faith."

I'd like to be able to say that my explorations of the Vatican strengthened my faith as a Catholic in the way, say, that touring the United States Capitol makes you proud to be an American. But that's not a good comparison. The monuments of Washington, D.C.—or even those of London or Paris—convey a grandeur that the Vatican, despite the glories of St. Peter's, really does not. If anything, spending time in the Vatican is a humbling experience. There is a lot *less* there than meets the eye.

A religion with a history as checkered as that of Christianity— inextricably tied up with Borgia popes, the Inquisition, and the Crusades—must speak its truth quietly. Like the people of Israel in the Old Testament—who continually broke their promises, abandoned or murdered their brothers, and worshipped the golden calf—Christians are, in the end, just as St. Paul said, hypocritical sinners. The Vatican teaches you that.

Thus, when my evangelical or atheist friends now taunt me, like Luther, with the ignominious blasphemies of the evil popes of Rome, I can now cheerfully respond, *"You don't know the half of it!"*

But that doesn't make me want to abandon my religion either. If anything, I find it tremendously comforting.

When I was in college, there was this particularly corrupt Jesuit priest who kept a Mercedes stashed on the side, who drank like an Irish longshoreman, and who occasionally slept with some of the more beautiful coeds in our dorm. He was a scandal. But strangely enough, he was the one priest to whom many students would go in a crisis, the one to whom they would listen. It's easier to take advice from a sinner than from a saint.

And unlike the more righteous young Jesuits of that period—who were so morally upright, they had to abandon the priesthood for other, more personally satisfying careers—this man is still a priest. The Jesuits wisely keep him away from young girls, of course, but he's still there. Despite his failings, his checkered past, he's still there.

And that, in the end, is why the Vatican is so important, for me and for any Catholic familiar with the Church's history.

It's still there.

Nations and empires come and go. Philosophies burn bright and then fade away. Science marches on. But so far, at least, despite the fervent hopes of many, the Vatican is still there, in the same spot, saying the same things.

For all its flaws, it is Catholicism's secret strength. It is our way of remembering.

Acknowledgments

I knew practically nothing about the Vatican before I started this book, so anything I say about it that happens to be true I learned either from personal interviews, direct observation, or a handful of good books.

The single greatest debt I owe is to Dr. Robert Moynihan and June Hager of *Inside the Vatican* magazine, whose cordiality, vast erudition, and knowledge of good drinking spots made the transition to life in Rome manageable. I also owe special thanks to Greg Burke of *Time* magazine; Jean-Marie Guenois and Blandine Becheras of I. Media; Jesùs Colina-Diez of ABC; Sr. Giovanna Gentile of the Vatican Press Office; Commandant Roland Buchs-Binz and Vice Corporal Frowin Bachmann of the Swiss Guards; His Eminence Angelo Cardinal Sodano, Vatican Secretary of State; freelance writer Martine Zaug; the staff of the Vatican Library and Vatican Secret Archives; Father Reginald Foster, OCD; Dr. Mauro Olivieri of the Vatican Philatelic and Numismatic Office; Father Sabino Maffeo, SJ, of the Vatican Observatory at Castel Gandolfo; The Equestrian Order of the Holy Sepulcher of Jerusalem; the staff of Vatican

Radio; and numerous priests, religious, bishops and cardinals who spoke to me off the record.

Although it probably isn't apparent, I actually did a lot of reading while researching this book. But a few books stand out and were invaluable sources of facts, anecdotes, gossip, quotations, and general know-how about the Vatican. For basic information about the holy places of Rome, you can't beat Stanley Luff's *The Christian's Guide to Rome* (published in Britain by Burns & Oats). For information about the Vatican itself, I relied primarily on two marvelous books—Jerrold M. Packard's *Peter's Kingdom: Inside the Papal City* (New York: Charles Scribner's Sons, 1985) and Paul Hofmann's hilarious *O Vatican! A Slightly Wicked View of the Holy See* (New York: Congdon & Weed, 1984). Both are now out of print. James-Charles Noonan, Jr.'s *The Church Visible: The Ceremonial Life and Protocol of the Roman Catholic Church* (New York: Viking, 1996) helped me remember the difference between crimson and scarlet and taught me the correct spelling for many of the weird get-ups worn by Vatican officials.

On a more personal note, I owe a lot to Anne Jäske, our Swedish assistant, translator, baby-sitter, guide, and friend during our stay in Rome. She made our life in Rome not merely bearable but fun. Also Luca De Meo, my translator and research assistant, was invaluable.

I should also thank my literary agent, Lisa Bankoff of ICM, for talking my editors at Doubleday, Bruce Tracy and Denell Downum, into taking on this project. Also, my West Coast agent, John Finn, helped with my financial affairs while we were in Rome, making sure our bank account always had money in it when we went to the ATM machine.

Finally, I owe more than I can say to my family. My mother, Mary Jane Hutchinson, who is the person primarily responsible for my Catholic upbringing and continuing faith, was scheduled to come with us to Rome. The month we were due to leave, however, she died suddenly of lung cancer. My wife, Glenn Ellen, who also lost her mother the same year, helped me go on with the project, as did my three sons, Robert,

James, and Kelly, who endured the rigors of international travel with stamina and good humor. My father, my brothers and sister, my father-in-law, John Duncan, and all of my numerous "outlaws" also provided moral support during a trying time. I can only hope they all know how much their continuing love and support have meant to me.

ROBERT J. HUTCHINSON, *Irvine, California*

Robert J. Hutchinson is the author of *The Book of Vices: A Collection of Classic Immoral Tales* and *The Absolute Beginner's Guide to Gambling*. He lives in Irvine, California, with his wife, Glenn Ellen, and their three sons, Robert John, James, and Kelly.